NOTHING IS US

A Memoir

E. David Brown

Published by Tu

ISBN: 978-1-998270-02-6

Tumbleweed Press Toronto, Canada

Printed in Canada

Cover design by Crayon Design & Communication
Photos: Barbara Kleinhans, Khaldoon Saleh, Miodrag Bogdanovic

To my daughter, Flannery

Now you know.

And

Jeff Brown (1954-2015)

"Non fui, Fui, Non sum, Non Curo."
Epicurus

"There was things which he stretched, but
mainly he told the truth."
Mark Twain from: "The Adventures of Huckleberry Finn"

Prologue

In January 1997 my father was lowered into a concrete grave liner in central Florida. A young female Air Force sergeant marched over to a bargain basement ghetto blaster and inserted a cassette. Dad, a retired Light Colonel, was the son of a former police chief of Birmingham, Alabama. His father had instilled in him a frightening dedication to country, authority, and God, provided the latter didn't interfere with one's obligation to the first two articles of allegiance.

Out of the speakers seeped a tinny version of Taps. The sergeant snapped off a salute to the family and turned to face three pimply-faced airmen shouldering rifles. They fired off three volleys seven times. The mini-honor guard folded "Old Glory" into a triangle and handed it awkwardly to my stepmother.

My father suffered from a litany of diseases running the gamut from kidney cancer to Parkinson's. On a 2 AM trek to the toilet, he stumbled, breaking his hip. While waiting for surgery he went into convulsions. The doctor uncovered a gash behind Dad's ear that he received when he fell against the bathroom vanity. His last words were, "Finally it's over."

As droplets of rain clung tenaciously to the tangle of Spanish moss dripping from the cemetery's live oaks, memories surfaced that I had tried to bury deeper than the grave in which my father was interred. Emotions as complex and loathsome as the most vile witches brew: shame, fear, anger, hatred, and self-loathing filled the hollow of my heart. Although these systemic poisons had permeated my life, I had refused to acknowledge the source.

Every day since Lt. Colonel E. H. Brown's funeral I have struggled to invent a memory that would redeem my father in my eyes and in turn allow the process of self-redemption to begin. A lot of people think they know the history of Noah but most fail to grasp that the real story begins after the floodwaters recede. Ham discovers his old man butt-naked and drunk. For his indiscretion he is cast out, banished to Canaan (or in my case Canada). Having resolved to uncover the nakedness of my father, the task is now to reconstruct the past as best I can. My siblings no doubt, have different, yet equally valid, interpretations of the past. I can only relate my version.

(1951-1964)

"I don't care if you love me or like me or call me Dad, but by God, call me Sir!"

Lt. Colonel E.H. Brown (U.S.A.F. Retired) 1925-1997

Chapter 1

In 1951 my mother was rushed to the Fort Benning infirmary in a military ambulance that had seen action in the First World War. In a puke yellow corridor lit by naked florescent ceiling lights, she gave birth to me in the deepest heat of a Georgia August.

Six months later Dad was posted to Metz, France. With two other junior officers, he rented a place in an 18th-century flour mill that had been converted into a quadruplex. The mill had a water wheel that moved through a sluggish stream, really just an open sewer. My mother arrived with my older sister and me in tow and was shown an apartment with one sink, a potbellied stove for heating and cooking, and an oversized laundry tub for stand-up baths. In the building's hallway was a WC used by all the quadruplex's occupants.

Finishing a two-year stint in Metz, we were transferred to Bitburg, Germany. Mom volunteered at a local health clinic and collected Hummel figurines and china teacups, the bulk of which failed to survive the trip back stateside. The most enduring token of our first tour in Germany was my brother. Born on February 9th, Jeff was an early Valentine's present, a far better gift, Mom would joke, than the Whitman Chocolate Sampler and nightgown Dad gave her every year.

We returned to the U.S.A. in 1956. Dad attended the Bethesda War College in Maryland and was promoted to Captain.

*

My sister had the enviable talent of attracting friends and quickly fell in with the neighborhood kids. Being less gregarious and a whiner I tagged along with her as an unwanted hanger-on. She tolerated my presence but only up to the point where my face did not jeopardize her social life. When she'd had enough of me, she'd whirl around and say, "Go home."

One miserably humid day I followed her all the way to her friend's house. The backyard gate swung open, and a red-haired girl jumped out and hugged Janet. She turned her eyes on me. Scowling, she twisted my ear and said, "You are not invited. It's a girl's only watermelon party. No boys allowed, especially crybabies."

Janet leaned down and whispered, "Go home, I'll bring you something if there's anything left."

The girl's house was about a block away from mine, twelve front yards at the most. It took me thirty minutes to make it halfway down the street. Every other footstep I wiped my tears and snot on the front of my T-shirt. With only a couple of more houses to go, I stopped at the corner, buried my nose in the hollow of a stop sign pole, and cried. Several fierce honeybees occupied the same space. Screaming, I ran home.

*

The Sunday after the stop sign incident my Uncle Jack and Aunt Jackie visited us. It was my Uncle Jack, a full bird

Colonel, who had convinced my father to sign on in the newly conceived Air Force as a regular and not reservist. His selling pitch, though pedestrian, was irrefutable. The government would take care of all our needs, providing housing, medical, and dental care, and would pay for Dad's schooling wherever he was stationed. Somehow the irony of protecting the free marketplace from the scourge of communism while existing in the socialistic cradle of the military never seemed incongruous to career lifers.

Jackie took us to the beach and crawled around on her hands and knees to dig for clams. Hard to believe she was Louise's sister, considering my paternal grandmother's most fervent passion was to make others crawl for her. On seeing my nose masquerading as a Zeppelin, Jackie bribed me with tabs of a Bit-of-Honey candy bar to recount my adventure.

"Tell me again how big that old bee was," she said.

I spread my hands about a foot apart. Jackie found this gesture hilarious and repeated, "Tell me again how big that old bee was."

Each time she prompted me I spread my hands further. Dad walked into the parlor, and Jackie egged me on. "Go on now, tell your Daddy how big that old bee was."

My father stood dead still with a glass of bourbon and water sweating in his palm. I giggled and stretched my arms their full width. He placed his tumbler on top of the coffee table and knelt down beside me. "David, how big was that bee?"

"This big, Daddy." As I started to extend my arms, he slapped me across the face. He sprung from his crouch like

3

a jack-in-the-box, pulled down my pants, and beat my bare bottom with the flat of his hand until Jackie grabbed me.

"That's what you get for lying. I hate liars worse than anything," he said.

I tried to bury myself in Jackie's bosom. Dad reached out to pull me away. "Be a man," he yelled. "Stop crying. Real men don't go around hugging and kissing. But I guess you're not a real man."

Chapter 2

In 1958 we were stationed at Selfridge Air base near Detroit, our sixth posting in seven years. The back wall of our apartment building was missing, the result of a tornado that had ripped through Detroit before our arrival. A plastic sheet covered the open rear of the kitchen and remained hanging there through the summer and well into the chilling dampness of autumn. Mom prepared meals on a Coleman stove and washed dishes in the bathtub. My father called her a real trooper.

The mile-and-a-half trek from home to school in winter was brutal. Being unable to drive restricted Mom's movements to the projects. She attempted to join a carpool, offering her babysitting services in lieu of a ride but got the cold shoulder from the other mothers. One day Janet walked Jeff and me home. We burrowed our way into her coat in an effort to stay warm and stave off ice pellets driven by a wind howling across Lake St. Claire. After treating our incipient cases of frostbite Mom brought up the subject of learning to drive over dinner. Dad said, "Norma, don't be an idiot. You can barely find your way around here on foot. How do you think you're going manage on the roads?"

"I'll manage," Mom said and walked over to the wall phone.

"Who are you calling?"

"A driving school Kathy told me about." Mom placed her hand over the mouthpiece. "Now, shush, honey."

Dad gritted his teeth. "You planned all along to do this without discussing it with me."

"There's nothing to discuss, Ernest."

Mom shifted into her Southern Belle telephone voice when the driving school answered. "Yes, I'd like to take driving lessons and I was wondering if y'all could make room for me. Certainly, I'll wait."

Dad slapped the table. "Damn it, Norma, we can't afford two cars."

"Honey, of course we can't. We'll just have to take turns."

Mom returned to the person at the other end of the line. "Tuesdays and Thursdays for the next six weeks? Why that sounds just fine to me. Alabama, why? Well, thank you, that's certainly kind of you. Although Vivian Leigh was not really from the South you know."

*

I took after my mother in more ways than looks. Just as she was a late starter driving, I learned to ride a bike at least a year after Jeff. I had received a second-hand three-speed for my eighth birthday. It remained chained to a no-parking sign while I mustered the courage to ride it. Jeff filched the lock key out of my sock drawer. Within an hour he was wheeling around the circle in front of our apartment building like a circus monkey. It made me furious, not because Jeff had learned to ride a bike before me, but because my father would expect me to follow suit. That evening Dad gave Jeff a pat on the head and told him what a natural athlete he was. He dug his fingers into my shoulder and promised that come Saturday he would teach me how to ride a bike.

Saturday arrived and I chewed my way through breakfast without tasting anything. Around eleven o'clock Dad marched me down the stairs and outside to my Raleigh.

"All you have to do is sit up straight and keep your eyes forward to maintain your balance," Dad instructed. He steadied the bicycle while I mounted it and walked beside me holding it upright. "Damn it, you have to peddle. The bike isn't going to peddle itself."

"Yes, Sir."

"Faster, the bike won't stay up if you don't peddle faster."

"Yes, Sir."

I turned the front wheel toward him and grabbed for his arm. He pushed me off. Again, I steered my way back to him and clutched at his shirt sleeve. He jumped in front of the bike and wrestled it by its handlebars to the ground like a cowboy bulldogging a steer. I rolled across the pavement and started crying.

My father's eyes narrowed into flinty slits. With one hand he snatched me up by my armpit while the other picked up the bike. Dragging it and me to the entrance of our apartment complex he stopped at the door. He could not bring both the Raleigh and me upstairs, so he flung the bike behind him. He toted me up the stairs in a fireman's carry. Once inside our apartment he pitched me on the couch and said in a calm voice, "You want to act like a baby, wet your bed and cry over falling off a bike, then you'll dress like one." He walked into the bathroom and returned with a large white bath towel.

My mother had retreated into a corner when Dad stormed into the room. She ventured out a few inches and called out to Jan and Jeff, "Go outside."

"No, stay," Dad ordered. "I want them to see their new baby brother." He bent over me and ripped off my cotton shorts. I struggled to get up. With the weight of his knee on my chest I could scarcely breathe. "Keep still or I'll give you something to cry about." Then he tucked the towel under my bum and pulled the front of it between my legs and fastened it with two large safety pins, creating a giant diaper.

"Ernest you've no right."

Dad stood up panting. "Keep out of this, Norma. If he wants to act like a baby, then by God he'll dress like one."He glanced at his wristwatch and told Jeff to turn on the television. He wanted to catch a National Geographic special on whales. I crawled off the couch and started to limp to the room I shared with Jeff. Dad ordered me to come back. "You might learn something if you watch this."

For two hours I sat on the couch next to my father with my brother and sister on the floor in front of me. My mother sat in an armchair with her legs curled under her, shielding her eyes behind a book. The doorbell rang.

"Go answer the door, David," Dad said.

I hesitated. My eyes darted around the room for a rescuer. Jeff and Jan sat frozen in front of the picture tube. Mom pressed her face closer to the pages of her book.

"I told you to answer the door," Dad repeated.

Later that afternoon I sat on the edge of my bed crying. Jeff tried to comfort me. "It was only Kathy. She's Mom's friend. She won't tell anyone."

Stone cold sober, all this had transpired before Dad's first evening Martini.

Chapter 3

Dad spent an excessive amount of time at the base hospital. He applied for every Temporary Tour of Duty posting (TDY) he could swing in an effort to better his chances of promotion. He logged assignments lasting anywhere from a few days to a few weeks in places as far away as Greenland and Newfoundland. Mom endured the loneliness endemic to a lifer's wife by disappearing into a book. She suffered from varicose veins and an excess of thyroid in Michigan. One moment she would be smoking a cigarette, calmly staring out of the window at the mostly hard-packed dirt yard of the project. Within a sigh she would launch into a cleaning frenzy, attacking every inch of the apartment with unrestrained ferocity. Smudge marks were an insult, each dust ball a mockery to be eradicated, as if by doing so the dark stain of despair spreading across her life could be Mr. Cleaned away.

Dad initiated a proactive approach to maintaining discipline during his absences. He made Jeff and me promise to mind Mom, keep out of trouble, and write to him. To impress on us the seriousness of his commands he beat us with a leather belt.

"That's it. Act like men," he lauded us for swallowing our cries while he flogged the back of our legs.

"Ernest, that's enough," Mom whimpered as she noticed that one of us, generally me, was about to scream.

Winded, Dad would draw us toward him and pat us on the back. "Take care of your mother and sister. You're the men of the family while I'm gone."

By Dad's standards, the whippings were therapeutic. By our measure, these farewell strappings were restrained.

One Sunday Jeff slinked into the kitchen where I was reading the funny pages. "We're in trouble. Help me," he whispered.

He dragged me to our bedroom, opened the door, and shoved me inside. Underneath the open window, flames leaped out of our toy box scorching the ceiling. The chemical smell of melting plastic and the synthetic fur of stuffed animals choked me. We rushed from the bathroom to the bedroom carrying glasses of water. In desperation, we ejected the toy box through the window. Dad must have looked outside and seen the flaming coffin of stuffed animals free fall to the ground. He pummeled us with his fists, kicked us, stood on our chests, and at one point picked up a small wooden baseball bat. If Mom had not intervened, he might have killed us.

Jeff and I remained at home for over a week. My mother waited for our cracked ribs, bruises, swollen lips, and blackened eyes to subside enough for us to return to school. "If anyone asks, say you were in a car accident," she said.

*

Shortly after the toy box incident, my father got into an argument with my mother. He put his fist through the locked bathroom door, connecting with Mom's jaw on the other side. The fight was the culmination of a series of skirmishes that had been going on for weeks revolving

12

around everything from the lousy Detroit weather to a costume my father wanted Mom to wear to the officer's club Halloween ball. It was a buckskin dress complete with fringes and beads. My Mother objected to the sign that Dad wanted to hang around her neck, "Big Chief Ernie's Squaw."

Three weeks before the Halloween ball I accidentally tore down a belt rack hanging on the inside of Dad's closet. The memory of the toy box beating induced me to lie to Dad on his discovering of the broken rack. He interrogated Jeff but my brother refused to speak. His silence was taken as an admission of guilt.

"If there's anything I hate more than a thief - it's a liar," Dad pronounced and struck my brother full-force with a closed fist in the face as I cringed in the corner. As I listened to the screams of my brother taking strap after strap against his bare legs vomit rose in my throat. I swallowed rather than admit my guilt.

Mom and Dad had a row after Jeff and I went to bed. They conducted it in true genteel Southern fashion in low but distinct voices.

"If you're that unhappy then why don't you leave?" my father asked.

"You and Louise would like that wouldn't you, Ernest?"

"Keep my mother out of this."

"How can I? Every time you open your mouth her words fall out."

My father's mother, an Old South dowager if there ever was one, frowned on their union, dedicating an extravagant amount of effort to reminding the family how her eldest son had married beneath his station.

Jeff climbed the ladder attached to the side of our bunk bed and slid in next to me. We held each other as the argument grew louder. Janet sneaked into our room after the front door slammed.

"They might get a divorce," Jan announced matter-of-factly.

Jeff sat up. "What's a divorce?"

"That's when Mom and Dad leave one another."

"What about us?" Jeff asked.

Janet shrugged, "We have to decide who we're going with."

My brother broke into a wide grin. "I'm going with Mom."

On Sunday morning Mom told Janet to help us pack our suitcases. She then called a cab. Mom sat in the front seat of the taxi and asked the driver to take us to the Greyhound terminal where we caught a bus to Birmingham.

Chapter 4

My Grandfather Agerton loaded our bags into the back of a 1940 paneled station wagon crammed with bushels of okra, snap beans, apples, and butternut squash.

We pulled up to the curb of a wood-shingled house. My grandmother's round face peeped out of a gabled window on the second story. Granddad turned off the ignition and slowly unloaded the car while Grandma dropped one plump leg at a time on the stairs leading down from the captain's porch that cased the front and right side of the house. She was as pale-skinned, short, and stout as my grandfather was olive-colored, tall and thin. As Grandma pressed our faces into her bosom, I inhaled the aroma of freshly baked biscuits.

Granddad placed a bushel of snap beans on the ground and asked Jeff and me to grab a handle and bring the basket into the house. We stepped inside the screened porch and dropped the basket. Suspended from a thick beam was a bench swing. It moved slightly in the breeze its shiny new chain catching glints of morning sunlight. We jumped into the swing and started pumping our legs to send it higher and higher. Jeff and I sailed the swing nearly up to the rafters.

Granddad raised his voice slightly, "You boys be careful." As he lifted his hand to the bridge of his nose to adjust his glasses, we flinched. "Boys, all I'm asking is to take care. Glass doesn't grow on trees."

We carried Mom's bags into the large room at the front of the house. A gas fireplace built into one salmon-pink wall faced a set of French doors and a span of windows that looked onto the side of the porch. Mom protested that she didn't want to take her sister's bedroom, but Grandma pursed her lips. "It's Jean's idea so don't go getting her all upset. Janet and her will have a fine old time yakking away upstairs."

Jeff and I took the room next to my sister's. We shared a bed that had belonged to Betty Faye, the youngest of my grandparent's three girls. It spooked us staying in Betty's room. Barely nineteen, she drowned while at a public beach with my Mom, Dad, and sister. An urgent call went out over the loudspeaker for medical assistance. Mom had completed nursing school in New Orleans and rushed over to the lifeguard's station to help with what she thought was routine first aid for some kid who had scraped his knee or been stung by a wasp. She entered the shed and saw the blue face of Betty Faye staring fish-eyed at her. A diver on his way into the water had clipped her neck.

My Aunt Jean arrived at half past six from the law office where she clerked. Mom sat in the swing with her legs curled under her smoking a cigarette. Jean walked by her and into the house without pausing.

Chapter 5

On Monday Mom put on her pillbox hat and white gloves, Deep South going out attire, and walked us down the street to Central Park Elementary & Junior High. Dating back to the turn of the century, the school's burnt brick structure was dilapidated back when Mom and her sisters had attended it.

Mr. Rush, the principal, smoothed back his thinning hair and straightened his polka-dot bow tie. He wheeled his chair away from the desk and stood. Hitching his pants up to his sternum he approached us. Janet scuffed the toe of her shoe on the floor and glanced up. Jeff, oblivious to Mr. Rush's presence, looked out the ancient sash windows at a squirrel jumping through the branches of an oak tree.

"Are you enrolling them for the whole academic year?"

"I don't know. At least until Christmas."

Mr. Rush slipped his hands into his trouser pockets and rocked on his heels. "Children, your mother was one of our best students. She won the civics writing scroll four times."

He spoke without pausing between sentences. "Four times y'all hear? That was remarkable. No one had done that up to then or has done it since. Four times, y'all understand the significance of that?" I watched his lips move without quite understanding his words. His accent was like the Dixiecrat Rooster from the Warner Brothers cartoon.

"Young man, you look like you should be in the fourth grade?"

I didn't know his answer required a response and stared straight ahead.

"I said you should be in the fourth grade," he said and leaned over into my face.

"Yes."

His spine cracked when he snapped into an upright position. He perched his hands on his hips. "Excuse me!"

I figured he was hard of hearing. I spoke louder. "I'm in the fourth grade."

His face lost its yellow pallor. His jowls transformed into a quivering mass of strawberry Jell-O. "Yes Sir, David. Down here we respond with sir when someone who is our elder or better speaks." He ended by looking at my mother. "Certainly, he must have learned that at home?"

The words of my father echoed in my head while I waited for my mother to respond. "I don't care if you love me or like me or call me Dad, but by God, call me, Sir!"

My mother smiled demurely and held up her white-gloved hands. "We have tried, Mr. Rush. But you know the children have lived up North for so long—"

Mr. Rush escorted Janet and Jeff to their classrooms first and then came back for me. "Norma Agerton, this one is the spittin' image of you. I hope he is half the student you were." He pinched my cheek between his sausage-sized thumb and forefinger. "Your mother was a real scholar. Don't let her down."

Mr. Rush held my hand, pulling me down the hall and up the stairs like an organ grinder leading a monkey. He stopped at the far end of a dingy plaster of Paris corridor and rapped on a glass pane in the center of a classroom door. Inside the room, a tall woman wearing a white blouse with a high-necked ruffled collar shook a pointer at the rigid students sitting in neat desk rows. She took long strides to the door. The movement of her ankle-length skirt revealed her black lace-up boots.

Mr. Rush opened the door, but she remained standing just inside the threshold. "Miss Maloney, this is your new student, David Brown."

She slid her Ben Franklin glasses to the tip of her nose. The smell of camphor and lavender clung to her like the inside of a spinster's hope chest.

"Where are you from, child?"

"Detroit."

"Detroit what, child?"

"Detroit, Michigan." I wondered if she was giving me a geography quiz.

"Are you deliberately being rude, child?"

"No."

"No, what?" Mr. Rush asked.

I thought back to the game of Alabama Jeopardy I had played in Mr. Rush's office and ventured a guess. "No, Mam?"

Mr. Rush twisted my cheek again and said, "He'll be alright, Miss Maloney. He's Norma Agerton's boy."

The hardness in Miss Maloney's eyes vanished. She gripped the top of my skull and used her talons to move my head from side to side. "Child, if you are half the student your mother was, you will do just fine."

As things turned out I was less than half the student my mother had been.

Aunt Jean worked with me every night to show me how to properly align long division columns in an appropriate, respectful manner for Miss Maloney. She told me she'd tutored Betty Faye as well. I asked her to tell me about Betty, her face went waxy.

"Never you mind about Betty Faye. You're the one having problems with old lady Maloney."

I never quite mastered the technique Jean taught me. Math remained a game of chance.

My real problem occurred when I turned in my first and only book report for Miss Maloney. In hindsight, "Uncle Tom's Cabin" was a poor choice of literature for a woman who winced every time she heard "the sewer intonations of northern gutter rats." It was Miss Maloney's conviction that the South in general and Alabama specifically were victims of the distorted retelling of the righteous rebellion of the southern states. When some child referred to this event as the Civil War, Miss Maloney would press her hand over her left breast and declare, "Grant and Sherman, with Lincoln's blessing, made certain there was nothing civil about the conflict."

She maintained that the Northern conquerors had spent a hundred years perpetuating a lie about the causes of the rebellion. "Slavery," she said, "had nothing to do with the war. Yankees fabricated the evils of that peculiar institution to keep its own downtrodden factory workers in check. The Negroes in comparison to the Irish and Polish tenement dwellers of New York and Boston were well-fed and happy. Why just listen to their spirituals? Do sad, mistreated people sing and praise the Lord if they are miserable?"

She would answer her own question with, "Only a happy heart can bring forth such a joyful sound."

To Miss Maloney, my selection of reading material bordered either on heresy or idiocy. She opted for the latter and "Norma's boy", thanks to Harriet Beecher-Stowe, was demoted from the fourth to the third grade. Before banishment from Miss Maloney's room, I exacted my revenge by composing a schoolyard jingle that rapidly became a hit.

Phony as baloney

Smelly as Cheese

Miss Maloney drinks her own pee

The third-grade teacher, a recent college graduate, mistakenly believed that by pairing me with my second cousin Buster, I would feel more comfortable in my new class. Buster let everyone know that my mother had abandoned her husband. He also used my demotion as irrefutable proof that despite what Yankees thought of themselves, they were in truth shit-house dumb. Buster's father, Walter, was a chronically out of kilt world-class complainer and racist. He took particular delight in peppering every conversation with, "Black son-of-a-bitch, papist traitors, commie perverts, degenerate outside agitators and goddamn Yankee hypocrites."

Chapter 6

The weekend before Halloween our third-grade teacher assigned Buster and me a joint project to report on the science and technology exhibit at the Alabama State Fair. We decided to see a matinee at a local theater before catching a bus to the fairgrounds.

We walked down a sidewalk of heaving slabs that hadn't been repaired since the depression. Passing a park, Buster stopped to take a sip from a drinking fountain. A sign affixed above it read "Whites." Off to the side was another fountain. It had two signs, "Coloreds" and "Out of Order". The only black person around was a tired-looking middle-aged man sitting on a bicycle ice cream wagon. It was too nippy for anyone to think of eating a Popsicle or Eskimo Pie so he just sat there as people walked by.

Several yards away from the street vendor Buster said, "Diddy told me never to buy an ice cream from one of them. They take the wrapper off and lick it and put it back on, then sells it to white folks."

At the theater, we watched "The Thirteen Ghosts". Because of an overwhelming aversion to people's heads popping into my lap, courtesy of the magic of 3-D, I spent most of the movie in the bathroom. When it was over Buster taunted me, "You sure a scaredy cat. Wait till I tell everyone 'bout you peeing yourself."

He bugged me all the way to the bus stop and as we waited forever for the bus to arrive. Even though the bus was mostly empty, the few whites riding it claimed more than half the seats while the blacks on board were squeezed into the last three or four rows. I reluctantly sat next to my cousin while he continued to taunt me. Four stops later I ripped loose with, "Shove it up your ass," and stormed to the back of the bus.

Buster's creamy complexion took on the tint of an undercooked pork chop. "I'm gonna tell your grandiddy."

I plopped down on the rear bench next to an ancient black man with a bamboo cane propped between his open knees. The old man stood up. Shaking his head and muttering something to himself, he held onto a strap dangling from the overhead handrail. When the bus came to a halt he hobbled down the aisle. He snatched his blue-striped railroad cap off his head and held it to his chest. Without looking directly at the driver, he spoke. The driver glanced over his shoulder and uncoiled his body from his seat. He patted the old man on his back, tore off a few bus tickets, and handed them to him. The old man retreated down the stairs, bobbing his head as he exited the bus.

The driver, an immense leather-faced man, stomped down the aisle. He nodded when a white person offered him a word of encouragement and glared at the blacks who looked directly at him. I turned in my seat to look out the rear window to see if we had run over something. When I faced forward he stood in front of me sucking his cheeks in and out. He lowered his hands onto my shoulders and jerking me off the bench, held me above the floor. "Just what do you think you are on about, son?"

"Sorry? I don't know what you mean." My clipped vowels betrayed my northern origin.

"Sorry! You sure are sorry. One sorry little pup that thinks he can just do what he likes, sit where he likes, and talk like he likes. Well, son, you gonna learn that we don't tolerate bothering and making trouble for hard-working decent colored folk. Now you get off of this vehicle before I call a policeman."

Buster came running to the back of the bus. "Sir, he didn't mean nothing by sitting there. He's my cousin and he doesn't understand."

"Don't understand, huh? Then get off here with your cousin and explain what he done wrong while you two are waiting for the next bus to come 'long."

When the bus drove off, Buster jabbed his finger into my chest. "Wait until I tell your grandiddy about this."

"Shut up asshole."

Buster broke into a smile. "Thank you for reminding me that I have to tell Norma how you talked dirty to me."

On the next bus, I took a seat behind the driver. The bus rumbled along its route monotonously toward the fairgrounds. It traveled through the commercial district, past strip malls, used car lots, and freestanding restaurants, every other one serving hickory-smoked barbecue. The bus turned onto a road that cut through Shantytown. A huge clown's face with a blinking red nose advertised TOM'S POTATO CHIPS to the poor blacks living under its shadow. Houses made of untreated lumber and covered with tarpaper squatted on grassless plots of land that turned into mud wallows with each downpour. Emaciated yard dogs snapped and growled at every passing car while infants and toddlers played in the only thing in abundance in their world, dirt.

Nearing suppertime, we entered the State Fair's Science and Technology pavilion. The aroma of hickory smoked barbecue caused Buster's stomach to growl. He latched onto my arm and walked in the direction of the smell. A large crowd looking up at four televisions on rotating pedestals impeded our pilgrimage to the barbecue pit outside the pavilion. The NBC peacock spread its rainbow plumage on all but one of the TVs. Periodically, Pa Cartwright, Little Joe, Adam, and Hoss, wearing white, blue, red, and green shirts, galloped into the bird's moment to plug Bonanza "airing on Sunday nights in glorious living color".

A considerably smaller group of viewers watched the remaining set broadcast in black and white. "Why, don't he just look like a movie star," an elderly woman standing right under the TV remarked. Someone chuckled. "The other one resembles a movie star too, like Pa Kettle in a stolen suit."

I followed the woman's eyes. A young, confident John F. Kennedy beamed from the screen. When Kennedy finished speaking the moderator posed a question to the then Vice-President of the United States. A jowly, badly shaven Richard M. Nixon dressed in a wrinkled charcoal suit responded by punctuating every sentence with "ah, ohm, or harrumph."

Miss Maloney's distinctive upper-crust southern accent stung my ears. "What is this world coming to when those two are running for the highest office in our land?"

*

I craned my neck to see her lecturing a few select students she'd taken to the fairgrounds. I wanted to set up a rousing chant of "Phony as baloney." With only three feet separating me from Miss Maloney, I remained mute and invisible. Miss Maloney despised J.F.K. in descending order of grievances because of his Catholicism, Boston accent, his prissy wife, and Nazi-supporting father. Nixon, she detested for a far simpler but more traditional reason. He was a Republican, as was Lincoln, as was Grant, and so on.

"No self-respecting Southerner will ever support the party which burned, pillaged, and has continued to violate our land for near a hundred years." Miss Maloney finished her tirade and led her gaggle of students to an exhibition of transistor radios. She paused briefly beside me. "Tell your mother hello for me. She was a very good student. I trust that where you are now will prepare you to do something useful someday."

*

Buster did not tell my Grandfather about my humiliation on the bus. He reserved that incident for the kids at recess. He especially relished relating the story to the boys in the older classes, embellishing the event with each retelling.

On the afternoon of Halloween Eve, several kids in the neighborhood got together for a game of touch football in a vacant lot down the street from my Grandfather's house. To liven things up Buster came up with the idea of pretending we were playing the annual Blue Gray Bowl to honor the only field of victory on which the South had ever won over the North.

Buster acted as referee. My sister, one of the strongest runners on the block, played fullback for the South on offense and guard on defense. The smallest, slowest, geekiest kids played for the North. I wound up as the center

27

on offense and tackle on defense for the North. Jeff played for both sides as a punt returner. The game went pretty well as expected. The South walked all over the North.

About thirty minutes into the game Mark Poulet and a couple of other sixth graders showed up. He pushed my sister aside to join the South's team without asking. Janet's face reddened but she retired to the sidelines and crossed her arms over her chest, keeping her cool even when Mark suggested that she could be a cheerleader.

I prepared to hike the football to our quarterback, Malcolm. Mark lined up opposite me. He grinned at me and leaped before Malcolm could say hike. He shoved my face into the field and mashed my nose in the sod.

From across the street, I heard, "You show 'em, son." I glanced over at Mark's father who wore both a belt and suspenders to hold up his pants. The screen door of his bungalow opened and a woman wearing a bathrobe stepped out.

Buster wagged his finger at Mark and shouted, "Five-yard penalty against the South for being offside."

When my side broke from its huddle Mark lined up against me again. Malcolm wanted me to hike the ball and drop back for a lateral. I didn't think it was such a hot idea. I was not that fast and had lousy hands.

Malcolm said, "That's the reason we're doing it- no one will expect me to give you the thing."

I hiked the ball on Malcolm's signal and dropped back. He ran past me and flipped the ball into my hands. No one anticipated the lateral. I had a wide-open field and took off, gaining about twenty yards before someone grabbed me by my shirt and pulled me down. When I started to push myself off the ground two hands forced my face into the turf. I crawfished forward, jumped to my feet, and spun around to see Mark grinning at me.

"Hey, this is supposed to be touch football," Janet yelled from the sidelines.

"Lookie there, the little nigger lover baby needs his big sister to stand up for him."

"Don't call me that again," I told Mark.

"Boy, I'll call you what I want, and I'll make you call yourself it or make you eat grass till you do."

Mark's parents crossed the street to get a better view of the game. I went back into the huddle, half-listening to Malcolm's strategy. "You got that, David?" Malcolm asked.

"Huh?"

"Never mind. Just keep Mark from blitzing me."

Mark didn't give me a chance to get into position. He pounced on me, drove his knee into my back when I went down. He rubbed my face in the grass. "Say it. Say you're a sissy Yankee nigger lover."

Mark's mother called feebly, "Mark you let that boy up; you're twice his size."

"Leave them alone," Mark's dad said. "Sometimes boys gotta get it out their system or their spleen will burst."

Mark shifted his weight, giving me enough space to roll out from under his knee and get to my feet. Janet ran up to me. She wiped the grass and dirt from my face with the sleeve of her shirt. I pushed her away and held back my tears as I trudged off the lot.

Janet said, "You guys are lucky my mother made David promise not to get in any fights."

Mark and his two buddies laughed. "Yeah, sure. Your baby brother near wet himself."

Janet looked at me. "It's okay. I'll tell Mom it wasn't your fault."

Mark glanced over his shoulder and put on a girly voice, "Right, I'll tell your Mommy it wasn't your fault and to change your diaper."

I charged down the field and leapt in the air slamming Mark full force in the stomach with my body. He flew back about three feet. He did not have the time to get up past his knees when I caught him in a sliding headlock. I pulled my forearm against his windpipe and pounded my free fist into his nose and right eye.

"Hit him with a stick!" Mr. Poulet yelled as the other kids formed a circle to prevent him from rescuing his son.

Mrs. Poulet screeched, "He's killin' my baby boy!"

Janet said, "That's enough, David."

"I'm sorry," Mark sobbed. "Don't hurt me no more. I'm a sissy Yankee nigger lover."

I loosened my hold on Mark. "What did you say?"

"I'm a sissy Yankee nigger lover."

I didn't care about his calling me that name. It was the memory of my father's knee crushing my chest as he forced me to wear a diaper that enraged me. I punched him in the eye one more time before releasing him.

Mark dashed through an opening in the circle and into the arms of his mother. She led him across the street back to their porch. His father fell in behind them swatting Mark on the back of his head with each step. "You let a boy half your size shame us on our own street."

My sister held my hand as we walked off the lot. Jeff trotted behind us. He kept reenacting my skirmish with Mark, punching holes in the air and making grunting noises, and yelling, "Ouch! Please don't hit me again."

When we passed Malcolm, he shoved the football into my arms. "Looks like the Blues won this one."

*

My Granddad Agerton was ending a conversation on the phone when we arrived at the house. "Yes Mam' you can be sure I'll talk to him. No, I don't think that'll be necessary, but I'll keep it in mind."

Granddad slipped his glasses down the bridge of his nose and looked over his frames at me. "That was Mrs. Poulet. I think you know her son."

I nodded.

"She says you gave her boy a nasty lickin'. That true?"

I nodded.

"He made Mark's nosebleed and gave him a black

eye," Jeff boasted.

"Mrs. Poulet believes it would be wise to keep you from trick-n-treatin' tonight as a punishment and as a means of protecting the other children in the neighborhood. She believes it might be a good idea to take you to the special ward down at Birmingham General before you hurt yourself or others."

"It wasn't his fault," Janet said.

"Well, what was it all about?"

"Mark kept picking on him," Janet answered.

"Mark's a lot bigger," Jeff piped up. "He made David eat grass."

"That what started the fight, David?" I raised my head. "No Sir."

Granddad pushed his dentures in and out of his mouth and blew out a gust of air from his nostrils. "I don't want to talk about this now. After we've finished supper and I'm done with the paper I will discuss this matter with you on the porch."

I barely chewed my food at supper. I knew I was in for it. My Grandma poked at me with an ear of corn. "Don't be telling me you're hungry later if you leave your supper."

After dinner, my grandfather settled into his armchair next to the oil furnace that stood in the center of the dining room like a bank safe. He finished the front page of his paper, flipped it closed at the crease, and stood up. I followed him to the front door. He held the door open for me and shut it behind us. He sat down on the porch swing and tilted his head to the empty space next to him.

"How'd the fight start?"

"He told me to say I was a Yankee nigger lover," I answered but left out the part about changing my diaper.

"Have colored people ever done anything to you to make you hate them?"

"No, Granddad."

"Then why did what that boy say bother you?"

"Because–"

"Because he called you a name. Well, David, there are worse things you will find in this life than being called a name- now shouldn't you be getting ready to go trick-or-treating?"

Chapter 7

Having the room directly over Mom's, I occasionally heard her sobbing. One night my grandmother's voice drifted through the floorboards. "It's not right, Norma. You've been here three months and you have not called Mr. and Mrs. Brown once to come see their grandchildren."

"I tried Mama, but you know how she feels about me."

"Norma, you can't wait here indefinitely for Ernest to come around. Swallow the pill and tell him you want to go back. The vow as I recall is for better or worse. With luck, this is the worst it will get. You got to call your husband now or decide how you're going to manage with three young ones on your own."

"I'm a trained nurse."

"So you are," Grandma said. "You can go back to caring for the sick, but who will care for your children? As much as I love my grandchildren, it will not be me."

*

Dad arrived in Birmingham December 20th. He made a show of kissing Mom in front of the in-laws, hugged Janet, and shook hands with Jeff and me. The days preceding the holiday Dad didn't shout or threaten to beat my brother or me even once.

Everything considered, my Grandparents were gracious, my Aunt Jean less so. She went to great lengths to ignore Dad, pausing as she walked by him and looking around him as she talked to us, her parents, herself, or in a pinch, to the furniture.

If Dad was offended, he didn't let on. He praised Grandma's cornbread and collard greens. He would pardon himself from Mr. and Mrs. Agerton's company to go out to the curb to smoke. He abstained from his pre-supper martini, after-dinner martini, and double-shot bourbon nightcap, downing vats of iced tea instead. A week of this took its toll. Dad attacked projects around the house rapaciously. He replaced perfectly good drainpipes with new ones and painted the porch swing even though Granddad told him it wasn't necessary. When not fixing stuff, Dad played catch with Jeff and me burning fastballs into our mitts. His frozen smile made it evident that he was wound as tight as a two-dollar watch.

Granddad had placed a pine tree no taller than a yardstick on the parlor coffee table. He disliked the crass ostentatiousness of the holiday season. Christmas in his opinion was a religious holiday that got waylaid by Thomas Nast and Coca-Cola. He had conceded the battle and went along with the holiday as far as his conscience would allow rather than have his grandchildren feel left out of the festival season. On Christmas morning Jeff and I tiptoed downstairs. I could not believe the haul of gifts piled higher than the coffee table tree. Jeff went straight for the Knucklehead dummy he'd been asking for since he saw a ventriloquist on Ed Sullivan. He tried to say "Boy oh boy" without moving his lips.

An Indy electric racecar set was prominently displayed in the center of the room. We fell to our knees and selected a car each and turned on the transformer. Completely engaged in the thrill of the race, we failed to sense our father's shadow fall across us. Jeff caught the full force of Dad's wrath first. He received a barefooted kick to his side which flipped him over the racecar track. Dad flogged us with the buckle end of his belt.

"Keep your voices down or I'll give you something to cry about," he warned through clenched teeth.

We scrambled on our hands and knees for cover and wedged ourselves behind the furnace. This move was a tactical error. We had sacrificed our mobility, trapped in a space where Dad could flail at us unceasingly.

Our screams awakened the house. Mom dashed into the dining room and whimpered, "Ernest, Ernest, stop."

"Norma, see what happens when you try to raise these boys without me? They have no respect, no decency." He continued to slap at us behind the cold furnace as he lectured Mom. "These worthless pieces of crap crept down here like thieves, depriving you of the joy of seeing their faces when they saw their gifts."

"Enough!" My granddad's voice echoed in the room. "Put that belt down and leave those boys alone."

My father spun on his heel. Granddad held Dad at bay with a look of disgust. Dad flung his belt at the wall.

"They are my boys, Mr. Agerton."

"That they are Ernest but it's my house."

By midday, Dad calmed down and tried to make amends. He talked about the University of Georgia's chances of winning the Orange Bowl. My grandparent's friends and relatives wandered in and out of the house all afternoon to share a cup of teetotalers' eggnog, pecan divinity, and fruitcake.

At 17:00 sharp Dad announced that it was time to gather up our things to go over to his parents' house. He ordered me to help him load the car with his oblations for his parents. Jeff made himself scarce. He sat upstairs in a corner cradling his dummy and sucking his thumb. Dad was uncharacteristically talkative, exuding warmth bordering on affection.

"Your Grandmother Brown will be pleased to see you all."

"Why didn't she call us?" I asked.

"Guess she saw no reason to invite your mother over until matters had been resolved to her satisfaction."

Chapter 8

We pulled up to a curb in a blue and white station wagon Swiss-cheesed with rust holes. A perfectly manicured lawn rolled down a small hill on which a large house sat. The Chief, a smoldering Hava-Tampa cigar gripped between his teeth, stood under a portico supported by antebellum colonnades that didn't match the mansion's Boston brickwork. We trudged up the stairs behind Dad.

The Chief stepped off the porch onto an oval flagstone landing. He removed the cigar from his mouth and extended his hand to my father. Sunlight glinted off a large diamond set in a square gold ring with three smaller diamonds on each side of the rock. Ernest Henry "Skinny" Brown wore the retirement gift from the city of Birmingham on his middle finger next to a wedding band made from a twenty-dollar gold double eagle and his Masonic signet.

Looking as round as a beer barrel and just as solid, he pumped Dad's hand, patted each grandchild on the head, and handed out silver dollars. He pointed to a white cellophane tree in the bay window of the living room. A floodlight covered with a tricolored rotating disc cast washed-out hues of blue, green, and red on the wall behind the tree.

"Damnedest thing isn't it, Ernest Junior? That tree will last a hundred years. Just dust it off and put it up every Christmas and it looks the same."

"Yes Sir," Dad said.

"It didn't come cheap if that's what you're thinking."

"I don't believe it did, Sir."

The Chief slipped his arm through Dad's and walked him to the holly-trimmed entrance of the house. The door flung open before the Chief touched the knob. Roberta, the family maid, greeted us. The elderly black woman had worked for Louise since Dad was a toddler. She placed both her arthritic hands on the sides of Dad's face. "My, my, Sir, Junior is the mirror image of Miss Louise."

"Roberta, dinner is growing cold!" a voice, icy, and shrill, announced from inside the house. "Quit your lollygagging and get them to the table."

My Dad raised his arm in a wagon train leader's forward-ho sweep. We dutifully fell into line and followed him into the house. My Grandmother Brown posed like Joan Crawford beside a doublewide staircase as we entered the foyer. Without expression, she studied the grocer's daughter and her brood. At her feet were two Pekinese. Kim, the chestnut-colored one, growled and hid behind her mistress. Toy, the white one, had one eye missing. Grandmother Brown grasped a knob on the balustrade. She beckoned us with a pale floating hand. My father, his posture noticeably stooped, moved toward Louise with small, cautious steps.

"Ernest Junior, you're late for Christmas Supper," Grandmother Brown said and added, "Norma, it must be difficult keeping to a schedule after such a long separation. I expected to hear from you sooner, but never-the-less, Happy Holidays."

"Mrs. Brown, I did telephone. Roberta answered. She said she'd tell you I called."

"Dear, now that things are back to normal, call me Mother Brown. Roberta must have failed to remember to give me your messages. Poor old woman would forget her head if it wasn't attached to her neck."

"Yes Mam."

"That is better. When you see your parents, give them my best wishes for the season."

Louise's eyes fell on Jeff and me. "Let's get to the table so we can eat and open the gifts." She addressed us in a flat voice. "You will like that, won't you boys?"

She draped her arm around Janet's shoulder and kissed her on the forehead, "I imagined you'd call, darling. I've really looked forward to seeing you." She cast a sideways glance at my mother. "But I understand the circumstances. It would have been awkward."

We marched behind Grandmother Brown toward a lavish Christmas feast, compliments of people owing or wanting favors of the Chief. Every Christmas Season he received smokes, bourbon, and enough food to dress a banquet table from judges, governors, and civic leaders ranging from Greek restaurant owners to white and black church and business leaders. His favorite adage was, "You don't get respect, you earn it."

A grand piano and a full-length suit of armor occupied the great hallway leading into the dining room. Since no one could play the piano, it collected dust. Jeff and I had found a use for the suit of armor. With rubber bands strung between our fingers, we fired off paper clips, spitballs, anything with enough weight to fly into the raised visor of the helmet.

In the center of the solid oak dining table was a turkey big enough to feed a Salvation Army Mission. Steam rose from a porcelain reindeer and sleigh gravy boat separating the turkey from a Virginia ham glazed with honey and studded with cloves and red currents. The Chief stood behind his chair at the head of the table. Louise occupied the chair to his right.

"Ernest Junior, sit beside your mother." The Chief pointed at the chairs at his left for Janet and Mom. He signaled my brother and me to sit down next to Dad.

Table settings were absent at our places. I glanced over at Jan; she had a holly-trimmed dinner plate, cut crystal water goblet, two forks, two knives, and soup and dessert spoons. My Grandfather Brown waited until we all clasped hands. He cleared his throat. "Ernest Junior, say grace."

My father's approach to giving thanks was economical. "Thank you for what we are about to receive. Amen."

"Okay, boys, off to the kitchen with you. Roberta has your plates ready," Louise ordered before the Amen faded.

"Why does Jan get to eat in the fancy dining room?" Jeff asked.

The slap aimed at my brother's face halted short of his cheek when the Chief coughed and said, "Not at the table, Ernest Junior. You can discipline the boy in the morning. It wouldn't be right to do it now. It's Christmas."

Jeff stood up and walked toward the double doors leading into the kitchen.

"Come back here," Dad said. "What do you have to say to your grandmother?"

My brother arched his eyebrows and said in a voice that dripped insincerity, "I am very, very sorry, Grandma. Merry, Merry Christmas and Happy, Happy New Year."

Dad shoved back his chair and leaped to his feet. Jeff raced for the double doors with my father in pursuit. Dad aborted the chase when he banged his kneecap against the corner of the serving trolley.

"Come back to the table Junior," the Chief ordered. "Sit down. You should not allow the boy to spoil this day for everyone else."

Louise exhaled, "With manners those boys have, it's a charity that I allow them to eat in the house at all. Oh well, it is the season of forgiveness. Besides, can I really blame them? Bad habits begin at home I am told."

My father sank further into his chair. His mint green eyes settled on me. "What are you still doing here? Get in there with your brother."

I knew better than to tarry and quickened my pace toward the kitchen. As I passed by her, Mom bowed her head and started shoveling candied yams into her mouth.

After dinner, the Chief shouted, "Boys join the family in the den."

When we entered the room Dad was pouring triple fingers of Jack Daniels into two tumblers. The Chief patted Dad on the back as he took his glass. He uncorked a china humidor on the coffee table and removed a cigar. Dad fetched an ashtray and held it while my Grandfather lit a match and inhaled the flame, taking care not to touch the cigar to the fire.

Around dusk, the doorbell rang. Charlie, my Dad's younger brother, swaggered into the room with his family. Dad retreated to the bar and fixed two more bourbons for the new arrivals. Charlie's wife was also named Jean to the other Jean's everlasting disapproval. A Southern belle down to her petite feet, Charlie's Jean had been a dancer and model. Her three children were blonde, blue-eyed, and beautiful. Jeff and I resembled gypsies standing next to them. Our olive skin turned dusty in the sun while Jean's children turned golden, and their hair became the color of corn silk. My Grandmother embraced Charlie's Jean, then gathered my cousins in her arms and smothered them in kisses. "Honey we have been waiting for y'all to arrive to open the gifts. We wanted to see the expressions on the children's faces."

The Chief motioned his sons to come over to him. He flopped an arm over each of their shoulders. "Junior, Charles, you boys don't see enough of each other."

"Hold that thought, Pap," Charlie interrupted and handed his father a gift-wrapped bottle.

My grandfather beamed when he tore off the silver foil and uncovered a decanter of Wild Turkey. "He knows what his daddy likes, doesn't he?" He put down the bottle. "If your brother ever tires of playing soldier you two could go into business. With my connections, your brains and charm, and Ernest Junior's bulldog persistence, you'd do real well for yourselves."

Dad flushed. Charlie picked up the Wild Turkey and switched it from hand to hand. "Come on Pap, Ernie made

Captain. When I was in the service, I was lucky to make sergeant and still luckier to keep my stripes. And you got to admit he was a hell-of-a-lot better fireman than I was a policeman. Your old pal, Bull, saw that right away."

When my father returned to Birmingham after WW II the chief had told him to join the fire department rather than the police force. The potential political fall-out inherent in charges of nepotism may have had something to do with the Chief's order. More likely his logic was different. One of my uncles swore between rare moments of sobriety that the Chief told my father, "If you do something to screw up it's better that it smears the fireboys than my boys."

"That cracker didn't know a good policeman from a mule," the Chief snarled.

"Pap, he did what he had to do," Charlie said.

This was true and was the cause of animosity between the Chief and Bull Connor. Connor dismissed my uncle from the police force after Charlie got drunk one night and drove through Birmingham firing his service revolver at the streetlights. The Chief never forgave Connor. Following the Selma march, he wrote a letter to the paper calling for his former friend's resignation as Public Safety Commissioner for exercising bad judgment and giving Birmingham a black eye internationally.

The Chief claimed that he had told Bull to issue Martin Luther King a parade permit. Connor ignored his advice and instead alternated between beating the marchers with weighted batons, sweeping them down the street with water cannons, and releasing attack dogs. The mayhem was broadcast across the globe. In the Soviet Union images of protesters being brutalized became definitive proof in their propaganda war against a corrupt, racist USA.

Louise stroked Charlie's cheek with the back of her knuckles. "Don't go putting yourself down, sweetheart. It just takes some boys a little longer to find themselves."

The next morning my father woke us up at 0:500. He ordered us to keep quiet because people were still sleeping. My Mother shuffled back and forth from the house to the car. At one point she stopped and asked in a monotone voice, "May we drop by my parents to say goodbye?"

"I'd have expected three months of being under the same roof as them would be enough to last you a lifetime."

By sunrise the car was packed, and we were ready to roll. Louise and the Chief walked us to the curb. Louise passed a grocery bag full of the previous night's leftovers through the window. "This should feed you until you get past Bowling Green. Don't see any reason why y'all should be spending good money in bad restaurants."

"Thank you Mrs. Bro..." Mom started to say, "I mean, Mother Brown."

Chapter 9

When we returned to Detroit my mother's arguments with my father ceased completely. And so my mother, who suppressed her rage to live, survived. Over the years she slipped in and out of bouts of profound depression, becoming invisible at one point, disappearing into a book, the written word offering her sanctuary from her bleak world.

Our family existed in this limbo for eighteen months then Dad received a transfer to Colorado Springs attached to the rank of Major. A couple of weeks before we left Detroit, Dad and Mom returned home at midnight from celebrating his promotion at the officer's club. He woke Janet, Jeff, and me and ordered us to report to the kitchen. Dad wore his dress blues and held in his palm a plush-covered box, the kind that rings come in. He flipped the lid of the box open. I gazed half asleep at two gold oak leaves secured to a piece of cardstock. Dad picked up Jan and stood her on a kitchen chair.

"David, give the leaves to your sister." Dad removed the silver double bars from his epaulets. Janet pinned the oak leaves in their place. She broke into a smile when he hugged her and kissed her on the cheek.

Mom said, "Jeffrey, David, tell your father congratulations."

We mouthed the words. Dad leaned over and extended his hand to shake. "Okay boys, hit the rack. We got a long drive ahead of us. It's Pikes Peak or bust for the Browns."

"What's Pikes Peak?" Jeff asked.

Dad rubbed Jeff's burr haircut. "That's the tallest mountain in Colorado, fourteen thousand one-hundred and eleven feet."

The drive from Detroit to Colorado was different than other long hauls we did over the years. Dad stopped at regular intervals to allow us to stretch our legs. He bought us tacky souvenirs and Stucky's pecan logs whenever he filled up with gas. The scenery through Michigan and Ohio remained remarkably the same, track home suburbs with only slight variations in the hues of industrial gray snow until we crossed the Kentucky border. The blue-green grass of Kentucky's rolling hills morphed into massive fir-covered mountains whose peaks disappeared in a dense coverage of clouds. Dad went impromptu on us and took an unscheduled trip up Smoky Mountain. When we reached the summit, he bought us an "I Climbed Old Smoky" pennant. He said, "This mountain is a molehill compared to what you'll see in Colorado."

*

The snow-capped mountain peaks sparkled under the Colorado sun. The movers came in and out of a white stucco house depositing brown boxes in the living room. Our furniture, an eclectic rummage sale mix of beds, dressers, couches, and tables had been placed haphazardly around the house. Mom's eyes brightened when she inspected each room. By our standards the house was palatial. It had three bedrooms; the master had its own bathroom, a closed kitchen, a living room, and a separate dining area.

Dad pulled Mom toward him and hugged her. "Norma, this is just a start. We're here for a while. No more moving around every two years. Who knows, we might buy our own place and settle down for good."

If it could be said that Dad was ever happy, then in Colorado he was happy. The mountains, clean air, and bountiful parklands acted as a tonic. When he arrived home from work he would go out into the front yard with a cup of coffee in hand and stare straight ahead without moving, watching as the pink rind of the sun dissolved behind Pikes Peak.

Dad's triple hospital administration assignment for ADC, NORAD, and SAC kept him away from home for about two weeks out of every month. When he did appear, he was a different guy. In Detroit dipping into his Martini olive jar had been an offense demanding the severest corporal punishment. But in Colorado Dad placed the olives stuffed with red pimentos out for us to eat.

He actually expressed an interest in what was happening in my life. I told him that I enjoyed exploring the sandstone buttes and mesas near our house with the BB gun he had given me for my eighth birthday. The truth of the matter was that I generally gave the BB rifle over to my brother to plink away at rodents. Meanwhile, I would locate a warm rock in the buttes and lie on my back looking up at the sun until red spots obscured my vision. I imagine Dad guessed something was amiss when he took us out to the rifle range. My sister and brother could outshoot me with ease.

"I thought you've been practicing," Dad said as Jeff banged the eyes out of his human-shaped targets.

One night during dinner Mom smiled and said, "A doctor at the clinic offered me a job while his nurse is off having a baby."

"Norma, my mother didn't have to work to help out my father and you're sure not going to either."

"Ernest, it'll only be temporary till the other nurse returns."

"Just make sure you don't go telling Mother."

On weekends we took family excursions into the mountains. On one such expedition, we traveled halfway through the state to look at the Royal Gorge and drove across a bridge suspended a mile above an open wound in the earth's crust. Another day trip we threaded our way along a narrow road and stopped at a clear lake sitting inside a bowl of mountains. Dad got out of the car and popped the trunk. He took out a Coleman cooler, a fishing rod, and a folding aluminum chair. He made potted meat sandwiches for all of us. After he distributed the sandwiches, he picked up his fishing rig and crouched near a boulder at the edge of the lake. I knelt next to him.

"Your mother really loves it here."

He tied off an artificial worm and handed me the rig. I rose and cast what seemed like a mile away from shore. It was chilly but I didn't mind. Dad pointed at a clearing on a mountain across the lake.

"We bought two lots over there. When I retire that's where we're going to settle down. Hell, it's an investment."

"What's an investment?"

"Something you put your time, money, and hope into, knowing that it will pay you back ten times in the future." He placed his arm over my back. "You kids are our biggest investment."

A year later Dad piled us in the car and drove to an empty lot surrounded by the skeleton frames of homes in a new development in Colorado Springs. Mom held Dad's hand as they paced off a rectangular boundary delineated by orange lengths of string attached to surveyor stakes.

"Boys, your room will be in the basement. Your sister's and the new baby's room will be upstairs," Mom said. "If it's a boy we will call him Thomas Ward Brown."

"What if it's a girl?" Jeff asked. "I haven't thought about it."

While my parents retired to one corner of the lot to describe an invisible family room, Janet smugly confessed that she knew about the baby before we did.

To pull in some extra cash Dad started signing up for more TDYs. Between running the household in Dad's absence and volunteering at the clinic, Mom appeared happier than anytime I could remember. When the new house neared completion Mom began to show her pregnancy. The new house was her domain. Dad was not around to put in his two cents on how to decorate it. She climbed a stepladder to hang drapes, pushed couches and chairs from one side of the living room to the other only to move them somewhere else again ten minutes later. The money she had saved working as a nurse went into purchasing furniture including a real mahogany dining room set and a matching china cabinet. With the leftover cash, she furnished the baby's nursery.

One evening while Dad inspected field hospitals in Canada along the DEW line I heard Louise shout into the telephone, "Norma, a woman of your age should know better. Even rabbits know when to stop."

Mom placed the receiver in its cradle and spread a large sheet of white butcher paper on the floor. She started to draw a forest and a menagerie of deer, beavers, raccoons, rabbits, and birds. She handed us colored markers.

"When I was younger I wanted to be a doctor or an artist. I was accepted to college to study science but your Grandfather said no. I pleaded with Daddy to let me go. I'd received a scholarship from a women's church group. He was proud of me but even with a scholarship he couldn't afford to send me to college. So I used the money to go to New Orleans to become a nurse. I returned to Birmingham the same time your father came back from the Second World War.

In the Aleutians, he carried a photograph of me dressed in my nursing uniform. His buddies said I looked like Elizabeth Taylor. He told them that I was ten times more beautiful than her. Your father may seem like an angry man, but remember he loves us all." She took the colored drawing into the nursery and taped it to the ceiling above the crib. I am not sure whether she was trying to convince us or herself about his love.

A week later my Grandmother Agerton arrived from Birmingham to help Mom during her last days of pregnancy. She stayed for a month. One afternoon when Jeff and I came home from school Janet met us at the door. Mom and my Grandmother were not there. Janet said Mom and Grandma had caught a cab to the hospital and that they were trying to locate Dad. Considering it was his hospital it should not have been all that hard to find him.

That evening Grandma came home with Dad and fixed us a dinner of deep southern fried chicken, collard greens, and biscuits. She apologized for not having had time to bake a pie. She would see to it that we had one for Mom when she returned from the hospital with our new baby brother. Grandma never had a chance to fulfill her promise. Dad thanked her for coming and put her on a plane by the weekend.

The renewal of the cycle of hit-and-run attacks by my father coincided with Tommy's birth. Jeff and I were beaten for infractions as small as failing to push the broom from the back of the garage to the front when we swept. Dad made it especially hard on Jeff. Once when the phone rang Jeff picked it up and said "Hello." Before he could say anything else my father snatched the receiver and pounded Jeff on his back with it.

"When you answer the telephone in my house you will say, Major Brown's residence. With whom do you wish to speak? Do I make myself clear or do I have to tattoo it on your hand?"

The Cuban Missile Crisis provided a brief respite for the family. Fidel Castro had encouraged Russia to place long-range missiles capable of delivering nuclear warheads to American targets on his island. This action outraged John Fitzgerald Kennedy, even though the USA had its own nukes aimed at the Soviet Union from Turkey, and also had one of its largest Navy bases located in Cuba.

Being a military town to the bone, everyone in Colorado Springs lived through those dangerous days of brinkmanship on a personal level. Colonel Fuller, Dad's friend and commander, would come over and talk about how things were going from bad to worse.

"Goddamn politicians. They start the crap and we gotta clean up after them. McNamara and Kennedy are determined to set the world on fire, Ernie."

"Hell, Batista is a rank bastard. If we hadn't supported him in the first place there wouldn't be any Castro," Dad said. Then he said something I would hear him repeat like an incantation over the ensuing years. "A dictator is a dictator but once you're engaged you better be committed."

Kennedy's blockade put Colorado Springs on full alert. Being the nerve center of North America's defense and retaliation network marked the sleepy little mountain town as a major burn zone. Fathers throughout the town started disappearing. Sometimes MPs would show up at houses and escort pilots and tactical field personnel to military cars with their engines running.

By late October the crisis registered in the schools. At my school, we went through daily nuclear attack drills. When the fire alarm bell rang my teacher clapped her hands and the kids rushed into the hall. We sat with backs against the wall, our heads trapped between our elbows. A joke circulated by older boys went, "In the case of a nuclear war, lean over, place your head between your legs, and kiss your sweet ass goodbye."

As I walked Jeff home after school the wailing of air raid sirens sounded from one end of the city to the other. We were several blocks away from our house and started running when a military police car pulled up next to us. He pointed at a drainage ditch beside the road, ordered us to lie face down in it until after the air raid sirens stopped, then drove off.

When the sirens went dead, we climbed out of the culvert. Our clothes were smeared with wet dirt, dog shit, and who knows what else. We had a painful case of tinnitus when we got back home. Mom was sitting in the front yard smoking a cigarette. The possibility of Colorado Springs and the rest of the world for that matter being obliterated did not dawn on me until years later.

That evening Dad failed to show up for dinner. He had been called away on short notice, sparing us the traditional farewell beating. Three weeks later we received postcards. Jeff got a picture of a Canadian goose from Labrador. Janet received a photo of the Northern Lights. My card featured frozen tundra with the words, Welcome to the Top of the World: Thule Greenland.

Jeff and I never shared in our friends 'concern for their displaced fathers. We had come to measure a good or bad duty assignment relative to the amount of time Dad was absent from home. Mom took us out to dinner and played Monopoly with us in front of the fireplace. My father sent us notes with loving comments like, "Mind your Mother. I will be back soon."

The Russians withdrew their missiles and military personnel trickled back into Colorado Springs. Dad came home. He kissed Mother and Janet and shook hands with Jeff and me.

He did not ask us if we had been bad or good. He sat down in an armchair, opened up his grip, and started pulling out gift after gift. I got a miniature stuffed wolverine, a knife carved out of whalebone, and several pictures Dad had taken of Greenland's white-on-white landscape from the air. He told Mom to mix them double Martinis.

"Colonel Fuller told me he's going to Cincinnati to head up a joint corps of engineering and emergency evacuation project for the Midwest."

"Oh, that's a shame," Mom said. "He and Mavis like it here so much."

"Yeah," Dad replied sullenly. "But it's the nature of the business we're in."

Mom turned on her heel and faced Dad with two Martinis in her hands. "What are you leading to Ernest?"

Dad took his drink. "What do you think I'm talking about?"

"But you promised."

"Goddamn Norma, don't be an idiot."

Dad was wrong about Pike's Peak. Mount Elbert is the Rocky Mountain State's tallest peak. By summer break the family was on the road headed for Ohio.

Chapter 10

Our first three months in Cincinnati we lived in the Stratford Apartments, a complex inhabited by a cross-section of professors and students from Xavier University. With so few kids around, Jeff and I learned to play together without bickering. I created a superhero character named Captain Stardust and wore red swimming trunks pulled over a pair of pajama bottoms, a white sleeveless undershirt, and a beach towel for a cape. Jeff's alter ego was Electric Man. He refused to wear a costume, saying it was bad enough we had to play this stupid game without looking like retards.

One afternoon I climbed a lamppost, jumped down, and landed on the pavement on my knees. In a panic I ran around in circles, creating a concentric spiral of blood on the cement. Jeff raced home to get Mom. Seeing the accident from her balcony a woman rushed out. She knelt beside me and stroked my hair as she inspected my gashed knees. She wore a sari. My hand brushed against her bronze stomach when she helped me stand. She led me toward her apartment building where she said she had plasters. As we arrived at her building's entrance Mom showed up holding a paperback in one hand and an unlit cigarette in the other.

"Thank you for your help but I can take it from here. I'm a nurse," Mom said.

"My husband is a medical student," the woman said tilting her head to read the book's title.

"Really," Mom said, "I wanted to be a Doctor, but you know how the times were."

The woman made a clucking sound with her tongue. Pierced through the side of her nose, a tiny diamond stud glinted in the sunlight.

Mom held up her book. "Have you read *My Cousin Rachel*?"

"Oh yes, I love Daphne du Maurier."

When I leaned closer to get a better look at the diamond, blood started flowing down my legs again. "Oh, I'm sorry," I said when I saw my blood on her sari. My mother stepped back and gestured with an all-encompassing sweep at my peculiar costume. "Have you lost your mind? You look like a rag picker. What have you been up to?"

I stumbled over my words as I tried to make a case for inventing a game to keep my brother entertained.

"I guess David takes after me. I used to act out scenes from stories I read when I was a child. My mother called me a bookworm."

"I also love books," The woman said then pushed open the door of her building.

Mom followed her and left me outside. For the rest of the summer, they took turns discussing literature over tea and cookies.

Jeff and I wandered back to our apartment. The curtains were drawn, and the living room was inkpot black. While we groped our way to the light switch Janet's voice pierced the darkness. "Oh God, hell-up me." A flashlight flicked on under her chin.

"Look what they've done to me!" She screeched. A luminous green face with black lips sucked breathless screams from us. We clung to each other like climbing ivy. The overhead light went on.

"Relax, it's only your sister," Martin, our upstairs neighbor, said.

Cindy, Martin's wife, sat on a stool with a charcoal pencil wavering in front of my sister's face. Jan wore a rubber cap with flaps that extended below her upper mandible.

Martin and Cindy attended the Cincinnati College of Mortuary Science. Martin's chosen profession may have been a calculated slap in the face of his father, a respected Kentucky cardiologist. Cindy was born into the trade. Her father's company ranked as one of the largest casket manufacturers in the Tri-State area. Cindy had given Jan a sweatshirt from her school with a smiling skull-and-crossbones placed inside a shield with a ribbon banner reading "CMS 1882" under the death's head.

On the coffee table were a makeup case and a large book opened to a gruesome photo of a person with the side of his face missing. Martin crossed the room quickly and flipped the book closed before I could get a better look.

"What's harder," Jan asked as Cindy helped her remove the rubber cap. "Fixing up a person who has been in a car accident or someone who shot himself through the head?"

"Depends on what kind of gun and how close the muzzle was to the person's head," Cindy answered.

"The type of ammunition makes a difference." Martin, a straight-A student when it came to restoration, looked with disdain at his wife. "Overall, I'd say car accidents are worse.

But you hardly ever have to do an open casket affair after a bad accident. For some reason people want you to put their loved ones back together like a jigsaw puzzle after they've blown their heads apart."

Cindy handed Janet two dollars for using her for their cosmetic restoration practice. "Nobody wants to admit their husband or kid committed suicide."

Chapter 11

The summer went by slowly. Mom had a friend; Janet had Martin and Cindy, and even Jeff found some kid his age to kick back with while I played out a solitary game of Captain Stardust. I felt grateful when Dad told us he had rented a split-level house in Sharonville, a rural community being gobbled up by urban refugees. We moved into our new house across the road from a working farm the day before my birthday.

The next morning Dad yelled for me to come to the backyard. "Happy birthday," he said.

A black and white border collie sat between a green plywood doghouse and an aluminum pole with a tetherball dangling from a rope.

A boy's best friend is his dog never rang true for me. Still, a present was a present, and at least Jet was an improvement over my previous year's gift, Fun with Math.

"Happy birthday," Dad repeated. "A dog's a responsibility. You'll feed, bathe, and clean up the pooch's shit every day. I warn you that spot checks will take place."

Like a magnet, the tetherball pole pulled kids from around the neighborhood to our yard. Part of the attraction was the game, but the actual draw was Jet. Dad sunk the pole into the ground a few yards away from the doghouse. Jet acted docile and behaved well as long as the local children stayed off his turf. Whenever some kid leaned against his doghouse, Jet peed on the intruder's leg.

Within a month word got around that the new kids had a really neat tetherball court and an even cooler dog. Randy Traynor, Paul Schepp, Freddie Hooper, and the local bullies, Clive and Zeke Fannon were regulars at the tetherball pole. Jet became so used to seeing them that he stopped lifting his leg when they leaned against his house.

I was lucky to have Randy as a friend. A lot of kids regarded him as one of the coolest boys in grade five. Though suffering from asthma, he held the record for the hundred-yard dash and was undefeated during gym period wrestling matches. He came from what was then known as a "broken family". Playground gossip had it that his Mom lived with some guy outside the matrimonial pen while his real father did major time in the State Pen. At first Randy detested me on the simple principle that I was the new kid on the block. I was used to that. Arrive at a school, get in a fight, make a couple of acquaintances, and move on.

During my second week in gym class, I was paired up against Randy on the mat. Most of the kids seemed disinterested in the match. They probably saw his victory as a foregone conclusion. Randy found himself flat on his back and counted out before he could tie up. The gym teacher must have assumed it was a fluke and had us go once more from standing position and twice from referee's position with the same results.

The coach pulled Randy and me aside after class. He wanted us to join the newly formed wrestling team. We'd wrestle against other elementary schools and clubs. With the skills we learned we would be shoo-ins to make the junior varsity team in middle school. We agreed without hesitation. This began my five-year cycle as an insufferable jock.

Paul Schepp, Jeff's friend, owned the largest comic book collection in the school. Dad considered comic books trash and ripped them apart in front of us when we left them lying around. Paul's memory was phenomenal. He could recall verbatim back issues of Spiderman, The Fantastic Four, Batman, and the Green Lantern. Paul ambled around the neighborhood with a rucksack filled with comics. He shared his treasures without wanting anything in return. However, like his favorite character, The Incredible Hulk, Paul transformed from a gentle boy into a raging psycho in a flash, his trigger, his own blood. Some people have a glass jaw. Paul had a crystal nose. The lightest tap on his snout called forth a gusher.

Clive and Zeke Fannon took special delight in smashing Paul in the face with the tetherball. Paul would clench his fist and howl in agony. He threw haymakers at the person or thing closest to him, usually losing his balance and landing on his ass.

When Randy wasn't around, the Fannons took over the yard giving us noogies and punches in the arm if we didn't do exactly what they told us. I complained to my mother and she said, as she looked up from her book, "You should feel sorry for them. They probably act the way they do because they have no friends."

"Of course, they don't have friends, Mom! They're assholes."

That evening I stood before Dad with a bar of soap stuffed in my mouth while he lectured me on talking disrespectfully to Mom. "You may think you are a hot shot but remember, anytime you are too big for me to handle, I'll use a goddamn baseball bat to keep you in line."

More of a hanger-on than a friend, Freddie Hooper from next door showed Jeff some chords on the guitar. Freddie had an uncanny ability to play any popular tune by ear after hearing it only once.

*

I tolerated Freddie to be close to his sister, Shirley. Well ahead of her classmates in developing breasts she'd perfected teasing to a science. Like her mother, Pearl, Shirley dyed her hair blonde, wore skintight pedal pushers, and men's button-down shirts knotted above her tummy like Tuesday Weld.

"The only way out of Kentucky is to either marry or die," Pearl joked when knocking down a beer with her latest husband in their front yard.

Carl Hooper spent most of the year between jobs. He possessed boundless generosity, offering to steal tools from his latest employer for my father. Dad always turned him down. Pearl invited my Mom to join her bowling team. At first, Mom declined, saying she was too busy what with volunteering at the hospital and keeping the house in order. Finally, Mom agreed to go out. After four weeks she quit, saying simply, "Pearl and her friends are not my type of people."

"Don't be a snob, Norma," Dad said. "Make friends. This new assignment is going to keep me away a lot, and I sure the hell don't intend to entertain you when I'm home."

Mom's rejection of Pearl's group started a feud. Mrs. Hooper threw trash over our fence. We also started receiving obscene phone calls in a woman's thinly disguised Kentucky briar-hopper accent.

"Major Brown's residence, to whom do you wish to speak?" I recited into the phone.

A voice spoke over the thunder of balls rolling down a polished alley and colliding with bowling pins, "Your bitch Mama thinks she's better than everyone. Maybe if she'd loosen up, her toy soldier would stay home more often." I hung up and never repeated what I had heard. The feud ended abruptly. Pearl came over to the house the day after New Year's bearing a tray of rice pudding. Mom sent me outside and invited Pearl into the living room for coffee. About an hour later Pearl came out. She glanced at me and said, "Treat your Mama good. She deserves it."

A month later Jan asked me out of nowhere, "I guess you're happy things have improved between Mom and Mrs. Hooper."

"Sure," I said. "Pearl is letting me see Shirley again."

Jan waited a few seconds before speaking. "Do you know why Mrs. Hooper brought that pudding over?"

"I guess it was a peace offering."

"Of sorts, Carl was laid off in July. Mom found out that the Hoopers were surviving on Spam and oatmeal. She bought a month's supply of groceries and had them delivered to Pearl. She went to Sears and bought clothes, toys, and books, had them gift-wrapped, and sent to their house. Pearl must have found out what Mom did."

Chapter 12

One day Dad assigned me to clean the garage. The task had to be completed before he got home. I started by stacking all the boxes and trunks that had littered the garage since our move from Colorado. I ran across a footlocker with Sgt. E.H. Brown stenciled on its lid.

Divided into an upper and lower section, the footlocker contained several long narrow jewelry boxes and some pamphlets. The gray booklets bore such titles as Treatment of Chemical Attack Victims, Medical Team Response to Nuclear Fallout, and Germ Warfare Treatment Protocol. Captain E.H. Brown had prepared them all for the Bethesda War College. Each of the jewelry boxes held a bronze, gold, or silver disk attached to a red, white, and blue striped bunting with various war theaters stamped on the medallions. I pinned the WWII Pacific Campaign 1941-1945 medal on my polo shirt. I continued to poke around through the tray, uncovering loose photos of a long-haired, younger version of my father.

In one photo he wore aviator shades, a slip of black hair carefully arranged above his eyebrows. With a snow-covered hill as a backdrop, he posed on a pair of skis, a rifle slung over his shoulder. In another picture, he and some of his friends passed around a brew.

With Dad's head tilted back, a buddy poured a can of beer into his open mouth. He smiled in every photograph, unlike the man who wore his uniform like a hair shirt and who told me to "Wipe that grin off your face. Only idiots and drunks smile all the time."

The last photo in the bunch was more recent. It was a black and white shot of Dad in his dress blues with his double captain bars. His youthful smile had disappeared, replaced by a straight line.

I lifted the tray. A wool coat covered the contents of the box. It was a vintage GI winter coat, the sort of coat that American soldiers wore in the European theater during the war. Underneath the coat was an empty flap holster sitting on top of a pile of khaki pants and a matching jacket. When I pulled the clothes out, I discovered two black photo albums at the bottom of the trunk and a velveteen souvenir book, Folies-Bergére (1952) embossed in gold letters on its cover.

On the first page of the souvenir book was a woman, naked from the waist up to her neck. Sequined bandoleers propped up her breasts as she walked down a white stairway. An enormous fan made of feathers was strapped to her back. Muscle men wearing leopard-spotted loincloths supported her fan on either side to prevent her from pitching forward and crashing through a chorus line of nude dancers. Presented on every glossy black and white page of the Folies book was a scene from history or mythology. Cleopatra, reclining on a divan, held what looked like a rubber snake to an exposed breast. Samson, his head resting in voluptuous Delilah's lap, slept as she waved a pair of shears over his thick mane of hair.

I placed the Folies-Bergére at the bottom of the trunk and picked up the photo albums. The first one contained pictures of my Dad from his teenage years. A lot of the pictures featured him with my mother. They smiled in all the shots, sometimes holding hands, never looking directly at the camera as though unaware of a phantom photographer preserving their youth.

The second collection held more of the same sort of photographs. As I flipped through it a green, legal-size folder fell out. My father's name appeared on a report entitled: Airman's Suicide (Selfridge Air Base, Michigan)- Investigating Officer Captain E. H. Brown. A photo attached to the thick document made me gasp. It was a close-up of a young man's head, or at least what remained of it. The left side of his face was gone. In its place were a jumble of broken bones, dangling strips of skin, and ropes of bloody muscle and tissue. Written at the bottom of the photograph, Exhibit A.

I thumbed past the lengthy, single-spaced description of the young man's service record and his futile attempt to be released from active duty. At the end of the report were more photographs. One picture featured the airman's body in what looked like a storage room. A close-up shot showed him with his feet flat on the floor, his knees in the air as though preparing to perform a set of stomach crunches. A standard military-issue rifle lay on his chest. A half smile crept across the intact part of his face. The smile ended in a puddle of blood and flesh pressed against the concrete.

*

The Folies-Bergére album and the photographs of the dead airman were valuable currency in the schoolyard. I concealed them in my backpack and brought them to school.

The naked French women, though admired on a puerile level, paled in comparison with the pictures of the young suicide circulating throughout the fifth and sixth grades. Clive and Zeke Fannon asked me if they could keep them over the weekend to show their cousins. I did not say yes but Clive stuffed them in his school bag. Come Monday I asked for the items. They shoved me aside and told me they would keep them as long as they wanted to.

After dinner that night Dad ordered Jeff and me to go to the garage. He pointed at his footlocker. "Which one of you was in my trunk? Never mind, it doesn't matter. I'm missing a book your mom and I bought when we visited Paris. I'm also minus a very sensitive folder that has some pictures of a young man who killed himself. I knew that boy pretty well. He pulled a couple of tours in Korea as a medic. He saw a lot but never talked about his experiences. Most men who have been to war don't talk about it. The ones who do were probably never on the front. I want both things back by the weekend, especially the folder." Dad walked back into the house.

The next day I confronted the Fannon brothers on their way home from school. Randy, Jeff, and Paul had come with me to lend moral support. "I need the album and photos back," I said.

Clive who was stupider and bigger than his bullet-headed brother laughed. "Let's make a crybaby sandwich."

Clive's grinning mug enraged me. I drove my knee into his groin. He whimpered going down. Zeke put a chokehold on me, but I grabbed his little finger and bent it until it cracked like a dry twig. He dropped to the grass and started bawling and rolling around.

Randy and Jeff tried to drag me away, but Paul blocked their way, giving me enough time to drop-kick Clive's chin. Paul got in a good one of his own, letting Zeke have a punch in the nose, payback for all the tetherballs slung in his face. I alternated kicking and slapping the brothers until even Paul tired of the sport and told me to stop.

Shaking my fists, I clenched my teeth like my father and said, "Give me back my stuff or I'll give you something to cry about."

I snatched the brothers' school bags and turned them upside down. Three-ringed binders, pencils, textbooks, and assorted junk food fell on the grass, but not the Folies-Bergére souvenir book or green document folder. Neither Jeff nor Randy was quick enough to stop me from rushing Clive. I kicked him in the stomach. "Listen, fat boy! If I don't have my stuff back by tonight, I'll beat you every day until you can't walk," I raged, channeling my father then spun around and whacked the side of Zeke's head. "That goes for you too."

That evening Jeff and I were in our bedroom when the doorbell rang. I continued doing my homework. Jeff sat on the upper bunk with his guitar, trying to figure out a set of chords. He parted the curtain with the neck of his instrument and looked out the window. "Mrs. Fannon," he said and plucked out the theme song of Peter Gunn.

"David, come here!" My father's voice boomed up the stairwell.

"Bring your brother too," my mother added.

I looked at Janet's closed door hoping that she would come out to act as a kind of public defender in the Supreme Court of Major Brown. No such luck.

Mrs. Fannon was inside the vestibule when I made the last step. With her fingertips barely touching Mrs. Fannon's elbow, Mom guided her to the living room. Dad offered his guest a winged back chair. He had stunned Mom with the Sears & Roebuck green checkered monstrosity on her birthday. Mrs. Fannon refused to be comfortable. She remained standing, trapping two books and a green folder against her chest with her Alice the Goon forearms. Then she spread her arms to the side. In her left hand, she held the folder and the Folies-Bergére album. In the other, she displayed a worn black leather Bible.

"I think these belong to you Mr. Brown," she said and tossed the album and folder into the winged back chair. "And this–" she waved the Bible like the hammer of Thor, "–is something your boys would be better off reading."

Dad picked up the folder and placed it on the coffee table. "How did you come to have these things, Mrs. Fannon?"

"My sons took them off your boy to keep him from showing them to children all over the playground."

"Is that true, David?"

"No Sir, they stole them off me and refused to return them."

"Listen to the lies coming out of that boy's mouth. My Clive and Zeke are sitting outside in the car as witnesses."

"Mrs. Fannon, go get them. I want to hear their version of what happened," Dad said.

Although she shook her head so hard that her glasses fell off, her shellacked helmet of hair remained motionless. "I will not bring my boys in here. They came home in tears

72

and hid in the basement. Your son and his friends gave them a beating."

"Did you and your friends gang up on her sons?"

"No Sir, I whipped them on my own."

"Mr. Brown, I've taught my boys the difference between right and wrong."

"Major Brown."

"I beg your pardon."

"I'm a Major, not a mister, Mrs. Fannon." His tone of voice was soft, deliberate, dangerously calm.

"When your family moved in, I made a point of telling the neighbors that your being a soldier was no reason to shun you, regardless of what tales have been spread on the licentiousness and immorality of military people. Let him who is without sin..."

Dad gave her a pencil-like smile. "I'm not quite up on the good book, Mrs. Fannon. What does he without sin do? Cast the first stone, lob the first grenade, or hail the first Mary?"

Mom cupped her hand over her mouth.

Mrs. Fannon plopped down in the Sears & Roebuck chair and nearly choked on her words. "You may think this all very funny Major Brown, but your son near crippled my Clive. He kneed him in his privates and then tried to break Zeke's finger."

"Is that true David?" Dad asked and lit up a cigarette.

"Yes, Sir."

"Did I teach you to fight dirty?"

"No Sir." I held back from saying, "No Sir, you taught me not to lose."

"Then why did you do it?"

"Because I couldn't fight both of them at the same time, Sir. I figured if I got Clive out of the way first, I could deal with Zeke."

Dad squeezed his eyelids shut and inhaled his cigarette, holding the fumes in his lungs as he pondered the situation. "Who was with you?" he asked, breathing out a plume of smoke from his nostrils.

"Jeff and some friends."

"Jeff and your friends let you fight two boys on your own?"

"Yes, Sir."

"Some friends, you got there," Dad said and turned to Mrs. Fannon. "Good night and thank you for returning my things."

"Major Brown, what are you going to do to make sure that this sort of thing never happens again?"

"I am going to tell David to stay away from your boys." Mrs. Fannon pushed herself out of the chair and dashed for the front door. My mother apologized for the misunderstanding as she breezed by her. Dad waited for the door to slam then lowered his hand to his waist and undid his belt buckle.

Chapter 13

Mr. Brahm, my sixth-grade English and Math teacher, saw me as an enigma. My reputation as an unrepentant thug who fought at the drop of a pin didn't square with my above-average school marks. His idea of teaching consisted of burying his students under complex math problems followed by a pop quiz virtually every other day. These tactics afforded him the leisure time during class to read detective novels. Mr. Brahm resembled his favorite gourmand literary idol, Nero Wolfe, at least physically. When he waddled down the school hallways, his flesh undulated like three hundred pounds of aspic squeezed into a condom.

Mr. Brahm made a point of hovering over my desk when we had an exam. When he handed back the graded tests, he'd pinch the corner of my paper between his meaty thumb and forefinger, making me play a game of tug-of-war for its possession.

"Got away with it again, but your time will come, Mr. Brown, your time will come."

This game would have gone on all year if it had not been for an admittedly poor joke Randy Traynor, and I pulled on a boy in our class who aspired to be a musician. Sherman, a talented cornet player, and gifted math student, looked like a miniature replica of Al Hirt sans beard.

Mini-Hirt also played teacher's pet and informer. If some kid let an "oh shit" or "fuck" slip from his lips, the rotund horn player took note of the infraction and passed it on to Mr. Brahm.

To make matters worse Sherman and Mr. Brahm attended the same non-denominational Christian Gospel Meeting House and sang in the choir that Mrs. Fannon directed.

Being a notorious curser, I was convinced that Mini-Hirt had informed on me because Mr. Brahm made me copy scripture passages for taking the Lord's name in vain. As I thumbed through the Bible, I discovered tales of rape and incest, pillage, and genocide all committed with the sanction of the Big Guy. For every "Love your neighbor" passage, there were ten slugs on slaughtering every living creature, including the goats and chickens, lest they corrupt you.

One recess Mini-Hirt sat next to Randy and me as we waited our turn to shoot hoops on the basketball court.

"Brown, did you hear that the PTA and school administration are so mad they're farting fire?" Randy asked.

"Big deal, they're always peeved about something."

"Believe me, this time it's different."

Thanks to Madalyn Murray O'Hair, teachers no longer could force students to say the Lord's Prayer. She had taken the city of Baltimore to the Supreme Court over the issue. The nation's highest court proclaimed that any expression of religious belief in school was a violation of the separation of church and state.

Without bothering to measure my words I said, "Fucking A! Now that fat dick head will lay off giving me all that Bible crap to copy."

No sooner was the sentence out of my mouth than Mini-Hirt dashed across the schoolyard and buttonholed Mr. Brahm. Brahm stared directly at me. He shook his head and blew his nose into a handkerchief before reentering the school.

Over the next month, Brahm became even more obsessed with my redemption. Since the Supreme Court ruling was not yet enforceable in the school corridors of America, he wasted no time in giving me page upon page from the books of Ezekiel and Revelations to transcribe.

In November Brahm announced that one of our fellow students had received a great honor. Sherman had been chosen to play a solo performance of hymns and popular songs at a recital sponsored by the Christian Gospel Meeting House. As a special treat, Sherman would bring his horn to school the next day and give us a private show.

When I came home the afternoon of Brahm's announcement, Mom put me to cleaning up the backyard. I scooped up mounds of Jet's excrement, dumped them into Glad kitchen bags, and stewed over the latest transcription Brahm had given me. Back in the house, I saw Mrs. Fannon sitting primly on the edge of the wing-backed chair.

"Don't run off," Mom chirped. "Mrs. Fannon came by to invite us to a recital at her church. I purchased four tickets so we can go hear her son play his trumpet."

I've heard people maintain that when anger gets the best of you, you see red, like drowning in a sea of blood. This is not true. When truly submerged in anger you see yellow like you're skin-diving in a pool of piss.

I ran into the backyard to the tetherball. I slung it around its pole so many times that its rope broke loose from the rubber grommet. The ball skipped across the yard, bowling over a metal trashcan. Out of the can spilled two plastic sacks of dog shit.

The next day I came to school with Jet's droppings double bagged at the top of my knapsack. Randy Traynor opened up his windbreaker and pulled a pack of Winstons from his breast pocket. I followed Randy behind the school.

Hiding beside a Dempsey dumpster, Randy lit up a smoke and passed it to me. I sucked at the filter, drenching it in my saliva. Randy threw the weed on the ground and crushed it under his heel.

"Jesus, Brown, smoke it, don't drown it."

Randy slipped another Winston from his pack and popped it into his mouth. When he started to light the cigarette, his eyes widened. A few yards away, clutching his cornet case, Sherman was spying on us.

"Oh man, I'm in for it now," Randy said with the desperation of a person who has seen the future and doesn't like the view. "I'm going to get suspended for sure once that jerk squeals on me." He saw me smiling. "What are you grinning about? We're both in for it."

Without commenting I placed my knapsack on the ground and opened it. I took out the two plastic bags and dangled them. "Randy, if we're gonna get suspended, we might as well give Brahm something really bad to kick us out for."

Randy and I dashed into class ahead of Sherman. When recess rolled around, we hung back as Sherman trotted down to the teachers' lounge, leaving his cornet case under his chair.

Randy acted quickly. He unlatched the case and pulled out the chromed horn. It smelled of oil and anchovies. I had the two bags of dog shit in my hand and began to undo the ties but stopped. The cornet had an intricate trademark engraved on its bell along with the date 1897. The horn bore the circular marks of thousands of hours of buffing and polishing, like a chalice that had been passed down from generation to generation. I heard the tramp of feet in the corridor.

Randy said, "Get on with it," but I hesitated too long. I stuffed the two bags in my knapsack.

"Chicken," Randy hissed.

I placed the cornet back in its case and was fumbling with the latches when Brahm strode into the room with Sherman.

"My instrument!" Sherman wailed.

For a tub of barely solidified lard, Mr. Brahm moved fast. He jerked me off my feet and slammed my ass down on a long folding table under the blackboard.

"You have gone too far this time Mr. Brown. Touching another boy's property without his permission is serious. It shows a lack of respect and bad breeding."

Randy was gone. He'd merged with the wave of kids returning from recess. I began to slide off the table when Mr. Brahm shouted, "Stay still. I have not given you permission to move from that spot."

He inserted a key in a beige storage cabinet and pulled at the door a couple of times until it sprang open. From inside the cabinet, a wooden board shaped like a beaver's tail with holes drilled through it appeared.

"David Brown," Mr. Brahm said. "I'm sorry it has to come to this, but it may actually prove to be your saving later on." He pushed me nose down on the table and swung the paddle dead center on my ass three times. I rose, my face burning, but tearless, and started back to my desk.

"I have not given you permission to leave." Mr. Brahm grabbed me by my collar and pulled me back. "Apologize to Sherman for touching his cornet without asking him."

For the fate I'd originally planned for the horn, I figured Mini-Hirt deserved an apology. "I'm sorry Sherman."

"Good," Mr. Brahm said. "Now thank me for the lesson you've learned today."

I actually considered caving in until Brahm added, "Perhaps if your own parents had taken to heart the admonition, spare the rod, and spoil the child I would not be required to administer this moral teaching."

I fought back the urge to gouge out Brahm's mossy eyes. Never again would I allow some fucking outsider to act as a surrogate in the role of loving fucking father.

"I don't have anything to thank you for," I snarled.

Mr. Brahm's sticky hand shoved me against his desk and held me there as he stood straddled-legged, winding up to hit a home run. The blows descended so rapidly that I lost count. I refused to cry out. The sweat from Mr. Brahm's palm dripped down the paddle's grip and onto my skin where my shirttail had ridden above my waistband. His breathing was labored. He stopped and staggered to his desk, slid open a drawer, and removed a baby blue inhalator. I straightened up and walked toward the door. After a few seconds of sucking on its tube, he wheezed, "Where do you think you're going?"

"None of your business." I slammed the door behind me as I marched out of his class.

When I arrived home, I saw Mom pacing up and down the sidewalk puffing on a cigarette. She rushed toward me, hugged me, and then slapped me so sharply that my teeth hurt. "Where have you been?"

"School."

"Don't lie to me!" She slapped me again. "Your teacher called and said you ran away after he disciplined you." I hadn't calculated that Mr. Brahm would recover from his asthma attack fast enough to call before I got home.

"He wants your father to come in to discuss your behavior this Friday."

A tombstone surfaced in my mind with my name chiseled on its face. "Have you told Dad yet?"

"Of course not, your father is in New Jersey. He won't be back until the twenty-second."

Mom must have detected my relief because she mussed my hair and said, "Maybe we can straighten this thing up before your father gets home. If we do, there's no reason why we should trouble him with it."

Mr. Brahm was unusually nice to me on Friday. The morning passed without a comment from him. At twelve-thirty, Mom appeared at the classroom door. Mr. Brahm released his students for lunch. I started to follow them but stopped when Mr. Brahm said, "David come back in here I want you present while I explain your misanthropic behavior."

Mr. Brahm gallantly slid his chair from behind his desk and with a sweep of his hand offered it to my mother.

The fat man began sweating when she touched his hairless forearm. "That's very kind of you, but I would rather remain standing." My spine tingled as her voice poured over him like syrup. "First of all, Mr. Broom," Mom began to say.

"My name is Mr. Brahm, Mrs. Brown."

"Of course, Mr. Broom," Mom replied, "I want to thank you for calling me the other day about the trouble. David told me what happened. I informed him that though your methods may be a bit extreme, they were for the most part justified. He has promised me he will not act up again."

"Mrs. Brown, you don't seem to understand the seriousness of what happened. Perhaps it would be better if we met again when your husband is present."

Mom glanced up at the clock; it read a quarter to one. "That might be difficult to arrange. My husband is in the Air Force and has somewhat irregular hours."

"Your husband's frequent absences may account for your son's attitude problems and moral lapses. Maybe if he spent more time looking after what happens at home–"

"You're right Mr. Broom. If Major Brown, spent more time at home taking care of his family instead of taking care of his duty to protect yours and other civilians' families, a lot of the problems you have alluded to would not have happened. But he's in the military, Mr. Broom, and has no choice. I'm sure that as a veteran you sympathize with us."

Brahm virtually had Four-F stamped on his forehead. He turned his face to the blackboard and said, "What goes on at your home isn't my concern. We're here to discuss the incident that occurred on Wednesday."

He was about to launch into a sermon when the intercom suspended above the door crackled. A solemn voice seeped through its speaker. "At 12:32 in Dallas Texas, John F. Kennedy, the President of the United States of America was shot. His condition is unknown. All students are dismissed for the remainder of the day."

*

My father arrived home at 18:00. We'd gathered around the flickering tube of the television. He ran upstairs, hardly acknowledging our presence. Drawers and doors opened and slammed. When Dad came down, minus his jacket but still wearing the rest of the uniform, he carried a large grip and a long suit bag. He parked his luggage near the front door and entered the living room. Pulling up a hassock, he sat next to Mom, his arm around her shoulder. She had not said much since the announcement of JFK's assassination except to order us to stay in the house. Disregarding her own rules on snacks before dinner she laid a spread of cookies, soft drinks, and bridge mix on the coffee table. Throughout the weekend our family, like so many others around the nation, leaned into the television screen trying to fathom the latest developments from Dallas and Washington. My father sat with the telephone on his lap.

On Sunday afternoon the doorbell rang. Three of my father's co-workers stood on the front stoop in their civvies.

A man with a red handlebar mustache asked me to get Major Brown. They spoke with my father in hushed tones then came into the living room.

Tommy was off to the side of the coffee table, rolling a yellow Tonka bulldozer back and forth on the carpet. Mom sat lotus style in front of the TV screen. She stood up to greet the men. "Please make yourselves comfortable while I go get y'all coffee." She glanced over her shoulder at the TV as she left the room.

My father turned down the television's volume. I retreated into a corner. Janet sat in the wing-backed chair. Jeff reclined on the couch, staring at the newscast. Dad cast an angry glance at them, and they leaped up to join me.

The man with the mustache said, "Ernie, have you packed your bags? The way it looks, some of us will be seeing Gitmo while others will be freezing their asses off at Gander"

"They're by the door, Colonel."

"Well, for what it's worth, I don't think the alert will last long."

A man wearing a baseball hat with a patch of an eagle clutching missiles in one talon and arrows in the other, said with casual familiarity, "Boys, we got a hell of a mess on our hands."

Dad smacked his palm with his fist. "McNamara didn't make things easier by shutting down those SAC and ADC bases last year."

"Major," the Colonel said, "we're not supposed to have opinions, only orders."

"Yes Sir," Dad answered.

My mother returned balancing a tray of four steaming cups of coffee, a creamer, sugar bowl, and a plateful of cookies. She kept her eyes directed at the screen as she set down the tray. "That's him," Mom said.

Live from Dallas, burly men in Stetsons escorted Lee Harvey Oswald through an underground parking garage. Dad increased the set's volume. On the television a broad-backed man wearing a poorly fitted suit and a gangster's fedora rushed forward, inserting himself between the deputies and their prisoner. A sound like a cap pistol came over the airwaves. Lee Harvey Oswald doubled over. He gathered the front of his white T-shirt in his hands, gaping open-mouthed at the camera. His lips formed a round vowel of indignation. The assassin of the alleged assassin disappeared under the heavy bodies of policemen and deputies piling on top of him like football players sacking a quarterback.

"Christ almighty!" the Colonel said and rushed out of the house with his fellow officers close behind.

At suppertime, the doorbell rang again. My father kissed my mother on the forehead as he got up from the table. Two MPs stood outside. Another one waited behind the wheel of a blue sedan parked at the curb. My father picked up his bags and left.

Mr. Brahm never had his meeting with my father. He eased up on me and even started to write comments like, "Keep up the good work" on my papers.

JFK's body lay in state in the Capitol Rotunda for a week. Thousands of people filed past the closed casket placing roses, poems, and slips of written prayers on its lid. A black horse wearing an empty saddle walked behind the caisson that transported the president's flag-draped coffin to Arlington cemetery. Men from all the branches of the military marched alongside the cart.

A home movie of Kennedy taking the headshot repeated itself on televisions around the world. In the film, fragments of Kennedy's skull and bits of his brain explode out of his head like confetti out of a Christmas cracker. When I viewed the McGruder film I did not think of JFK, the statesman, or of John-John snapping off a salute. My thoughts went back to a green folder containing the photograph of a soldier who blew off the side of his own face. As I reassembled the image in my mind, I understood why the lid of Kennedy's coffin was closed. Martin was right. The type of ammunition makes a difference.

(1964-1968)

"Assassination is the extreme form of censorship."
George Bernard Shaw

"I will kill you myself before I let you shame this uniform or disgrace this family."

Lt. Colonel E.H. Brown (U.S.A.F. Retired) 1925-1997

Chapter 14

At the start of eighth grade, my father received a transfer to Germany. We moved in with my mother's parents and waited for him to send for us. Birmingham had gone from regarding itself as a beacon of culture and enlightenment to seeing itself as the world did, a racist decaying steel town. White supremacists had succeeded in indelibly stamping the images of burning crosses and the tortured remains of civil rights activists on the collective consciousness. Most of the kids who teased me about my Yankee accent in the fourth grade were now trying to flatten their own so they could pass for the Main Street Midwesterners they saw on the tube.

My Uncle Walter came over to my grandfather's twice while we were there. Granddad Agerton barely shared the time of day with him. Walter chortled at the news of blacks or idealistic white civil rights activists getting their heads caved in by local yokel cops and the state police. Things came to a head when Walter gloated over the bombing of the 16th Street Baptist Church near my granddad's store. My grandfather, furious, stuffed his hands in his pockets, probably to keep himself from strangling my uncle.

"Walter, the coloreds who go to that church are my customers and decent people. You may not know it now; you may never be smart enough to know it but one day your children will have to lie about where they came from. Now get out of my house and don't come back until you can clean up your mind or at least shut your mouth."

Native Alabamians, as much as they protested their innocence, could not distance themselves from the blackened timber skeleton of the church and the charred bodies of four young girls. For several years I made a point of informing people that I was from Colorado, Ohio, Michigan, anywhere but the South.

*

At the end of October Dad sent for us to join him. He was waiting for us inside the Frankfurt airport terminal. He dropped his lit cigarette and waved at us. He hugged and kissed Mom and Janet and shook hands with Jeff and me.

"Is there anything I should know about before we go boys? I would rather take care of business here. It's a long drive and I don't want to be thinking about disciplining you. I should be concentrating on staying alive."

"Oh Ernest, don't tease them. For the most part, they were good."

"That's what worries me, the other parts."

Dad gathered up our luggage and herded us out into a crisp November evening. Parked by the curb was a green 1957 VW beetle. He opened the front hood and tossed in our bags. It was a tight squeeze, but everyone managed to fit inside.

He bombed out of the airport, merging on the autobahn with a swarm of mini-European cars moving like cartoon insects at hyper-speed. Mom held onto a strap above the door, her knuckles turned white. Dad raced along the autobahn and then took an exit onto a narrow road that wound through the Taunus Mountains.

The glow of the lights of Frankfurt disappeared as the VW climbed into the mist. The road twisted sharply. A fog enveloped the Volkswagen as it drove higher into the mountains. The engine sputtered, seeming to gasp for air. Automobile fog lights headed in the opposite direction twinkled like amber fireflies. Dad rolled down his window and wiped off droplets of water from his side mirror.

My ears popped as the elevation rose. After a couple of hours, Dad turned off onto a country road, its strip of pavement so narrow that the side mirrors of cars speeding past almost touched. The smell of pine needles, moldering hay, smoky manure, and coal fires filled my nostrils. Dad cruised by a white three-story structure with a peaked roof. A Teutonic-lettered sign dangled from an angle iron. A large overhanging light illuminated the sign, Neuhof Gasthaus.

He hung a right onto teeth-jarring cobblestones and navigated through a labyrinth of streets lined on both sides by 18th-century row houses. The VW rolled smoothly on asphalt entering a modern housing development that looked down on the old village. Past midnight, we pulled into the driveway of an eggshell white duplex and tumbled out of the car. Less than a hundred meters away from the house was a cemetery. A streetlight that resembled a bishop's crosier cast an eerie glow over immaculately kept graves and mottled tombstones.

The next day was Saturday. Jeff and I got permission to investigate the village. Janet stayed behind to help Mom sort through the boxes that had been sent ahead of us. Outside, an old woman swept the curb in front of her house. She ceased sweeping and said, "Güten Morgen."

Jeff smiled and said the only German word he knew "Danke schön."

She ran into the house and returned with a banana. She thrust it at Jeff. Again, he said, "Danke schön." For the eighteen months we 'lived in the village the old woman dashed out into the street to give Jeff a banana. Jeff and I continued down the street, past the sterile modern houses perched above the old part of the town. The houses faced back-to-back. Each dwelling had a small garden that sloped toward the street. No kids were to be seen. Later I learned German students attended school half-day on Saturdays.

As we entered the old part of Neuhof the asphalt under our feet turned into cobblestone. The houses' wooden beams embedded in yellowing plaster had not deteriorated over two centuries. We stopped to look at a hand-hewn stone church flanked by two Gothic spires. Two old women walking up from the narrow streets glanced our way. They could barely totter up the hill, their legs bowed like wishbones from rickets. The women carried net shopping bags overflowing with packages wrapped in brown paper.

The aroma of freshly baked bread and spiced salami wafted from the old town. Jeff and I turned onto a street scarcely wide enough to permit the passage of an Isetta, the bubble car that provided economical transportation in a fuel-starved Germany. The sky appeared as a gunmetal blue ribbon above the peaked rooftops.

On both sides of the street were small shops. The stores had samples of their wares displayed in their windows. In one shop a large ham dangled above an assortment of cold cuts and sausages. As the door opened, I could taste the tangy spices.

Jeff peered through the window of a bakery. Mounds of cookies, sweet rolls, and hard Laugen Brötchen spilled out of wicker baskets. A white chocolate Sankt Nikolaus accompanied by a dark chocolate Knecht Rupert stood guard over the trove of pastries and breads. A bell tinkled and two boys stepped out of the bakery. One was a gangly redhead. The other had caramel-colored skin. He wore a burgundy shirt buttoned up to his neck, shiny black pants and pointed Beatle boots. A girl about my age walked out of the store after the boys. Her hair was a dried-out version of the redhead's mop. They had identical Cyrano de Bergerac noses. She waved at some older German boys exiting a tobacconist down the street and raced off to meet them. Her micro-mini skirt hugged her thighs as she bounced down the cobblestones.

"What are you looking at?" the redhead asked.

"Noth-noth-nothing," I stammered.

"I'm not talking to you. I know what you're looking at. You're staring at my sister's knockers and ass." The kid poked Jeff. "I'm talking to him."

"You speak American!" Jeff exclaimed.

"Of course he speaks English," the other kid said. His accent was a weird mixture of Middle American and something European. "You think you're the only Yanks living here?"

"I'm looking at that thing on the counter that looks like a giant chocolate drop," Jeff said.

"It's called a Sheiß Kopf," the redhead said.

"What's a Sheiß Kopf?"

"Pete's a Sheiß Kopf," the other boy said.

"Shut up Yanny. I'm trying to teach him German." Pete put his arm around Jeff. "That's what that chocolate-covered thing is called. They cost only five pfifings. That's about 2 cents."

"We don't have any money."

"I'll give you some geld. I'll even go in there with you. All you have to say is, Du bist eine Sheiß Kopf."

"Don't listen to him," Yanny said. "Sheiß Kopf means shit head."

"Ah man," Pete whined.

Jeff laughed. "Hey that's pretty cool. Can you teach me some words?"

"Sure, I'll give you words you'll never learn at school."

After Jeff and Pete walked away Yanny asked me, "Do you play sports?"

"In Ohio, I was on the wrestling team and I took judo."

"Ever played fußball, soccer? The village is inviting boys to try out for the local teams."

"No, but I'm willing to give it a shot."

"It's going to be great to have someone to hang around with besides that goofball." Yanny nodded in the direction of Pete. "Kathy's okay but he's a jerk-off."

Around 19:00 my father answered the doorbell. He stared at Yanny until the boy said, "I'm Captain Ridley's son."

"The dentist?"

"Yes Sir. I told David I'd take him to the community center."

"And do what?"

94

"Excuse me?"

"It's a simple enough question. What do you plan to do once you get there?"

"They have tryouts for the village soccer team."

"David can hardly walk a straight line much less dribble a soccer ball. Maybe you should bring Jeff along. He's the natural athlete. David works hard but he's no Pele. But I reckon it'll be an opportunity for him to get to know some locals and maybe pick up a little German." He dropped his hand on my shoulder and dug his fingers into the muscle. It was a ritual I was familiar with and did my best not to show any pain or he would squeeze harder.

"I don't want it getting back that you did anything to embarrass me. Remember that you not only represent your family but your country as well."

Dad dipped into his pant pocket and pulled out a ten Deutschmark bill. He stuffed the money in my shirt pocket and whispered, "I will kill you myself before I let you shame this uniform or disgrace this family."

Inside the sports center males ranging from eight to twenty-five performed soccer drills. They bounced balls off the tops of their shoes and knees and headed them with the same ease as kids in the US playing catch.

At the other end of the Geimeindehalle beneath a basketball hoop were six goal nets. Boys lined up single file at half court. They attempted to drive the black-and-white sphere past grim-faced goalies.

Yanny spoke with a man dressed in a neon blue sweatsuit. The man looked at me and then nodded. Before I could react, he kicked a ball in my direction. It slammed into my gut with the force of a cannonball. I drop-kicked the ball back to him. He motioned me to come over and grabbed my hand and started pumping it up and down. He turned to Yanny and said something.

"Herr Vogel thinks your ball-handling skills stink but since you're not afraid he'll give you a shot playing fullback. Your job is to stop the strikers from getting to the goalie."

The first part of the evening was a joke. No matter how hard I tried, kids of all ages, shapes, and sizes rushed past me. It finally dawned on me to play the man and not the ball. By night's end, I'd scraped my knees and elbows raw from slide-tackling strikers.

Yanny came to get me as the lights in the Geimeindehalle flicked off and on. A blonde girl and her stocky brunette friend accompanied him. He had talked to them all evening without joining practice.

"How come you didn't play?" I asked.

"I had other things on my mind. Besides with this," he lifted his pant leg and revealed a metal brace coming out of a high-top orthopedic boot, "I don't do a lot of dribbling."

"Sorry."

He shrugged. "This is Gertrude." The blonde smiled.

Her front teeth jutted out like a horse taking a bit.

"Ich bin Doris," the dark-haired girl said.

"She says her name—"

"I got it. Ich bin David."

A thick-necked man in green coveralls and billy boots appeared out of nowhere. Reeking of schnapps, he barked out an order, "Jezt, Raus!"

Without understanding a lick of German, it was clear to me he was kicking us out. Doris stayed behind as Yanny, Gertrude, and I left. I waved at her. The man shoved her toward a set of stairs leading up to a balcony.

"What gives with that guy?"

"He's her old man. Her family lives above the Geimeindehalle."

"That's too bad."

"Yeah." He pulled out a flat pack of cigarettes. I shook my head when he offered me one. He pushed open the box from the bottom and withdrew a smoke with his teeth. "She likes you." He slipped his hand under the back of Gertrude's coat.

"How do you know?"

"She said so. She thinks you're cute."

I wanted to ask more but didn't want to seem too interested. "Do you think I'll make the team?"

"Everybody makes the team. How much you'll play is the real question."

"She really said she likes me?"

"Yeah."

Chapter 15

Each weekday at 6 A.M. a school bus painted Air Force blue picked up the American kids living throughout the Taunus Mountains. It took us to General H.H. Arnold Middle School and Senior High School in Wiesbaden. The Neuhofers lived near the end of the route, a trip of 80 kilometers. A surly German named Fritz, at least that's what everyone called him, drove the bus when he wasn't screaming at us to shut up and sit down.

For a few weeks Janet, Pete, Jeff, Kathy, and I walked together to the Gasthaus to wait for the bus. Yanny sometimes joined us as far as the butcher shop. He attended a school in the village. Yanny's father planned to stay in Germany when his tour was up. There was no way he'd take his family back to the small North Carolina town he came from. It was bad enough being an educated black man in the South, but it would be much worse with his blonde wife and strawberry-skinned son.

If the school bus was a few minutes late it fell behind a caravan of tractors leaving for the farm fields outside the villages. I didn't mind. It gave me a chance to stare out the window and take in the sheep and cows grazing in front of a backdrop of rolling hills and picture book forests. After a couple of weeks of having a seat to myself a tall kid dressed in a Boy Scout uniform plopped down next to me. Merit badges covered his sash and he wore an Eagle Scout patch on his sleeve.

"That concrete bunker in the field," he said, "is probably left over from the Second World War. Most of these woodlands were destroyed during the war but they came back. Pretty amazing, huh?"

I scooted closer to the window. A huge wooden barrel on wheels pulled by a horse blocked the road in front of us. The stench of liquid manure spilling out of a poorly sealed tap saturated the atmosphere.

The scout said, "Do you know they call that thing a honey wagon?"

"Who calls it a honey wagon?"

"The Germans, that's how it's translated into English. I think it's actually a universal term for a liquid manure wagon."

A shorter but more muscular version of the Boy Scout leaned across the aisle. His upper mouth was cleft. "He's right. In most European languages it is referred to as a honey wagon."

The Boy Scout folded his legs under him in the lotus position. "My name's Kyle Bains and this is my brother Millard."

Although Kyle and I were in the same grade, I rarely bumped into him during my first month since he was taking all advanced subjects. I had been a respectable junior high student in Ohio and Alabama but the cadre who controlled placement in Germany decided that being a respectable student anywhere near the Mason-Dixon Line was an academic liability. By the next semester, I was kicked upstairs and joined Kyle in his World History, Biochemistry, and European Literature classes. Fortunately, there was no room in the accelerated math section so I was spared the embarrassment of demonstrating my profound ignorance of algebra and geometry until the ninth grade.

Kyle introduced me to a lot of people. Most of these individuals became the popular clique at General H.H. Arnold Senior High. Ironically, Kyle never went out of his way to join the in-group though he was considered ultra-cool.

Kyle claimed to be an iconoclast. I had to take him at his word as I didn't know what an iconoclast was. His father had instilled in him a sense of pride and duty to push over sacred cows. Major Bains was in the reserves, viewed by the regular military as a civilian in uniform. Kyle said that his father had set his mind on becoming a bush pilot and teaching at a university as soon as his reserve time was up.

"My father's going to let his students know the USA has its head up its ass when it comes to South East Asia," he kept repeating.

I yawned before asking him, "Don't you think our government knows what's it's doing?"

On a wet February day, Kyle stayed after school with me while I tried out for the high school wrestling team. The coach was ex-military. For two hours Coach had us run sprints, do pushups, shoot moves, and work from both standing and referee positions on takedowns and escapes. In the final hour, each boy had to wrestle for three periods with not only the guys in his weight division but the class above as well. Kyle was sitting in the hallway when I left the gym, a book perched on his knees.

"Did you make the team?" Kyle asked.

"Yeah, but Coach says I have to wrestle off every week to keep my spot."

A few guys who knew Kyle as a superlative athlete needled him to try out for the wrestling team. Kyle politely refused, saying it would be too hard to make arrangements on a regular basis to stay after school and get a ride home.

The pressure to join moved from flattery to name-calling. When someone taped a drawing to his locker of a Boy Scout humping a chicken Kyle walked into the gym unannounced during practice.

The coach squinted. "I told you last time you were here either suit up or get out."

Kyle peeled off his shirt. His upper body was cut like a gymnast. "I want to try out for the team."

"Go away you'll get hurt. These boys have been learning and perfecting moves for weeks."

Kyle stepped onto the mat. He pointed at Jim Zale who had been bugging him the most. I'd wrestled him a few times and he was good. Jim weighed in about twenty pounds heavier than Kyle, so I expected to see my friend get pinned in the first period. Jim tied up with Kyle and tried to muscle him. Kyle slipped under Jim's arm and lifted him in a tight waist from behind and drove him shoulder-first into the mat, pinning him in ten seconds. We were shocked.

"That's pretty impressive," the coach said. "See me after practice and I'll put you on the roster."

Kyle helped Jim to his feet. "No thank you. Sticking my nose into someone's armpit isn't my thing."

Chapter 16

One day when walking up the hill with Yanny I saw a circle of kids near the old church. I ran to the crowd and was surprised to see Jeff duking it out with Dieter, a big farmer's kid with whom I had become friendly. Someone pushed my brother from behind and he fell on the ground. Before Dieter could do any serious damage, I jumped inside the circle. Dieter could really hit hard but his rubber muck boots made him clumsy and slow. I did a basic leg takedown, pressed Dieter's cheek to the cobblestones, and pulled his arm in a hammerlock behind his back.

"What's going on?"

"I asked Pete how do say do you want to goof around. The next thing I know Dieter's pounding on me," Jeff answered.

"What did you say?"

"Hast du kanoodle auf dem box?"

"Let go of Dieter," Yanny said. "Your brother asked if he had turds in his pants."

"Great gag," Dupree howled and took off.

Jeff chased after Pete. There was no way he could catch him. The redhead had to be fast to survive the practical jokes he pulled on friends and foes alike.

Following the fight, Dieter and Yanny became my after-school companions. When we weren't playing soccer or hanging around the Gasthaus we gabbed about the local girls. Actually, I listened while they bragged about their sexual prowess. My exploits consisted of a few awkward attempts at talking to Doris. Dieter said, "She's interested in you. She dates Ami soldiers, even Schwartzes, so if she wants to see you this is good."

"Her father hates Americans. What do you think he'd do if he caught us together?"

"Kennsch de Wayne!"

"Who the fuck cares? I care. Her father slapped Lothar for just looking at her."

"Lothar ist einer Busengrapscher."

"A what?"

Dieter raised both his hands to chest level and pretended he was squeezing an invisible pair of boobs.

"Busengrapscher," he articulated very slowly.

With Dieter's prodding, I finally got the courage to ask Doris for a movie. We caught a bus to Van, a village about 7 km from Neuhof. During the ride, I kept my hands in my lap and looked straight ahead. Doris sat so close to me that it was impossible to slip a piece of notebook paper between our hips.

"You like me to be seine feste Freundin?" she asked.

"My what?"

"Your garl frond."

"My girlfriend?"

"Ja, gurl frund."

The theater was above a store. When we entered the lobby the ticket seller took my money and nodded at some folding chairs leaning against a wall. I carried our chairs into a large rectangular room. The screen, made of a piece of canvas, was stretched between a wood frame.

Before the movie rolled the ticket seller entered the theater and passed down the aisle holding a box containing candy bars, boiled eggs, cookies, and orange soda pop. Doris stopped him and took one of each item in his collection.

She smiled and placed her hand on my lap. Every minute on the minute she squeezed so hard that my balls throbbed under her palm. Part way into the movie I realized I was watching a dubbed version of "Cat Ballou". It was weird hearing Lee Marvin speak German.

When we arrived back in Neuhof, Doris reminded me that I'd promised to buy her an ice cream. I only had enough money left to buy one cone. She offered to let me lick one side of the swirly soft ice.

"Nein danke."

"Warum nicht?"

"It gives me a headache," I lied.

On the way back to the Geimeindehalle we stopped to watch a carnival set up tents and trailers in a camping plazt. Doris curled her plump lips as she looked at the dark-skinned Gypsies. We hurried past a group of young girls tending to even younger children while the adults busied themselves with cards and cigarettes.

"Die Zigeuners sind verdammter Schweinehunds," she said and dropped her ice cream. It splattered on her sweater. She pinched her nose, feigning a gagging sound.

When we arrived at the Geimeindehalle Doris hooked her arm through my elbow and led me upstairs to the apartment where her family lived. Her parents were out. She motioned me to sit down on a yellow couch with the foam poking through its cushions then disappeared into her bedroom. When she returned, she carried two blouses, one white and the other sheer. She removed her stained sweater. Her breasts overflowed a bra that she must have bought years earlier. She alternated holding each blouse against her torso. I was unable to take my eyes off her. I pointed at the sheer top. She grinned and put on the blouse, leaving it open.

She lifted my hands and helped me button the first two buttons then left me on my own. As I continued buttoning, approaching her breasts, I asked why the Gypsies were only allowed to stay in town for two weeks.

Doris shrugged. "Sie sind die Diebe."

"Not all can be thieves."

"Alles sind die Diebe," she disagreed.

"What if they can't move on?"

"Sie müssen."

"That doesn't seem fair."

"Er geht ihnen besser als uns!" Her eyes bored through me when she switched to heavily accented English. "We pay gypsies and other Auslanders for what happened to them in the war. You call that fair?"

My fingers slipped into the cup of her bra to touch her nipples. "I don't know," I said.

"Deutschland suffered too. My vater lost his leg in the war but who is paying him?"

She backed away, quickly finished buttoning her blouse, then flung the apartment door open. "Goodbye. You must go."

I learned a valuable lesson about the politics of sexuality. Foreplay does not require conversation. The next day when Yanny and Dieter caught up with me they teased me. Dieter said that Doris was going around the village telling her girlfriends that I was sweet and didn't touch her even though she stood in front of me almost naked.

"Is it true you saw her Kiste?" Dieter asked.

"Her what?"

"Her tits, her boobs," Yanny said.

I had inherited the parochial belief that one did not kiss and tell, not that there was anything to tell.

"You must do something when you see her again," Dieter said.

"Like what?"

"Die Ische is saying to everyone you are sweet."

"What's wrong with being considered nice?"

Yanny hesitated then backed well out of my reach. "Doris is telling everyone you're queer."

"Ja, she says du bist eine Tunte." Before Dieter could finish his sentence, I popped him in the nose.

For a few days after the incident, I stayed in the house. I did not go to the door when Dieter came over to apologize. I also did not attend soccer practice for a week.

Yanny telephoned. "You're going to be kicked off the team if you skip practice one more time."

"Big deal."

"Herr Vogel's disappointed. He gave you a chance."

"I don't care."

"The worst thing you can do is stay away. People will take it as proof of what she's been saying. If you come most of the guys will pass off her remarks as just more lies from the fat whore."

"She's not that fat," I said.

I returned to the Geimeindehalle but avoided Doris and made a point of leaving immediately after practice. I also refused to socialize with anyone on the bus ride to school. For a week I sat next to Kyle without letting a word pass between us.

He eventually said, "You've been really surly. Did you get cut from the wrestling team?"

"No."

"So what gives?"

"A girl in Neuhof is spreading lies about me."

"So?"

"I'm ashamed to show my face in the village."

"That's it?"

"What do you mean is that it? She's going around telling people I'm queer."

"So?"

"I'm not."

"Grow up, Brown. There are worse things than being called a homosexual."

"Like what!"

"Like being one of the people who care what people think."

Chapter 17

I loved the perks given to athletes; being able to leave class early and getting extensions on homework and postponements on exams. At pep rallies, each member of the basketball and wrestling team was called to the center of the gym floor by name. We listened with ultra-cool indifference to the cheers of the student body. The team traveled to meets all over Germany. We also had tournaments against other dependent schools from England, France, and Italy. My first three matches went well. After winning one match by a pin in thirteen seconds my face and scrawny body appeared on the sports page of the base paper.

Once you made junior or senior varsity you got excused from having to take physical education. Like most jocks, I considered the guys who took PE to be geeks. Two boys especially fit that definition, Udo and Curt. They were in my gym class on the junior high side. It was hard to say which one was the bigger nerd. I think they became friends because they had no other choice, having been marked as losers even by other losers. Both had pear-shaped bodies and the muscle tone of Jell-O. They snorted and whinnied when they laughed at each other's lame jokes. The PE teachers picked on them without mercy. The other boys persecuted them.

On one occasion Udo was reduced to tears after a shower. Someone slung Udo's soaking pants at his face with enough velocity to knock him off his feet. He squatted on the floor like a hairless squirrel, trying unsuccessfully to untie his pant legs, which had been jerked into a knot.

Curt came running out of the shower. He helped his friend to his feet. "You guys are really stupid. Really idiots." He picked up the trousers and threw them underhand at one of Udo's laughing tormentors.

Kyle pushed his way through the gathering. He handed Udo his own slacks. "Wear these."

"What are you going to wear?"

Kyle took a pair of sweatpants from his gym bag. He wore them and a sweatshirt with an MIT decal on its front the rest of the day.

*

Most of the guys on the wrestling and basketball teams took the same classes. It was a nightmare for our unfortunate teachers. We were the princes of General H.H. Arnold and as such got away with stuff for which any ordinary student would have been expelled.

Mr. Champagne, my English composition, and world literature instructor had three strikes against him, his name, his effeminate voice, and his theatrical mannerisms. He made a point of standing by the door and greeting each of his students. When everyone was seated, he'd throw his head back and flounce to the blackboard where he had written some bit of poetry. His two great passions were Percy Bysshe Shelley and the eccentric 1880s Bavarian ruler, Ludwig the II, who built chateaus throughout the German Alps. After finishing a lecture, Mr. Champagne would go on and on about his favorite subject, the Herrenchiemsee.

"Though the castle was never completed it was meant to surpass Versailles in ostentation." Mr. Champagne glowed as he spoke. "Ludwig financed his glorious projects by taxing his subjects into ruin. His bruised body washed up on the shores of Lake Starnberg shortly after his ministers declared him insane and stripped him of his throne. Ludwig may have lived longer if he had read Ozymandias instead of trying to create monuments to assure his immortality."

Bubbles, as the jocks called Mr. Champagne, encouraged me to read more and to pursue writing. Based on a maudlin short story I wrote for his class he became convinced that I was a budding author. I tried to slough off his compliments, but he persisted. He asked me to work on the school's literary magazine.

"Yeah, that'll go over real well with the team and my coach," I said.

"Mr. Brown, there is no shame in having an imagination."

Without asking me he published one of my stories in the H.H. Arnold literary journal.

The story was called The Pact. It was about an old man and his wife of fifty years. They shuffle down a leaf-strewn path in a forest and reminisce about their life together. At the end of the path, they sit down on a bench and perform the ultimate act of love; they share a plate of poison mushrooms.

I dreaded going to wrestling practice.

The coach was especially creative in his jibes, "Get out there and practice your escapes, Shakespeare. Drive his face into the mat. What do you think you're doing writing a love poem?"

One afternoon when Mr. Champagne entered the classroom, I stuck my finger inside my mouth and pulled it out making a popping sound. The trick was picked up by the other jocks in the room. For about five minutes mock champagne cork explosions filled the class.

"That is enough! I demand respect!" Mr. Champagne wailed and stamped into the book closet. "I will remain in here until you're prepared to act like civilized humans."

I am not sure who got the idea to jam the door closed with a wooden block, but it happened. Mr. Champagne screamed and beat on the door with his tiny fists. I wish I could say that I paused to open the door as the entire class filed out of the room and headed for the snack bar down the hill from the school. But I didn't. I may have even led the Exodus. Two more classes came and went without letting him out. The following day Mr. Champagne was absent. In his place was a stocky bristle-haired ex-marine named Mr. Gillette. His actual field of teaching was algebra and geometry.

"Your teacher is on sick leave. He may or may not come back," Gillette said. "Let it be known, gentlemen that what happened to Mr. Champagne won't happen to me. Furthermore, though I hate poetry, I have been assigned to teach you poetry. If I have to teach it, you'll learn to appreciate it. Do I make myself clear?"

Chapter 18

I kept playing fußall at the Geimeindehalle. Gerhard, Doris's former boyfriend, constantly ragged on me. Three years older than me, Gerhard was a man in size and strength. I suspected that he was responsible for drawing swastikas paired with racist messages against Americans, Schwartzes, and Jüden on our driveway. I got holy shit from my father.

"It is your job to protect this property when I'm gone," Dad said and punched me in the stomach before ordering me to scrub off the graffiti.

My fight with Gerhard started because of Peter Dupree. Pete drove a soccer ball into the nuts of a kid named Lothar. He threatened to go after Pete but calmed down when Dupree apologized. Pete waited until Lothar's back was turned and then aimed a ball at his head. The ball struck Lothar with such force that he fell to his knees. It bounced and crashed through a window. I tried to help Lothar to his feet, but he pushed me away and went after Pete with justifiable homicide in mind. I stepped between them to defuse the situation and ended up on the wrong side of both camps.

As I held Lothar back Pete sucker-punched him. At that point, Gerhard joined the fracas. He lifted me off the floor and dragged me into the entrance hall of the Geimeindehalle. I did a leg sweep sending him sliding across the floor. What had been a skirmish turned into a serious fight where the objective was to hurt the other person so badly that he could not get up.

His elbow smashed across the nape of my neck. I toppled over and yelled when he drove a knee into my back then booted me in the side. Picking me up again he kicked open the double doors of the entrance and tossed me down the stairs into the snow. Sometimes common sense arrives too late. I charged back into the sports hall.

Gerhard beat me from one end of the building to the next before throwing me through the doors and into the snow again. Sometimes common sense never arrives. Three more times I struggled back into the sports hall. Three more times Gerhard beat me up and threw me outside. On the fourth and last time, Gerhard, who'd been trying to make a game out of it, noticed his friends. They were no longer laughing. He could no more stop than I could. I wonder if we were driven by our duty to our respective fatherlands or fathers to fight it out. Gerhard kneed me in the stomach. He slammed me into the wall. The impact drove the wind out of me. I heard a click and caught the glint of a switchblade gripped in Gerhard's fist. He pricked me under the chin with the tip of the blade.

Jorge, a cadet at the police academy, snatched the knife from Gerhard's hand. He forced him to the floor and shook his head in disgust. Gerhard wheezed. I sucked back the snot dribbling from my nose.

"I should arrest both of you."

Jorge forced us to shake hands, draped an arm over each of us, and walked us to the Gasthaus. He bought us a beer followed by a shot of schnapps. The beer washed over my swollen lips and the molten schnapps burned my throat. At midnight my father stood in the doorway with his arms folded over his chest. Jorge related in Wagnerian tones the battle that had taken place in the sports hall. My father thanked Jorge and did not say anything except, "It's a good thing tomorrow is Saturday." Dad let me sleep in until 9:00 and did not mention the previous night's event.

*

A month after the fight Lothar choked to death on his own vomit while recuperating from the flu. His single mother could barely afford to bury him. Jeff, Pete, and I delivered flowers to Lothar's mother. She lived in a small apartment above the local butcher shop.

She flung open a window and stretched out her neck when we rang the doorbell. Her eyes settled on us. A smile crept across her pale face like a centipede. She invited us in. The narrow stairway smelled sickly sweet. I thought that the odor came from the butcher shop. As we approached her apartment the smell became even more cloying. Lothar's mother opened the door. A sliver of light passed between two panels of faded green drapes. A teakettle on the boil in a cubbyhole kitchenette wailed in harmony with Lothar's mother when she fell on my neck and soaked my collar with her tears. She swallowed and mumbled something. Pete for once did not play the clown. He told her how sorry we were and how much we missed Lothar. I handed her a bouquet of white carnations. She nodded in the charitable way of the grieving. She walked into the kitchen. The teakettle ceased its keening.

The smell in the apartment was overbearing. She tilted her head to a door that led into the only bedroom. Jeff and Pete walked behind her. The door screamed on its rusted

117

hinges. Several candles illuminated the room. A cube of lavender incense smoked in an ashtray. Lothar, dressed in his Sunday suit and new black plastic shoes, lay on the bed. A thick layer of pancake makeup could not cover the green tint of his face and hands. His lips curled over his teeth. His face was bloated as if he were strangling from the string tie pulled tight against his windpipe.

Peter and Jeff glanced at one another. Their morbid curiosity overcame their revulsion, and they entered the room. Alternating between bad German and English, I retreated from the apartment. I shook my head and muttered "Ich tut mir leid, I am sorry," over and over. Outside on the street, I stared at the cobblestones. I was ashamed. My father had pounded into me that I was supposed to fear nothing, nothing but him.

Chapter 19

After eighteen months of living in Neuhof, a three-bedroom apartment became available in the officers' housing complex in Wiesbaden. My parents leaped at the chance to upgrade their standard of living. Cigarettes and booze were to be had for a song at the base exchange. The officer's club served great meals on the cheap so they could go out more often than they ever had while in the States. The added bonus of the conversion rate being four Deustche Marks to the American dollar allowed my parents to get off by themselves and play the role of well-heeled tourists.

When Dad was not touring NATO and SEATO hospitals in exotic locales like Turkey, Pakistan, Greece, Italy, and Lebanon, he seemed content living in Wiesbaden. He expressed an interest in the things we did. He went to a couple of my wrestling meets and encouraged me to go out for the high school soccer team. He gave Janet permission to work as a chambermaid with one of her friends in Holland over the summer break. He even complimented my brother on his progress playing the guitar and sprang for classical lessons.

One weekend he took Jeff on a trip to a base near the Czech border. They ate at the officers' club and stayed in a swank hotel. After pouring himself a drink Dad told my brother that he was the first one to know that he'd made Lieutenant Colonel. Not even Mom was aware of the promotion. When Jeff got back, I asked him how it felt to be in on the news before anyone else.

"Dad told me that he respected me because I took whatever punishment he dealt out without flinching or hiding behind Mom's skirt."

I was pissed off at the obvious reference but held back.

"Know what?"

"What?"

"I'm his favorite," Jeff said. He rolled up his sleeve and showed me a nasty purple bruise. "His favorite fucking punching bag."

In the spring Dad arrived home from a trip to Athens and shouted, "Boys, come here." Jeff and I rushed into the living room and stood at attention. He leaned back in a kitchen chair. Mom brought over two chilled cocktail glasses.

My father plucked an olive stuffed with an anchovy from his martini and popped it in his mouth. "Guess what? I've accumulated so much time off that we are going to start seeing more of Europe."

"That's great, Ernest. The last time here you were too busy setting up hospitals and writing reports to be a tourist."

"What did you expect? It was only six years after the war."

"I'm just saying it will be wonderful to see Europe as a family now that kids are old enough to appreciate it."

Dad sipped the frigid mixture of three parts vodka to one part vermouth. "Norma, these trips are more than just about sightseeing. I'm worried these knuckleheads are being exposed to the wrong messages over here."

"You know they're fine."

"I know no such thing."

"Oh stop it, Ernest."

"Don't you ever tell me to stop it. Have you heard the crap they listen to on the radio?"

Barry McGuire had just released the "Eve of Destruction". I tuned it in on Radio Caroline, a pirate station broadcasting from a ship that floated in the English Channel.

McGuire, along with Bob Dylan and other anti-war musicians, were purged from the American Armed Forces airwaves, and their albums were pulled from the shelves of base exchanges across the world.

Dad slammed his glass on the table. "If I ever discover either of you listening to that faggot, commie music I'll put you out of your misery." He slugged me in the arm. "I'm talking to you. Do you hear me? Do you understand?"

"Yes, Sir."

"Good, throw away those Dylan and Beatles records

I found hidden in your bedroom."

"I'm not hiding them, Dad, they're on my desk in plain sight."

A calm came over my father. He took the second cocktail glass from the tray. "That's true. You didn't hide them. That's the only reason I didn't break them over your skull."

Mom spoke up. "Ernest, if today's generation saw what happened here in both world wars they wouldn't be so quick to condemn us."

"Brilliant observation. Now go sweeten my drink."

*

On Memorial Day weekend, Dad loaded us into a Volkswagen camping bus and embarked on Phase I of Ernest H. Brown's History of Europe Tour. The first stop was at Trier near the German-French border. Dad scheduled an hour and forty-five minutes to see the ancient Roman city's famed Porte Nigra. The double-arched entry gate flanked on both sides by towers that rose over ninety feet into the clear sky was all that remained of the wall that once surrounded the city.

My parents decided to take lunch at a sidewalk café with a garden. The heavy perfume of flowers planted throughout the medieval town saturated the atmosphere. The café was located under a street sign on which the word Jüdengasse was printed. A group of young adults strummed guitars in front of a three-story house across the street. The windows of the house were framed with brown shutters secured to plaster walls that had not seen a coat of whitewash since 1918.

An American voice sang out "Workers Unite" followed by a unified cry of "Down with USA imperialists".

My father dropped his fork and crossed the road. He trained his eyes on a brass plate screwed into the wall next to the entrance of the home.

"Come here, David."

"In a minute Sir." I forked a piece of wiener schnitzel into my mouth.

"You come when I call you if you want to have enough teeth left to finish your meal."

I crossed the street still chewing.

"Swallow and translate this plaque."

The piece of veal went down my throat like a wad of cardboard. "I think it says that this was the home of Karl Marx. Also, there is something about his 150th birthday."

A young woman stood beside me; her breasts were pushing out of the armholes of her sleeveless undershirt. The guy she was with had a fisted arm thrust in the air. His free hand was shoved down the back of her hip-hugger jeans. His hair hung below his collar. He wore an army fatigue jacket with a peace symbol crudely drawn on its back.

"Yeah man! Karl Marx, the most important person since Jesus Christ," the guy said.

My father raised his head from the plaque. "You're right, Marx was the most influential man since Christ. Without him, we wouldn't have had Hitler or Stalin."

"I don't know about that," the young man said. He withered under Dad's murderous glare.

"That's an Airborne jacket, son."

"I was Airborne. But then again so is bird shit until it hits the ground."

"When did you get out?"

"Two years ago. I went stateside and came back to where people know what's going on. I am free."

"You're damn right you are." Dad started to walk away.

The guy clicked his heels and snapped off an exaggerated salute. "Yes fucking Sir!"

Dad did an about-face and quietly said, "See that table at the café? My wife and children are sitting there. Do you understand?"

The young man's bravado evaporated. "Yes Sir. I'm sorry I used that kind of language in front of your family."

A cold smile appeared on my father's face. "I hope you find what you're looking for boy, before trouble finds you." Dad went back to the café.

The young guy looked at me. "Hey kid, is that prick your old man?"

"Yes."

"Ever considered deserting?"

*

We stood on a hill in Verdun and looked down at the endless rows of white crosses. Dad spread out his arms as if to gather in the battleground where men had lived and in some cases were buried alive in muddy trenches filled with human waste and the waste of humans.

It had been nearly half a century since a million men had perished, fighting over a plot of farmland. Shell craters lined with grass pocked the landscape. Barbed wire strung along the forested margins of the battleground prevented tourists from straying into the woods. There, the mementos of war were still trip-wired to maim and kill.

*

My father whispered to himself as he trudged over the landscape from one monument to the next. He marched across a broad expanse of lawn that was as finely manicured as a golf course. At the end of the green space were stairs that led up to an immense monument, the Ossuaire de Douaumont. A Gothic steeple was centered on a concrete tube that stretched out an equal distance from either side of the entrance like a half-buried subway car. The elaborate steeple resembled a Roman candle stuck in a loaf of white bread. I knelt at one of the numerous windows built into the sides of the tube. I jumped back when I saw a fissured skull smiling for eternity, sightlessly peering into the future. It was resting on a slagheap of bones piled the depth and width of the building from one end to the other. As homage to man's stupidity, the remains of over 130,000 French and German soldiers' femurs, pelvises, and ulnas were deposited in a jumbled mass.

My father, who served in three wars before he died, pushed his glasses up the bridge of his nose and thumbed away a tear from the corner of his eye. He sat on a stair, lit a cigarette, and held in the smoke long enough to sear his lungs. He smoked down to the filter then crushed the red-tipped butt against the sole of his shoe and slipped it inside his cigarette pack.

Chapter 20

Phase II of Ernest H. Brown's History of Europe Tour commenced July 1966 when he returned from Turkey bearing gifts. Mom got a white galabia decorated with gold stars and silver moons. My sister received a pair of curly-toed satin slippers. Jeff and I both were handed miniature scimitar letter openers complete with brass sheaths. Tommy got nothing. Dad also gave me a book on Ataturk. He believed it worthwhile to read something about the First World War without a European slant.

"There are two sides to every coin," Dad said.

'Sure,' I thought, 'your side and the wrong side.'

Dad cracked an ice cube under his molars. "I've booked us a week at Garmisch and Chiemsee."

*

July was a beautiful month to tour the Bavarian Alps. Whenever an especially breathtaking scene came into view my father pulled over and got out to admire the scenery. On his orders, the family remained sitting in the car, caught in the wake of speeding trucks and automobiles.

Dad stopped in Munich for lunch. We strolled through the old part of the city passing buildings trimmed in gingerbread moldings. We ate on an outdoor patio attached to the famous Hofbrau Haus.

Men in Lederhosen sat on a raised stage and played oom-pah-pah music. Pigtailed waitresses squeezed into tight green Bavarian peasant dresses rushed around toting four giant steins in each hand.

"This place was a shell when I came here in 52. Most of Munich had been reduced to rubble by our bombers," Dad said and took a sip of beer. "In 1933 Heinrich Himmler established the first concentration camp on a hill overlooking a village called Dachau, twenty minutes away from Munich by car. We'll be going there after lunch."

Dad held up his empty mug to a passing waitress and continued. "I visited Dachau in 1953 and again in 1955 to substantiate rumors that former inmates were still living in the camp." He gulped down the beer the waitress set in front of him. "I knew something about the camps from military films I'd seen. They hanged the commandant for crimes against humanity. His excuse, he was just following orders." Dad paused. "Sometimes you have to ignore orders."

*

The flower-bedecked market center of the village of Dachau was built around a fountain. Stone images of dancing farmers and wives in typical 17th-century garb adorned its pillars. There was nothing to indicate what had occurred just a couple of kilometers away from the quaint little town.

On Dad's instructions, I asked the first person we encountered, a man around my grandfather's age, "Woh sind die Konzentrationslager Dachau?" He snorted and pulled down the brim of his green felt hat. He marched off without answering.

"Ernest," Mom spoke up. She'd been silent since Munich. "Maybe we should just forget about it and go back to our vacation if you don't remember where the place is."

"I know where the camp is. I want to see if the people have changed since I was last here. They haven't."

Dad ordered me to continue asking people until I got a reply. Young, old, fat, slim, I got the same nothing response or at most a shrug until one man stopped and pointed at a road going up a hill outside the village. The man spoke to me in English with a heavy Eastern European accent.

"If you are going you should leave soon. They close the camp at 16:00."

Outside the entrance of Dachau, a perky blonde said, "Please join the tour."

"That won't be necessary," Dad answered. "I've been here before."

A sparkling expanse of white gravel created a sanitary boundary between the present and the past. Equipped with benches, flower gardens, and smooth monoliths inscribed with the names of the victims of Dachau, Deutschland's image reformers had allowed a few buildings to remain standing. Most prominent was a long crematorium that had been scrubbed spotless inside and out. The red brick building could have passed for a bakery if not for the black and white photos sandwiched between glass display signs. The images captured smoldering corpses in ovens resembling half-done lumps of dough on rolling trays.

"What the hell," my father cursed, pounding his fists against his thighs as he turned toward a guide in the midst of misinforming a group of Americans that Dachau had been the first internment camp, "an experiment to see how far the Reich could go without arousing protest from their citizens."

"Dachau was a concentration camp," Dad interrupted.

"There is truth to what this gentleman says but you must remember that Germany was in the midst of a depression so the imprisonment of potential revolutionists may have been perceived as a stabilizing influence."

Dad closed his eyes. "The SS knew the Americans were only twenty miles away and still the lousy bastards were killing and incinerating people until a few hours before the 42nd arrived. The crematorium was still warm from the last batch of half-burned corpses."

A plump woman wearing plastic orange hoops for earrings and bobbing like a walrus in a herd of other plump women said, "Mister, this girl is doing her best to educate us. Unless you have personal experience, please let her continue."

"How personal do you want my husband's experience to be? He was here right after the war before they had time to make everything spic-and-span."

"You were here?"

"I saw men squatting inside those barracks without anyone around who even cared if they existed. They survived by scrounging scraps from the local garbage dump."

He nodded in the direction of a wall. "There were bullet holes there from where the Germans lined up prisoners three or four deep and shot them point blank to save ammunition."

The tour guide interjected, "What we must understand is that it was the SS who ran the camps."

"Over there beyond the crematorium was the infirmary. People who entered were not always sick. The prisoners were used as guinea pigs in so-called medical experiments."

The guide stiffened her spine. "Ja, Ja there were horrible things that happened here. We have a section in the museum dedicated to this."

"Young lady, this is not a museum. This is Dachau."

"You cannot blame my whole country for the actions of madmen. Most Germans did not know what was happening. How could they?"

Dad looked up at the chimney stacks of the crematorium. "They saw the smoke. They smelled the burning flesh."

"Don't you think you're being a little hard on this girl? After all, she isn't to blame. She wasn't even born then," the plump woman said.

"I don't blame her. I just want her to know what happened here."

Chapter 21

There were a few minor inconveniences associated with being on the wrestling team. I was five-foot-ten and since the start of the season had lost twenty-five pounds to make weight at 121. Two seniors who wrestled at 130 and 135 were guaranteed their place in their respective weight classes even though I had beaten both consistently in practice. Still, I was on the team, and I was not about to chuck it out of pride. Like most wrestlers I starved myself before meets, living on celery, clear broth, and salted ice cubes. After a match, I joined my fellow teammates in a binge-eating session where we gorged ourselves all night on triple thick milkshakes, double patty hamburgers, and plates of fries. The next morning, we started the dieting cycle again. The most extreme weight loss routine was called purge and surge. It consisted of taking a laxative three days prior to a meet, vomiting on the day of the meet, and working out in a steam room wearing a sweat suit to lose the few extra ounces needed to right the scales.

I gave it my all in practice, often volunteering when the coach or one of the other senior wrestlers wanted to demonstrate a move. After one such demonstration, I ended up in traction for five days. While I was in the hospital the coach sent Mario Michelieni to my house for my uniform.

I detested Mario. Every practice he challenged me in an attempt to take my place on the team. It became a tedious ritual pinning him and hearing him mumble under his breath how he'd get me next time.

My first week out of the hospital, the coach allowed me to come to practice as a helper. Watching Mario strut like a rooster in my togs infuriated me. He tossed a towel in my lap after faking his way through some takedowns and said, "Brownie, anytime you want your position back I'll let you wrestle me for it."

I went home and tore off my neck brace and tossed it in the trash. The next day my mother caught me putting my wrestling shoes in my gym bag.

"The team needs me," I insisted. "Coach said if I beat Mario I get my place back on the team."

"Is your coach going to stay up all night with you when you break your neck or worse? No, he'll just send some other undernourished moron over to claim your uniform."

We were still arguing when Dad arrived. "This had better be about something important," he said.

"Your idiot son thinks he's going off to wrestling practice to see what other part of his anatomy he can destroy."

"I gotta admire your enthusiasm even if I think you're nuts."

"If I don't think I can do it I'll quit Sir. But I have to wipe the smirk off Mario's face first."

"Who's Mario?"

"He's that nice boy who brought over a box of chocolate when he picked up David's uniform."

"I didn't like him," Dad said.

"But Ernest, what if he breaks his neck?"

"His coach is a fool but it's his neck," Dad said and opened the liquor cabinet.

At practice the next day, the coach asked who wanted to challenge for Mario's weight class. I stepped onto the mat. Mario turned to the coach. "This can't be for real."

My neck injury did not permit me to grapple on the mat. I could not bridge, and any pressure applied to my shoulders or upper back sent me into muscle spasms. As soon as the coach blew the whistle, I stiff-armed Mario. He lost his balance I dove into his midsection like a tackle sacking a quarterback. He landed on his back, his head bouncing off the mat. I was back on the team.

The exhilaration of that match faded over the next few meets. Win or lose, I barely managed to walk off the mat. Incessant pain traveled from my neck to my legs. I swallowed dozens of aspirins to make it through the day. Maintaining weight was no problem. I was unable to eat anything that required vigorous chewing.

When I discovered all I needed to get my varsity letter was to participate in two more matches, I set my teeth to tough it out. My final meet was a quadrangle tournament. Teams from across Germany would wrestle for three days in Ludwigsburg. Four matches at a time were to take place. The team that scored the most points would emerge as a contender for the European Championship to be held in Lakenheath, England. As I packed for the trip my mother stood in my bedroom doorway, begging me not to go.

The first day of the meet I wrestled within my own weight class and won on points. The next morning over the loudspeakers a voice called out "Jerome from Munich, Stacey from Wiesbaden center mat." I looked up and down the bench but did not see our 145 wrestler. The coach lifted his arm and waved me over.

"Yeah coach?"

"Get out there."

"Where's Stacey?"

"Back at the hotel spewing his guts out. You're in for him."

"Jerome from Munich, Stacey from Wiesbaden center mat," the loudspeaker announced with more force.

I felt elated being called on to bail the team out of trouble. When I stepped onto the mat and saw my opponent my confidence dissolved. He was big, really big. He flexed his arms for my benefit. His biceps were thicker than my calves.

The referee ran his hands over our outstretched hands to ensure our nails were cut short. The boy from Munich adjusted his headgear and cracked his neck as he moved it from side to side. We shook and backed away from one another. He got behind me and slipped a half-nelson on me. I twisted, rammed my hip into the hollow of his pelvis, and threw him over my thigh. I was all over him, but it was futile. He was so strong that he crawled out of the circle with me on his back. The referee called us back. I elected to go down to my knees and let him take the top. As soon as the ref blew the whistle I sat out and scrambled to my feet. Before I could turn around to face him the kid slipped another standing half on me. Again, I went for the throw. As he sailed over me, I flipped under him and landed on my left arm.

A sound like a rifle shot echoed through the gym. I glanced at my arm and thought it strange that my elbow should be facing in the opposite direction. My opponent had landed on his face. He stood up, blood gushing from his nose. He raced across the mat and slid across my arm driving one broken bone through another.

The referee pulled the kid off me and quickly inspected his face to see where all the blood was coming from. I tried to push myself to my knees but couldn't.

"Holy shit. Keep him down. Medic, medic!" I heard shouting.

A guy in a white tunic stabbed me with a needle. I grew woozy. Morphine coursed through my system. I looked at my left arm. The arm was bent in four places, pieces of jagged bone pressing but not protruding through the skin.

There was no hospital in Ludwigsburg, so I was transported in a moss-green ambulance to Stuttgart. A medic kept telling me on the way down the bumpy road that it wasn't so bad, that bones heal.

Stuttgart was not equipped to deal with my kind of injury, their hospital being little more than an infirmary. The weekend staff consisted of two medics and an on-call general practitioner. When I lifted my head and saw my mangled arm cradled in a makeshift splint, I screamed. Someone gave me another shot of morphine. It was dark when the doctor showed up. He used his bare hands to snap my bones into some semblance of alignment and told the corpsman to plaster me. I was kept under sedation throughout the night.

"Your coach called us," Dad said when I awoke the next morning to find my parents at my bedside.

My lips, covered in a bitter-tasting gummy substance, crackled when I opened my mouth. "How'd we do?"

"I don't know about the team but your arm is broken in four places, your elbow is shattered and you sprained your wrist. By any measure, you lost."

My cast, an L-shaped affair, went from my knuckles to my shoulder. My fingers poked out of it like plump black sausages. Two days after arriving home Mom convinced Dad to rush me to emergency. The cast was soggy at the elbow. When the medic cut away the cast, he almost gagged. The putrid stench of wet plaster, pus, and blood filled the treatment room.

"Christ, who the hell set this arm?" the orthopedic surgeon said. "A few more days and you might have lost it. They set the son-of-gun without cleaning it or letting the swelling go down."

I was hospitalized for the balance of the week. Mario Michelieni appeared at my room and rapped on the doorframe.

"Hey Brown, how's it going?"

I was still groggy from the combined effects of antibiotics and painkillers and could just squeak out, "Fine and you?"

"I ain't got time to shoot the shit. I came to see if you brought back my uniform."

"I think they threw it away in Stuttgart."

"It was getting pretty ripe anyway," he said and left.

The coach came by the same day. He dropped a box of chocolates on the bedtable. "The team says get well soon." He lifted the lid off the chocolates. On top of the first layer of candy was a yellow fabric W with a gold pin in the shape of a wrestler on all fours attached to it. "I thought it best to present your letter here."

The coach drummed his fingers on the dinner tray. "Brown I got a favor to ask you. I talked to the doctor, and he said he has never seen a break like yours. Your ulna and radius snapped in two like breadsticks. Next semester I'm teaching health science and I'd like to borrow your x-rays to show the class what a compound fracture looks like."

My last day in the hospital I received an unexpected visit from Kyle. I had not seen him for a long time. The first few minutes were strained. Finally, he said, "Tough break."

"No kidding."

"Hang in there. Things are going to be a bit dicey at first-adjusting to being just another student and not a super jock."

"Give me a break, Kyle."

"No can do, someone already beat me to it."

"Funny."

"My Dad's time is up. We're going to live either in New Mexico or Alaska depending on where he decides to teach."

"Great, I guess you'll be getting your pilot license now."

Kyle looked around the room. "Do you remember when you asked me what was worse than being a homosexual?"

"Sure."

"Have you heard about Udo and Curt?"

"What about them?"

"Things got even worse for them. Some creep said Udo was caught giving Curt a blowjob in the dorms. Of course, it's a lie. If it was true, they would have been expelled in an eye blink. But nevertheless, Udo and Curt couldn't walk down the hall together without someone calling them cocksuckers or faggots."

"That's rough," I rasped and licked my dry lips.

Kyle handed me a plastic cup filled with water and crooked its straw, so I was able to take a sip.

"Udo is dead. Curt found him when he went to his room. He'd tied his bed sheet to the water heater pipe that runs along the ceiling and hung himself."

Chapter 22

I remained in a cast for six months before the doctor came to the realization that my arm was not healing. I underwent two bone graft operations. Dad must have felt sorry for me because he consented to let me take one of the empty maid's rooms in the basement of our housing complex. I liked living apart from the family. I suppose I could have taken advantage of the situation to sneak out at night, but I did not. I was content to sink into my bed and read or listen to British pirate radio.

It was not a newfound love of academia that motivated me to hit the books. I figured if I kept my marks above average and became more active in school affairs, I would gain some sparkle points and secure my rung on the popularity ladder. It wasn't easy. I had made more than a few enemies as a cocksure jock and quasi-tough.

*

On a lark, I enrolled in a public speaking course. My teacher was a dead ringer for Joan Baez. Like many of the teachers at H.H. Arnold, she had run out of cash in Germany as she hitchhiked around the world. Miss Kastner, a Radcliffe graduate, carried her blue blood pedigree into class but parked her left-of-Mao political sentiments in the coffee clubs downtown. She was not an easy person to charm. For my first oration and dramatic reading, I mouthed Lincoln's "Gettysburg Address" and recited Robert Frost's "Stopping by Woods on a Snowy Evening."

"Have you no imagination people!" Miss Klastner leaped out of her chair and stuck a pencil inside her ear. "Be forewarned, if I listen to one more insipid version of Lincoln, Frost, or Poe I will drive this pencil through my ear drum and into my brain."

For five classes she made us listen to recorded speeches and prose and poetry readings. At first, I affected the smarmy indifference of my former crowd of jocks. Then she played Jonathan Edwards' "Sinners in the Hands of an Angry God" and won me over. I envisioned black-garbed New England Puritans weeping and crawling on the ground as Edwards hurled their souls into the inferno.

"The God that holds you over the pit of hell, much as one holds a spider, or some loathsome insect over the fire, abhors you, and is dreadfully provoked: his wrath towards you burns like fire; he looks upon you as worthy of nothing else, but to be cast into the fire; he is of purer eyes than to bear to have you in his sight; you are ten thousand times more abominable in his eyes, than the most hateful venomous serpent is in ours."

If Edwards's ability to scare the shit out of emotionless New Englanders was not enough to win me over, listening to the boozy nicotine-stained intonations of Dylan Thomas reading from his works clinched the deal.

"And you, my father, there on the sad height, Curse, bless me now with your fierce tears, I pray. Do not go gentle into that good night. Rage, rage against the dying of the light."

On my first foray into the European American Dependent School Public Speaking Challenge, I placed third in extemporaneous speaking and got an honorable mention for my oration on a theme Miss Klastner chose for me, "Vietnam Now, or World War III Later".

A bit confused by her recommendation I said, "Miss Klastner, I thought you were against the war."

"That's true. But I'm in favor of winning. This is a hot-button topic and can't fail to impress the judges."

Even though I had no informed opinion about the US involvement in Southeast Asia I garnered applause by flicking on the "save the world for democracy" switch. Within the space of a few months, I went from being a B-minus student and middling athlete to being on the student council. By the end of grade 10, I had served as class representative, been elected as student of the month, and made the dean's list.

Chapter 23

We toured Italy in June of 1967, dragging a Nimrod tent trailer behind us. I think my father enjoyed the planning phase of the trips more than the actual destination. He gathered the family in his study, where he placed a card table next to his desk so he could spread out his large map of Europe and the more detailed maps of the countries on his trip itinerary. Slips of paper on which he had written "Things to Do & See, Primary Routes, Contingency Plans, Places to Bivouac" were thumbtacked to a cork bulletin board. He employed a color-coding system on his vacation briefing board (yellow = must see, green = would like to see, and pink = alternative or if time allows).

"Alright listen up! Here is the plan of action," he announced. "We'll go through Austria and Switzerland to enter Italy. That way we'll be able to see Salzburg and camp a couple of nights at Lake Lucerne. Next, we drive through northern Italy to Venice and then on to Pisa. When we're finished there, it's on to Florence. We'll make Rome with several days to spare giving us a chance to stop and camp at someplace on the Mediterranean. Any questions? Good. We'll decide who will be responsible for keeping track of the agenda of things we want to do and see in each country later."

Inevitably a monkey wrench jammed the cogs of Dad's vacation machine. We never made Venice. Roadwork detoured us too far south to justify turning back to the city's plazas and waterways.

"It's really no great loss to miss Venice," Dad said. "The canals are just open sewers. No telling what kind of disease you could catch."

We drove to Pisa arriving just as the famous tower was being cordoned off for repairs. Florence was a repeat of Venice and Pisa. Dante's famed city was recovering from the previous year's flood. Most galleries and museums were closed to the public while restoration work was underway. If Mom had not charmed a guard at the Uffizi, we might have been the only people to visit Florence and not see Michelangelo's David. The pattern was consistent. While in Rome we failed to see the Sistine Chapel and the Vatican. We had arrived while the holy city was closed due to the investiture of new cardinals.

We ate pasta and gelato and suffered the heat while we vainly sought out things to do. There are only so many visits one can make to the Coliseum. We spent the last three days of the Italian vacation in a campground watching the waves of the Mediterranean lap against a garbage-strewn beach. The authorities closed the beach to bathers when they discovered raw sewage being flushed into the sea.

*

Janet begged to stay home rather than join our next family vacation to Strasbourg in June of 1967. She had been accepted to several top-flight schools but opted to attend the University of Alabama. She said she wanted to pack. Dad caved and told Jan to have a good weekend. She won and lost at the same time.

Our experience in Strasbourg differed little from our Italian one. We arrived in a downpour. Jeff and I raised the tent trailer in a camping platz situated beside a mosquito-infested bog then spent three days not seeing the local sights. Museums, churches, and even the famous chateau were closed. A nationwide civil servants strike had paralyzed the country.

Throughout the month of July, Janet alternated between being morose or nauseous. One night Mom and Dad retreated to the furthest corners of the house with Jan and waged a battle of wills.

"You don't have a choice," Dad said. "You will get rid of it one way or another."

"Yes, I do have a choice, Daddy." Janet's voice was resolute. She had always been the strongest of us. When Dad started to spank her when she was eleven, Jan snatched the leather belt out of his hand. She raced outside and raged, "I won't let you. And if you try, I will scream and keep screaming." It was the last time my father ever laid a hand on her.

"I'm keeping it."

"You made your bed now you are going to have to lie in it," Dad growled.

"How could you?" Mom wailed.

"I didn't mean for it to happen."

"It's a little too late to think about that now."

"Don't you speak to your brothers about this."

"How can I hide it from them?"

"You and your boyfriend will be long gone before anyone has a chance to notice," Dad said.

*

At the beginning of August Janet flew to Birmingham. Dad insisted on shipping the steamer trunk in which she packed her clothes and mementos of her time in Germany separately because it was too big for the plane.

It never arrived. It was stolen from the post office and found floating in the river. Her graduation yearbook, souvenirs of the various places she visited in Europe, a photo album of happy times spent with her friends, and letters of acceptance from numerous colleges were ruined. It was as though Jan's past along with her future had drowned in the Rhine.

Two weeks after Jan left, my father followed her to Birmingham. Around that same time her boyfriend, Fred, also disappeared from Wiesbaden. Later I learned the three of them had stood through a discreet church wedding, sans ring, sans cake, sans hugs and kisses.

One evening my mother said, "Jan won't be coming home again for a while."

I said, "Yeah, I guess she'll have a lot to do, studying and all."

Mom broke into tears. My Dad's response was predictable when I pulled the same ploy on him.

"How's Jan doing in school, Dad?"

He grabbed me by the throat and slammed me against the wall. "I'm fed up with your questions. You have no right to ask a goddamn thing. Do you understand?"

"Yes."

He slapped me across the face. "Yes! Yes what?"

"Yes Sir."

"Go blow your nose and wipe your face. You have no right to cry either. Your mother is doing enough of that shit for the whole building."

Chapter 24

While we hardly talked about Janet's absence at home, the rumor mill was working overtime at school. Jeff and I were quizzed by some kids as to "how she got knocked up." Generally, I ignored the comments. I had too much to lose by knuckle diplomacy.

On the surface at least it was business as usual with my chums. Nate Crumpler, Jim Zale, Duane Dewy, and me were like the fabled four horsemen, the epitome of junior Joe Americans. We were sure that our all-around good guy attitudes would ensure us a place in any college. Duane, the only black kid in the Speech Club, had already secured letters of recommendation for the Air Force Academy. Though laced with a faint flavor of Deep South paternalism, my father held up Duane's family as what was possible with a little luck and a lot of work. Mom added that our people, especially a member of our own family, should hang their heads for rejecting the gifts and advantages they'd been given. After such an observation Mom would retire to a corner and spend the next few hours sighing and wringing her hands.

Sometimes I heard her wailing late at night. "If you had no respect for yourself you should have thought of your family."

"Shut up and go to sleep. You want the whole building to know, Norma?"

Choking sobs replaced Mom's curses.

Mrs. Norbert, from upstairs, became a regular unwanted guest in our living room.

Her entry line was always the same. "Hello Norma, I came down to see if you need any comforting."

"Why would I?"

"I don't know. Maybe you want to talk about it."

"No, I don't."

"How is your daughter doing in school."

"She's doing fine."

A true Mississippian, Mrs. Norbert lugged around a black leather bible when she came to speak to my mother. One day I walked in from school with Duane. She looked up and wrinkled her nose as though something had been left out to rot.

"Have it your way. You told me that some of your people were not born into the faith. I read somewhere that there is retribution unto the seventh generation. How far are you removed from those ancestors?"

My mother fanned herself wearily with a magazine. In Colorado Mom had taken up and later abandoned Martin Luther's hard-assed interpretation of Catholicism as her doctrine of the moment. She vacillated between several belief systems before finally settling on her own peculiar version of Judaic Christian rationalism, which took in both her Puritan background and her real or imagined ancestral Jewish connections.

Mrs. Norbert scowled when I grabbed Duane's half-eaten Oreo and took a bite.

"You better open your eyes Norma before you're sent another tribulation."

Mom's cheekbones already angular and high became more pronounced as she struggled to hold her peace. "Mrs. Norbert, maybe it would be best if you leave."

"Why Norma I hardly got here. I have so much more to help you with."

"I don't think I'll be needing any more of your help."

That evening Mom exhibited an unaccustomed composure. "Ernest, it's time to stop this nonsense. It's time to stop mourning and be upfront with it all."

Dad stomped off to the balcony where he smoked one cigarette after another. Then he called Jeff and me to his office. Tommy came too and sat in Mom's lap. "Boys, at the end of June we'll be going to Omaha, Nebraska. I am going to take six months off to finish my degree."

I was stunned. My friends had prodded me to run for junior class president the next year. I believed that I would graduate from H. H. Arnold. "Six months and then what, Sir?"

"What do you mean and then what?"

"Where do we go from there; will you be stationed in Omaha?"

Mom coughed.

"No, we'll be moving to Texas. Your sister lives there now."

"I thought she enrolled at the University of Alabama," Jeff said knowing full well that she had not gone there.

Mom issued one of her rare orders. "Ernest, tell them."

153

Dad gritted his teeth. "You boys are going to be uncles."

Chapter 25

Things started getting increasingly bizarre on the home front. Late at night my mother would walk into the pantry and close the door behind her. Curses, small, shrill, and repetitive, seeped under the doorway. "Slut! Whore! Whose child are you? You're mine! I love you. I have to love you. Love you and the little boy you made." Mom stopped socializing with the base wives. She spent hours away from Wiesbaden visiting Frau Angerman in Neuhof. Imegard, Mom's best and perhaps only true lifelong friend, was a Hausfrau of Brünhilde proportions. They were an odd pairing. Frau Angerman lived to eat, drink, party, and dance. Mom adored flowers, walks through the countryside, history, and culture.

Dad went out of his way to be friendly and charming with Jeff and me. He gave Jeff a twelve-string guitar and me a new Remington 22 caliber over/under 20-gauge shotgun. He made an effort to take us to the skeet range to shoot clay pigeons. He came home with a shotgun shell loading kit and spent the evening teaching us how to fill the empty shells. Jeff found a covert way of getting his revenge on the old man. He packed the shells with everything except the shot. At the range when Dad yelled, "Pull!" he fired confetti at the clay plates.

Now that Dad had made the announcement official, I could not ignore the not-so-veiled innuendoes about Janet. Things completely fell apart in Algebra class. As I approached my desk, I saw a felt-tip drawing of a naked woman. She was on her back, her open legs in the air. Cartoon figures with their pants around their knees and erect dicks were lined up in front of her. The caption under the drawing read, "Greetings from your loving sister."

Scott Ferland, the class comedian, waved a black marker at me and laughed. "Hey Brown," he shouted. "I thought you were an art lover."

Prematurely balding, Ferland was too fat to extricate himself from his desk. The edge of my math book caught him above his eyebrows. As his hands went up to protect his face, I flipped his desk over. My fists and feet sunk into him.

Algebra was not the best class to choose to lose my temper. While I slapped Scott across the face, he blubbered out an apology. Mr. Gillette jerked me up by my collar. "I don't know who started this. I don't know what is going on. I don't care. But it better stop!"

I sat down. Gillette passed out the marked exams from the previous week. When he handed me my test, I looked at the D- and fixed my face into a concrete block of apathy.

Gillette said, "Mr. Brown, your marks have been slipping lately. Maybe you should spend more time studying and less time playing patty-cake with Mr. Ferland."

I crumpled the exam, aimed it at the trash basket, stood up, and took two steps to leave. Mr. Gillette may have been shorter than me, but his neck was as big around as my thighs and his biceps stretched the seams of his cheap poly-cotton sleeves to near bursting.

He lowered his head, drove his shoulder into my midsection, and lifted me up. He kicked open the door and dashed into the hallway. Flipping me off his shoulder, he kept a hand behind my head to keep me from cracking my skull against the wall.

"What is your problem, Mister? I gave you a break in there and this is how you pay me back?"

My fists were clenched as solid as a ball pin hammer.

"Back off. Leave me alone. Touch me again and I'll..."

Gillette released his hold on me and held his arms in the air, palms facing out. "Calm down, boy. You're not a bad kid. What's going on?"

"Nothing."

"My only concern is to make sure you learn what I got to teach you."

"I don't need to learn what you have to offer," I shouted back.

"Christ kid, you can't even deliver pizzas if you can't do a simple math problem."

"I don't need this class. I don't need your crap."

"You're crossing the line, Brown. You're going to get a B out of my course or you are going to be expelled for making wise to me and for pounding that moron in there. If you get a B the matter will be forgotten. What do you say?"

I wiped the back of my hand under my cheekbones. I had been crying without realizing it.

"Go for a walk Brown."

As I started down the hallway Gillette said, "Dave, your sister was a good student and a nice girl. Things have a way of working themselves out in the end."

Chapter 26

I pulled a B in algebra and made the Dean's list, making me eligible to enter the US Dependent School Forensic Speech Tournament along with Duane.

The speech competitions were held at H.H. Arnold. When I looked at the front row of the auditorium, I saw Kyle. His father had postponed his return to the States to do a family tour of Europe. Kyle had aced his advanced placement exams and had graduated early. He worked as a volunteer at the base library and tutored German kids from his village in English while awaiting his acceptance to MIT. I had learned all this from Duane who kept in contact with Kyle. They had been in the scouts together. Following the summer riots in Detroit, they organized an interracial dialogue that no one went to as it coincided with Oktober Fest.

I did not make it past the first round. Just as I hit the key line on why legalizing euthanasia was a slippery slope that could lead us back to the horrors of Nazi Germany I started stuttering nervously.

Kyle walked up to me after I left the stage. "It was a good speech," he said.

"Thanks," I said coldly recalling the last time we had met in the hospital. "It's the topic Miss Klastner said I would score the most points with."

"Maybe that's the problem. You're too concerned with scoring points." He waved at Duane who had delivered a moving recitation of Martin Luther King's "I have been to the mountain" sermon.

By the time the big tournament rolled around in April, I'd rebounded and represented H.H. Arnold in the extemporaneous and oration categories. Duane also made the cut. In my American literature class, I had finished reading Henry David Thoreau's Essay on Civil Disobedience. Miss Klastner remarked that Gandhi and Martin Luther King had used Thoreau's writings as a basis for their non-violent protests. She had me push the idea further and contrast it with Oliver Wendell Holmes's statement that one does not have the right to yell fire in a crowded theater.

My speech was called "Dr. King, civil disobedience or civil unrest, license or freedom?" It was a hit. I coasted through the first day and made the cut as one of the four finalists. On the third day of the tournament, as I prepared to go on stage, Miss Klastner entered the auditorium from the wings. Her face was paler than the manila folder she carried. She climbed onto the stage and waved off the girl giving a speech on the Peace Corps. She flicked the microphone with her red lacquered fingernails and announced, "I regret to inform you that Dr. Martin Luther King was murdered at 6:01 P.M. on Thursday in Memphis Tennessee. In respect for Dr. King, we will curtail the remainder of today's speeches."

*

On Monday a notice was posted on the front doors of H.H. Arnold. It was a directive from the base commander that disallowed the gathering of more than four black airmen or students until the potential for violence ended.

Duane passed out of my circle of friends, choosing to hang exclusively with other black kids.

The truth, I learned, contrary to Mr. Gillette's words, is that most things do not have a way of working themselves out.

(1968-1969)

"History repeats itself, first as tragedy, second as farce."
Karl Marx

"Whippings and abuse are like laudanum; you have to double the dose as the sensibilities decline."
Harriet Beecher Stowe

"Do you think I'm telling you all this to hear myself talk? My history is the result of taking on a lot of scar tissue. I just want you to avoid whatever mistakes I made in the past. The first thing you have to learn is that if you ever get too big for me to handle with my fists, I'll use a baseball bat."
Lt. Colonel E.H. Brown (U.S.A.F. Retired) 1925-1997

Chapter 27

We flew out of Frankfurt on June 5th, 1968. Somewhere over the Atlantic, the pilot announced that Robert Kennedy had been gunned down by a busboy in the lobby of the Ambassador Hotel in Los Angeles.

Dad had shipped the VW camper, tent trailer, and station wagon to New Jersey a month before we left Germany. After deplaning in Trenton, we packed into the two cars and hit the highway. Dad was determined to make the drive from New Jersey to Florida non-stop. The plan was to visit the Chief and Louise at their motel. Time permitting and Dad willing, we would make a short stopover in Birmingham to see Mom's parents.

Dad pulled the Nimrod behind the VW bus. Mom followed in the station wagon with Jeff and Tom. I rode shotgun with Dad. My parents kept in contact via Dad's latest brush with technology, a long-range walkie-talkie.

"Ah, this is Yellow Top to Pretty Mama, do you copy? Over."

Static then a faint, "Hello, Ernest."

"Pretty Mama this is Yellow Top how far are you behind me? Over."

More static and a giggle passed through the walkie-talkie. "Ernest, if you'd slow down, you would know I am just right behind you."

"For Christ's sake Norma, follow the protocol. Do you copy? Over."

"Yellow Top, I copy."

The heat became more and more intolerable the further south we traveled. Despite the airtight atmosphere, Dad puffed steadily on pack after pack of Robert Burn's cigarillos. The stench, the humidity, the closed windows of the VW bus made me car sick.

Forty minutes passed before Dad pulled into a Stuckeys to get gas and a complimentary pecan log. When I returned from vomiting in the men's room, he commended me for exercising self-restraint and acting like a man. Eighteen hours had passed since we had landed in New Jersey and coasted into my grandparent's motel in the swampland of central Florida. Louise and the Chief were not at the flamingo pink motel. They were at their new house on the West Coast, replete with a swimming pool and central air. Of the motel's thirteen units only the office/living quarters had a high enough ceiling for the heat to rise and escape through a whirling turbo vent. Each unit was supplied with a barely functioning swamp cooler. My parents slept in the office unit until the Chief and Louise returned, whereupon, they were banished to one of the motel rooms.

I took three worthless showers a day to try to keep cool. As soon as I stepped out of the shower a humid air blanket smelling of decay and Lysol enveloped me. I wheezed constantly. Sleep was impossible. The gators croaked all night long and thrashed around when they caught a bird or rodent.

One afternoon I saw my father standing on the dock. "Come here, I want to talk to you," he said, staring down the length of a fishing rod. The tangled line hung from its end like a spider web.

Propped precariously against a folding chair was a rifle. Dad said, "Go ahead pick it up. I brought it down to snap off a few rounds to scare off turtles and alligators. The damn things are eating all the fish."

I picked up the 22 as Dad leaned over the handrail, holding a glass of bourbon and water in one hand and cradling a photograph in the other. He dropped the photo in the lake. It floated face down among the lily pads and swamp grasses.

"Fire a shot over by that dead cypress."

I rested the rifle on its butt end against a wooden bench.

"Go on. Don't you want to scare off some gators?" He groaned as he squatted to take a bottle of Jack Daniels from under the lawn chair. "Want a drink?"

"No Sir. I only like beer."

"Picked up that taste over in Germany, didn't you?" I nodded.

"Guess we picked up a lot over there. More than we bargained for."

"Yes Sir."

"Did you like it over there, like seeing all those places?"

"I liked it, Sir."

"Me too. You've done a lot more things than most kids your age. Maybe too many things."

I lowered my eyes and studied the dock's aging planks of wood.

He played with the tangle of fishing line fouling the reel. "David?"

"Yes Sir?"

"You ever thought you were in love?" I didn't know what he wanted.

"Have you? I know damn well you must have tried to light up the outfield with some girl. But have you ever been in love?"

"I'm not sure what you mean, Sir."

"It's not that damn hard to understand. Unless you're a sissy."

I concentrated on the image of my father in the lake's black surface. His watery reflection stretched from the dock to the middle of the lake. My eyes wandered from the lake and settled on the rifle. "It would be so easy," I thought.

"Well, have you ever been in l-o-v-e?"

"No."

"Good! Love is the word most abused in the English language. It holds as much substance as a snowball in hell."

"Love?"

"Yes. Take your mother and me. We've been married twenty-one years. But we were probably only in l-o-v-e one, two, maybe ten years at the most. That's not to say I don't care for her. I do. Truth is, we both would have been just as happy with someone else." Dad put his drink on the top of the railing and picked up the rifle. He aimed it at the water bubbles that popped to the surface of the lake and then handed it to me. He pointed at a turtle swimming near the dying cypress tree.

"You know what really gets to me? I never took Janet for being careless. Hell, how can you grow up in the military without having the sense to take precautions?" He wrapped his arm around me. I pretended to place the turtle in my sights. Dad's breath smelled of bourbon and cherry cigarillos. He leaned over the rifle stock.

"Never ball on an impulse. Plan your moves well in advance. Make sure that it's purely biological. Emotion screws up judgment. Count to ten, unwrap your little friend, slip it on, and go for it. It may not be as pleasurable as skin to skin, but it sure beats the hell out of playing Mommy and Daddy at eighteen."

His arm lay across my neck like a sack of cornmeal. I tried to roll out from under its weight. Dad's green eyes went glassy. He gritted his teeth and pinched my cheek so hard that droplets of blood burst to the surface of my skin. "I'm not finished. I'll tell you when I'm finished. If you ever do to some poor girl what Fred did to Jan, you're history. The girl's father won't have to deal with you because I'll kill you myself. Do I make myself clear?" He pushed himself away from me and walked a perfectly straight line back to the motel, leaving a half bottle of Jack Daniels on the dock.

I jammed the butt of the rifle into the hollow of my shoulder and squeezed off round after round. The turtle I aimed for leaped into the air as a bullet blew off its head.

Chapter 28

Dad was given a six-month leave of absence to finish a degree in Administration at Creighton University. Arriving in Omaha in mid-July of 1968 we camped in a trailer park on the banks of the Missouri River. At the time, the skyline of Omaha consisted of a solitary office building that rose above the wind-stunted trees of the campground like a giant middle finger flipping neighboring Iowa the bird.

Offutt airbase, where B-52s stood on the ready to lift off and drop their payload of nuclear bombs on the Soviets, kept Omaha's economy afloat. On this base, the Enola Gay was produced. The plane eventually flew on to obliterate Hiroshima. The other staple of Omaha was the insurance industry.

In the trailer park, we fended off mosquitoes and held our noses to block the stench of algae and water scum that proliferated in the most intense heat wave Omaha had experienced in a quarter of a century. Mom and Dad disappeared after breakfast every morning and did not return to the campground until sundown. They were searching for an affordable house near Creighton University. Affordable was the operative word. Dad had to take a pay cut while he finished his MBA.

We moved into a duplex the second week of August. The duplex was one of four located at the end of a dirt road between a cornfield and a railroad track. The dwellings looked substantial, but it became quickly apparent that they had been thrown up to house seasonal workers.

They were constructed of cinder blocks that were painted sea green outside and were not insulated. The windows, single pane sliders, were more suited for the tropics than the minus twenty winters of the Nebraska plains. My parents and baby brother slept upstairs. Jeff and I occupied a room in a bare basement next to an alcove that sheltered the furnace and water heater. The furnace gasped whenever the temperature dipped below sixty degrees. It operated on two cycles, barely on and dead. The 20-gallon hot water tank never brought the water temperature beyond tepid. Still, the house was an improvement over the campground.

With the exception of two crates containing our clothing, dishware, a typewriter, and my father's arsenal of pistols, rifles, and shotguns, everything we owned was in storage at our next duty station in Texas. The only acquisition Dad made in Omaha was a portable black-and-white television.

For seven days in August, my father and I sat in front of the Zenith, mesmerized by the scenes of chaos played out in Chicago. Mayor Daley's cops swept through the streets and parks of the windy city like the Czar's Cossacks ridding Moscow of Bolsheviks. Only this time the Cossacks were armed with water cannons, cattle prods, and teargas. The insurgents smoked pot, wore headbands and beads, listened to the Jefferson Airplane and the Hendrix Experience, and nominated a pig as their presidential candidate.

On my birthday, Tom Hayden, Jerry Rubin, Abbie Hoffman, and thousands of other bell-bottomed, tie-dyed youths took control of the airwaves. They let their fathers know that John Wayne belonged to Hollywood and Vietnam belonged to Ho Chi Minh.

Dad spent my birthday switching television stations as if searching for an image to balance out the pictures of mayhem, the chanting of peaceniks, and the jeers of militants. His eyes moved from the flickering screen to Jeff and me. He sat so close to the TV that his face glowed from its beams. After the tear gas settled and the Chicago 7 were led away flashing V-fingered peace signs and giving the finger, Dad said, "Tomorrow you two get a goddamn haircut."

*

When my father last attended university, the colleges of America were packed with young men recently returned from Korea, many of whom had also served in WWII. Eisenhower was president, Nixon was harmless, and James Dean had not yet been elevated to mythic dimensions. Now slogans like "saving the world for democracy, a just and lasting peace, my country right or wrong," mantras to my father, were openly derided in class by students and professors alike.

At Creighton Dad's resolve to face the enemy head-on became an obsession. He staggered into the house every evening exhausted from defending his uniform and country. He challenged students too young to have remembered the sacrifice his generation had made and professors too enamored with left-wing academia to care. Traitors had taken over the college corridors; this was an immutable truth in my father's mind.

When Lt. Colonel Brown, as he insisted on being called, returned from a particularly grueling day of contending with views different than his own, he buried himself in his studies. With a notepad and coffee cup full of pens and pencils in front of him and a drinking glass of bourbon and water within reach of his left hand, he blocked out everything and everybody.

"What are you reading?" he asked me one evening on his way to the kitchen to get a cup of coffee. I held up a dog-eared copy of The Jungle. He took it from me and recounted the apocryphal tale of how upon reading Upton Sinclair's novel at breakfast, Teddy Roosevelt pushed aside his sausage and eggs and later that afternoon enacted legislation to inspect slaughterhouses.

"People rarely see past the surface of an issue," Dad said. "The Jungle used the stockyards of Chicago to symbolize the exploitation of immigrant workers in America."

Dad railed against the student protesters and University professors who were blinded by their own oratory on the US involvement in Vietnam. In the next breath, he would let it drop that Truman should have followed F.D.R.'s position that no American blood should be shed in Indochina. "If we'd backed Ho Chi Minh instead of De Gaulle, Vietnam would have been our strongest ally against China. But we didn't. Just as we didn't read the writing on the wall in Cuba. We backed that bastard Batista and now we got Castro. A dictator is a dictator. But once your nation is engaged, you stand down. There is no room for dissent when you are at war even if it is a stupid war. You're either in or out."

As the weeks passed a new dynamic emerged in family relations. The hostility and abuse that Dad had previously directed at Jeff shifted more and more to me. The only explanation I have for this transfer is that I was closer to the age of the protesters he saw on television. One evening, on the way to the bathroom I made the mistake of pausing to listen to Dad and my brother. Jeff's teacher had asked his students to write a story from a Vietnamese child's point of view. My father cranked up the complexity of the Asian conflicts starting with Mao's great march to the sea. At some point, Dad dredged up the Domino Theory.

"Hey Jeff," I quipped, "I got an idea. How about writing about some kid in a hospital bed? Have the kid say the Americans are talking about dominoes, the Vietcong are worrying about Chinese checkers and all I want to do is go home and play bingo with my friends."

I should have watched Dad's hands. I should have seen him remove his Bulova watch from his left wrist and slip it over the knuckles of his dominant right. This was Lt. Colonel E.H. Brown's version of anger management, a subtle reminder to himself that breaking my face would also damage the crystal of his beloved watch, a gift from his co-workers when he was promoted to Major back in Detroit. His punch glanced off the side of my head. I did not wait for a second blow and retreated into the bathroom but wasn't quick enough to close and lock the door.

Dad burst into the bathroom yelling, "A game, a fucking game! Is that what your pinko teachers are feeding you?" He flailed the air as he backed me up to the edge of the tub. "Maybe I should drag your pansy ass down to the Marine recruiting station to enlist. You can explain the game to some Gunny Sergeant in boot camp, faggot!"

I shoved him away. "You don't have to drag my ass down there! I'll go myself if it means getting away from you!"

Dad snatched my throat with his left hand and threw me into the tub while his right fist caught me once in the solar plexus and once in the forehead. Slivers of the shattered watch crystal embedded the skin above my eyebrows. He continued to pummel me as I slumped into the tub.

My mother treaded carefully into the bathroom. The porcelain tub was splattered with blood. She tugged at my father's arm half-heartedly as he lifted one leg over the edge of the tub and held me down with his foot.

"Don't ever talk to me like that again. If I can't get respect out of you, I'll beat it into you. Do you think I'm telling you all this to hear myself talk? My history is the result of taking on a lot of scar tissue. I just want you to avoid whatever mistakes I made in the past. The first thing you have to learn is that if you ever get too big for me to handle with my fists, I'll use a baseball bat."

After he walked out of the bathroom my mother helped me from the tub, then turned on the tap and stood there, watching the diluted mixture of blood and water swirl down the drain. She picked up a Louis L'Amour pocketbook off the lid of the toilet and asked me if I had read it. I shook my head.

"Of course not. Westerns are what your father likes." Mom tossed the book on the floor and walked out of the bathroom.

Chapter 29

We left Omaha before the Christmas break. It was ten below zero. Dad picked me up as I walked home from wrestling practice. The vicious Nebraska wind howled down from Canada with no obstacles to deflect its intensity. The VW camping bus and Ford station wagon were loaded. Dad's AAA trip ticket was on the dashboard. He had plotted out every stop from Omaha to Dallas based on the average fuel consumption of the Ford. He was determined to make it to Kansas City with only three fill-ups along the way. As we drove south of the city limits, the solitary skyscraper of Omaha protruded through the frosted landscape. Tufts of clouds drifting above the building made it resemble a birthday candle after someone had made a wish.

By the time we arrived in Lincoln, Mom had buried the walkie-talkie in a half-eaten bag of chips. Dad slowed down to 50 mph to keep her in his rearview mirror. In Kansas City Dad veered off into a filling station. He entered a phone booth to call his brother for directions to his house.

Mom scanned the neighborhood. A Greyhound bus terminal faced the Texaco. Next to the terminal, a squat red-brick hotel boasted its best features, 4 Dollars and Lounge, Ladies Welcome.

In front of the bus terminal stood a man wearing a torn parka. Spots of orange, the garment's original color, peeked through the grime. He was taking a leak against the wall. When he finished, he doubled over and tossed his cookies on the sidewalk beside an overflowing wire garbage basket.

He wove his way down the block and lined up with his fellow derelicts at the liquor store. A large black woman wearing a sunbonnet and a towel wrapped around her face pushed a shopping cart across the street. She pulled up next to Mom's side of the car and rapped on the glass with swollen knuckles. Mom rolled down the window a matchbook's width.

The woman pointed at the fully extended stem of the door lock and said, "Honey, be best if you keep your doors locked." She pressed her face to the crack. "Used to be a good neighborhood."

Mom passed a dollar bill through the slit of the window.

The bag lady mouthed "God bless you" and pushed her cart toward a doublewide trailer that sat on a bare lot. A sign in front of the trailer beckoned the public, Mighty Redeemer Pentecostal Assembly. Sunday Services 10 AM/ Noontime fellowship and lunch Wednesdays. All sinners welcome.

Dad said, "Charlie's place is on the other side of town. He says we should hightail it out of here and don't look back. See if you can keep up with me this time. I don't want to go back and hunt for you."

Mom's hand dove into the bag of chips and came out grasping the walkie-talkie. She wiped the crumbs and oil off with a napkin and held it up for Dad to see. "Don't worry, Ernest, if I get lost I'll shout yoo-hoo, I'm over here."

"Norma, don't get cute. Just make sure you sign off properly this time."

We drove through block after block of garbage-strewn streets and neglected housing projects until we picked up the cross-town freeway. It was after dinnertime when we rolled into Uncle Charlie's townhouse complex. Lincolns, Cadillacs, Buicks, and Oldsmobiles were moored like battleships under a covered carport.

My father stopped midway down the row of cars without signaling. Mom slammed on her brakes and avoided rear-ending him. Uncle Charlie was leaning against the trunk of a candy apple red Coupe de Ville convertible. He held two highball glasses filled to the rim. As soon as Dad stepped out of the mini-bus Charlie handed him one. Dad followed Charlie to Mom's car. My uncle opened the door for my mother. She slid out of her seat without taking his hand. Charlie stepped back and flashed his mass marketing smile.

"Ernie," Charlie said turning away from my mother. "Let's finish off these Long Island Ice Teas. After dinner, we'll get serious. Pap sent me a decanter of 12-year-old sipping whiskey."

In his tailor-made slacks, yellow shirt, and cashmere sweater, Charlie stood in sharp contrast to my father. Aside from a Tweed sports coat, blue blazer, and double-knit polyester trousers, my Dad owned nothing that could be classified as dressy.

"New car?" Dad asked.

Charlie tilted his head toward the Coupe de Ville. "Yeah, they're not much on mileage. But who cares? It's a company car. Jean hates the damn thing. She only drives the Buick, says she wants a hardtop in case there's an accident or some kid heaves a brick off an overpass."

My mother walked ten paces behind Charlie and Dad. "Where is Jean?"

"Inside with the kids. She went out earlier and bought quite a spread – Kentucky fried chicken, salads, and a pecan and cherry pie. She still can't cook but she's a genie out of the bottle when it comes to arranging a party."

Dad and Uncle Charlie emptied their tumblers before they reached the front stoop of the townhouse. Jean Brown waited inside an open doorway trimmed with blinking lights shaped like poinsettias.

A plastic wreath decorated with pinecones and red and white polka dot mushrooms hung on the door. Thumb tacked to the lintel was a Seasons Greetings banner. A sprig of mistletoe dangled above Jean's head. She pecked Dad on the cheek and handed him a martini poured into a margarita goblet. A swollen olive rolled around the bottom of the glass like an eyeball.

"I made them extra dry for you, just waved the Vermouth bottle over the gin. Norma, honey, I made us Manhattans, proper lady drinks," Jean said. "You boys must be famished. Go on in the kitchen and get something while there is still something left."

"Well Ernie, now that you're a Colonel you should think of opening your own franchise," Charlie quipped. My mother pursed her lips and folded her arms over her chest. Perhaps she was biting her tongue, waiting for her husband to come back with a clever remark that would put young Charlie in his place. The return zinger never came.

My mother lived by the maxim, "If you can't say something nice to or about someone it is better to say nothing at all." If she disliked a person she might say, "She's a good hostess or her dog is well trained."

Mom was almost mute the three days we spent in Kansas City. She cleaned the kitchen, dusted the furniture, scrubbed the toilets and bathtubs, and made the beds. She wore a hurt smile while Charlie and Dad reminisced and traded barbs. After dinner, she stayed upstairs and read.

One evening as Jeff and I sat in the den watching a Perry Como holiday special, Jean found an opening in Charlie and Dad's conversation and recounted her past history as a debutante, model, dancer, and femme fatale of Birmingham's crusty upper caste.

She fanned herself in the best tradition of a blushing daughter of the confederacy and breathlessly said, "Oh my goodness, Miss Louise was so delighted. She shone like a sunbeam when Charles marched up to the pulpit in his tuxedo and waited for me to sashay down the aisle in the gown my own mother had worn at her wedding. I knew that Mother Brown was overjoyed to see her baby boy find happiness and herself find a daughter."

Fortunately, Mom was safely out of earshot, sequestered in the guest room. My father looked toward the hallway leading to the guest room. He said in a low voice, "We got married by a justice of the peace, couldn't afford the big show what with my just being out the army and Norma finishing nursing school."

Charlie drained his drink and scooped out an ice cube with his tongue, sucking on it as he responded. "Ernie, Ma, and Pap understood. A grocer's daughter doesn't bring a lot to a marriage much less be able to pay for one."

My mother entered the den as Charlie concluded his observation. If she heard anything it was not obvious. She walked straight past her husband to the television. "Boys time for bed," Mom said. "We got to get up early if we're to keep to your father's time schedule. I want to see both of you bright-eyed and bushy-tailed in the morning."

At seven o'clock the next morning, we sat around the kitchen table for breakfast. Jean was sitting next to Dad. Charlie was still in bed and Mom was at the sink washing the dishes. Jean poured Dad a cup of coffee out of a Dunkin' Donuts thermos. She asked, "Norma, will you be seeing Janet when you get to Texas?"

My mother began wringing the dishcloth with a determination reserved for live chickens. "Yes, I suppose we will. Janet's husband got a job in North Dallas with Sears and Roebuck as a department manager."

"You must be looking forward to seeing that new grandchild of yours. What is it?"

"It?" Mom squeezed out whatever moisture remained in the dishrag.

"Boy or girl?"

Mom stammered, "It's a ba-boy."

"It has a name, doesn't it?"

"Christopher," Mother sang out and fled out the patio doors into the frosty Kansas City morning to light a cigarette.

Chapter 30

I don't know what Dad's rush was to get to Irving. Bereft of visual stimuli, the most outstanding features of this Dallas suburb were the Cowboy Stadium and a multi-lane interstate slab of concrete running from North Texas to Galveston like an immense drag strip.

Our first place was a rental cookie-cutter house. A single live oak tree was planted beside its bay window. The day we arrived Dad told Jeff and me to find a store and bring back milk and a loaf of bread. We walked up the quiet residential street past virtually identical ranch houses footed on cement slabs. The dominant form of grass, a creeping mass of tendrils and small tough blades made Astroturf seem lush. The color theme of the neighborhood was brown. The roofs were brown, the front doors were brown, the yards were brown, and the evergreen shrubs were brown.

A horrible rendition of Wild Thing reached our ears. A chubby kid sitting on a folding chair was bent over an acoustic guitar. His tongue lolled out the side of his mouth as he concentrated on fretting and plucking the strings. Despite the fifty-plus-degree day, he was wearing a parka.

"That really stinks," Jeff said.

The boy got up and handed the guitar to Jeff. Albert was burned into its leather shoulder strap.

"Can you do any better?"

Jeff picked out Green Sleeves followed by Tom Dooley.

Monday morning, I walked to MacArthur High. I left before Jeff so I could be in my new homeroom early. I wanted to avoid being escorted into class and introduced as the new kid. I entered the halls of an immense airless building that resembled a concrete bunker. A buck-toothed woman standing inside the doorway cleared her throat. She wore a broach in the shape of a horseshoe with a crucifix inside the arch. She pointed a pencil at me. "Where do you think you're going? The first one hasn't rung."

"The first what?"

"Bell."

"I came early so I could get all the enrollment stuff out of the way first thing."

Mr. Berk, the senior principal, had his back to the door when I entered the office. He was built like a defensive tackle, broad-backed and square. Next to a file cabinet stood Vice-principal Eugene Lesman, a sickly thin, freckle-faced, pasty man. Lesman's concave chest and curvature of the spine made him resemble a ferret standing on two legs. He kept his arms close to his sides. His fingers curled into his palms.

Mr. Berk didn't turn around. "Take a seat," he said and held up a folder. "Been reading your file, Ernest."

"David, I prefer to be called David."

"Didn't hear him asking how you preferred to be called," Lesman said.

"That's okay Eugene. If he wants to be called David, that's what we'll call him."

Mr. Berk turned to face me. "From your transcript, it looks like you got all the credits to graduate, except for Texas History and Civics."

I was pleased by the prospect of getting out of high school a year early.

Mr. Berk grinned. "The education board is clear about all students having to take these courses and since they are offered only at the start of the school year, you'll have to take them next year."

"What am I supposed to do the rest of this year?"

"You will be taught and you will learn. Although your records here show you as a good student, I question just how good the schooling you did in Germany could have been."

"And Nebraska," Lesman chimed in, wrinkling his nose at the name of that state.

"That's right. MacArthur prides itself in the number of students it graduates who go on to junior college and beyond."

"A lot," Lesman added.

Mr. Berk circled behind my chair and dropped his hands on my shoulders. "Things are done differently here in Texas than you may be used to. We pride ourselves on producing good citizens. Transforming boys into men who aren't afraid to stand up for God and country."

Mr. Berk stepped in front of me and slapped the folder down on his desk. "You know what this is?" he asked. "It's your school history, what the French call a dossier. And it tells me a story. It tells me that you got to learn what side of the block you want to walk on. On the surface, everything looks fine. You are an above-average student, though your math skills could stand improvement. You have been on the student council. Lettered in sports, though I hardly classify cross-country and soccer as real sports. Rasslin is good. Mr. Worell, our head coach, is fixing to start a team of our own. It's the other stuff, the speech club, drama, and the humanities courses that concern me."

"Sir, they were not electives at my other high schools. I needed them to graduate."

"Make it clear to him what our expectations are Mr. Berk."

"I'm getting to it Eugene. The way I see it, son, you got to understand what's important and learn to concentrate on those things. Join the ROTC or Key Club. Go out for real sports teams like baseball, football, or golf. Of course, you got to prove to your physical education instructor in gym class that you are fit for a sports team."

This last comment set my teeth. "Excuse me? Are you telling me that I not only have to stay in school another year but I also have to take gym class?"

"Seems you don't have a problem in the hearing department," Lesman said. "But you appear to have a problem in the respect department."

"I don't have a problem in the respect department," I said in a nasal twang imitation of Lesman's voice. "I don't have a problem with having to take the extra year either, as I didn't expect to graduate until next year. I do have a problem with having to take gym class."

Mr. Berk's scalp reddened under his flattop haircut. "So what's the problem?"

"In your handbook, it states that students who have lettered in a varsity sport are exempt from Phys-Ed."

"Weren't on my teams that you lettered," Mr. Berk countered. "This here crying about having to take gym confirms my initial judgment about you not knowing what side is the right side to walk on. You are all over the board, son, academically, socially, and otherwise. You take speech-making and then want me to believe that you're just a good old boy who loves sports. It's perplexing, almost like you don't know whether to suck or blow. You understand me?"

"No, I don't understand."

"No! Did you just say, no?"

"Calm down, Eugene, David is new here so he hasn't caught onto what's proper yet," Mr. Berk said.

Lesman leaned over my chair. "Boy, you are digging yourself a hole. You best listen up when we speak. Mr. Berk told you, we don't have no rasslin, soccer, or long-distance running team. What we got is baseball, football, basketball, tennis and golf. If you ain't on one of those teams, then you are in gym class." Lesman jabbed his bony fist into the hollow of my shoulder. "You will be tickled pink, no doubt, to learn we got a drama, art, and Latin club. I question the type of boy who goes in for that sort of thing but I'm pretty sure you'll fit right in with the sorts that goes in for those things."

I covered the bottom of my face with my hand and chewed on my lower lip. The chewing I could hide, but my anger was impossible to conceal.

"Don't go giving me the eye," Lesman screeched and ran out of the room. He returned a few seconds later with what looked like a cricket paddle with holes drilled through it. The board was painted to resemble the lone star flag of Texas. "Come here," Lesman barked. "I want to introduce you to the great equalizer. It brings boys who think they are high and mighty down to where they belong. Now get up and bend over."

I stood nose to nose with Lesman. "No Sir, I'm not bending over. I did nothing wrong."

"What did you say?" Lesman's little ears twitched.

"Eugene, the boy's right. He hasn't done anything, but if he doesn't form a better attitude right quick, I'll guarantee he'll be in here for an introduction to the board before you know it. Now David, you may think we're picking on you, but we're not. Mr. Lesman and I just wanted to let you know that things here are different from what you may be used to." He opened his office door. and extended his hand toward me. I looked down at it and realized that he wanted me to shake. I shook.

The secretary brought me to Miss Kirsch, my homeroom and sociology teacher's class. I was in a daze after my bizarre encounter with Berk and Lesman and barely acknowledged her greeting. Miss Kirsch crooked her finger at a boy who bore a remarkable resemblance to a young Abe Lincoln. "Mort, this is David Brown. He's from Germany and Nebraska and will be finishing his schooling with us." She gave him a duplicate copy of my course schedule. "I want you to act as his guide and mentor. I think you're in many of the same classes."

Mort broke into a wide grin. "So you lived in Germany? I'm quite a world traveler myself. I go to Rome about four times a year." He plucked at his permanent cowlick and laughed before he gave the punch line. "Rome Texas that is," and stabbed the air with his extraordinarily long index finger.

Mort Ewing was an anomaly, a fun-loving fundamentalist Christian. He adored the Beatles and Oral Roberts in equal portions. He introduced me at lunch to his inseparable friends: Sammy Marsh, a triple letterman and a member of the Young Republicans, and Mike Chan, a convert to Mort's First Church of Christ the Savior.

When I arrived home from school, I found Jeff sitting on the curb.

"How'd it go?" I asked.

"You wouldn't believe me if I told you."

"Try me."

Jeff related essentially the same story. I say essentially because he immediately fell into favor with Berk and Lesman when he said he was interested in going out for the football team.

"Did that prick Lesman tell you to bend over?"

"Yeah, it's some kind of initiation thing."

"What did you do?"

"I bent over. I don't want it to get back to the guys on the football team that I wimped out. What did you do?"

I walked into the house without answering him.

Chapter 31

My first experience of fair play in Texas came through Coach Worell. A scowl was a permanent fixture on his pink face. After several losing seasons as the lead football coach, he had been demoted to head of phys-ed and driver's-ed. His assistant scampered up and down the line repeating everything Worell said. Monkey Man Sims had acquired his nickname because of his uncanny resemblance to Curious George.

"Count off, sound off!" Worell shouted.

"Y'all heard the man," Sims's Gomer Pyle voice chipped in, "Count off, sound off!"

When it came my time to say, "Number seven, Brown," Worell pushed past Sims and bumped me so hard with his stomach that I fell on my ass.

Monkey Man smiled broadly. "Ya get up." He popped me on my head with his clipboard. "This here is David Brown, Coach Worell. Mr. Berk says he thinks he's too good to be taking this class."

"Mr. Lesman told me to keep an eye on you. He informed me that you're a varsity man." Worell said.

"Yes Sir. I did cross-country, and wrestling and played soccer for my village's team in Germany."

"Let me get this straight. You think you should get a buy because you played these so-called sports?"

"Not anymore, Sir."

191

"Good thing Mr. Berk set you straight, Brownie. Because I don't consider prancing and dancing to be real sports. I will admit, however, that we have our own version of rasslin and soccer here. Don't we Tory."

A guy my height but considerably more muscled chuckled showing his Skoal stained teeth. "Tha's a fact, Coach. We'll show the new boy how we do thangs in Texas."

Tory always hung around Vernon, a tall, sponge-haired kid. Both boys belonged to a click that consisted of a no-neck junior bull rider named Hamilton Duncan, and Roy Peavey, a stock car enthusiast. The gang wore straw cowboy hats, pointed boots, and belt buckles as round as dessert plates. Because of their willingness to stomp hippies and sissies with the tacit approval of Mr. Berk and Lesman, most kids in the school feared them. "Looks like you made a friend," Coach Worell cracked. "In honor of your first day, we'll go outside and play a game of soccer, Texas style."

"Say Coach, we got real blue Norther' blowin'," Mort said.

"I don't recall asking for no dang weather report Ewing. Now hustle on out of here," Worell bellowed.

The class double-timed it onto the football practice field.

"Mort, Tory, you pick your teams," Worell said.

Monkey Man Sims walked behind him carrying a scuffed basketball. "We got no genuine soccer ball so this will have to do."

"I'll take the new boy," Mort said and slapped me on the back when I came on side. Pretty soon the two teams were completed.

Monkey Man bared his teeth. "Ya'll line up, line up now. I'll say go and you go."

Coach Worell grunted as he lowered his body over a bench and zipped up his windbreaker. "Get on with it. I ain't got all day."

I asked Mort what position he wanted me to play.

"Position? Well, I know that Chan likes to play goalie because he doesn't like to run. As for other positions, I didn't know there are any. We just kick the ball and go for it."

"Quit your jawin'," Sims said. He had me face off against Tory. He blew his whistle and rolled the basketball in between us. Tory braced a forearm against my chest and pushed me down. He took possession of the ball. He had zilch control and flipped onto his back when the ball rolled under his feet. I caught up with the ball and dribbled downfield. I passed it to a kid on my right side who scooped it up in his arms. Sims rightfully blew the whistle for the foul and brought us back to center field. I headed the ball when Sims kicked it at me. When the ball came down, I instinctively trapped it between my feet and then started showing off, bouncing it off the top of my shoe and knee a couple of times.

"Get over here Brownie," Sims shouted. "Tha's good tha's real good, boy." He hooked an arm around my neck and rubbed his knuckles into my scalp. "Generally speakin', Brownie, we play genuine American football, so we don't got your footsy skills. That being the case we gonna do drills so you can show us some of the fancy steps the Krauts use."

I wanted to get in their good graces. "Sure Mr. Sims that will be fun."

"Glad you see it that way. Our boys is real poor at ball handling, you know running with the thang, passing it and all that sort of stuff." He picked up the ball, catching me off guard, and slammed it into my gut. I gasped.

"Now here's what I want you to do," Sims said. "Dribble down to the south side goal post. Put this thang between the posts. Clear?"

I took off down field zigzagging back and forth as I dribbled the ball. About ten yards before the post, I improvised and did a slide kick and drove the basketball through the huge space between the two uprights.

"Atta boy," Sims yelled out. "Now get back down here and go for the north side posts." He called to the sidelines, "Tory, Vernon, Ham, Roy." They ambled onto the field.

"Brownie, these boys' job is to stop you before you make it past the twenty-yard line. Go get 'em boys!"

They rushed me whooping and screeching. Ham reached me first. He went for the ball, but I did a backkick. Ham's foot struck empty space and he lost his footing. He landed on his ass and muttered something about taking care of me. The other three guys dove for the ball but ended up chewing turf as I sidestepped them.

The goalposts loomed before me. "Home free," I thought.

"For the love of Mike," Coach Worell shouted. He heaved his three hundred pounds off the bench, waved Tory and his gang over, and tore into them, "What in tittysville do you girly boys think you are doing? Mr. Sims told you to get out there and stop this priss from scoring. If you don't stop him, I'll have you doing laps around this field until you puke."

"You heard the man," Sims said and rolled the ball at my feet. I trapped it and started toward the goalposts. The boys chased after me but could not manage to get control of the ball. I was on a high. I spun, back-dribbled, and cut sideways to confuse them. The thrill was especially rewarding since back in Neuhof I was considered a lousy middle and long field player. My lead feet had relegated me to fullback whose only job was to intercept the strikers and protect the goalkeeper.

The word "score" filled my head. It was knocked from my thoughts when an elbow crashed into the side of my jaw followed by a blow to my kidneys. I dropped to my knees. Ham stood above me, his clenched fists hanging at his sides. He laughed when Tory joined him, picked up the ball, and bounced it off my forehead.

I got up slowly and started walking off the field.

"Where do you think you are going," Worell screamed. "I didn't hear myself tell you class is over. Get back there and do it again."

"Yeah," Monkey Man's falsetto sang. "You run out of steam or guts?"

"Jesus, boy, I thought you was good," Tory said.

I had had enough, enough of Worell and Monkey Man and most certainly enough of this goat roper and his buckaroo buddies. My foot slipped under the ball. It went airborne, spiraling into Tory's face with so much spin that it split his lip open. "I am good," I said.

Monkey Man raced over. "What do you think you're doing?"

"Guess I lost ball control."

"That does it. It's time for you to go inside and touch your toes."

I understood that Sims intended to paddle me in front of the entire class. He grabbed my wrist, but I twisted out of his grip. Worell blocked my retreat. "You deaf, son? Mr. Sims told you to get inside. Maybe after he gets through, you'll learn who the lead dog is around here."

It was relatively easy to elude Worell's fleshy arm as he tried to haul me in.

I struggled to maintain my composure. "They fouled me, broke the rules. You saw them do it. You go for the ball, not the man, Sir."

"Who said you're a man?" Worell laughed. His triple flaps of chin wobbled. "I'll let it go this time. Chalk it up to a learning experience Brownie."

"You ain't been in Texas long enough to understand we play by our own set of rules," Sims said.

"Then it's not soccer." I was careful to end my sentence with, "Sir."

"Sure it is. It's Lone Star sock her. And girl, you got socked good."

I stripped off my T-shirt in the locker room and turned around when four shadows fell across the locker door. My path of escape was blocked. Tory and Ham were still pale from our encounter. They let Roy and Vernon do the talking.

"You played my friends dirty," Roy said and shoved me against the cold surface of the locker door.

Vernon hooted, "Faggot, you're in for a real ass stompin'." He threw the weight of his shoulder against me and drove the handle of the door into my naked back. He held me while Roy extended his arm and touched my nose, measuring off the distance to break my face. My eyes wandered to the entrance of the locker room and fell on Sims. He was propped up against the wall near the light switch, watching but not moving.

Before Roy could land his blow, Mort Ewing and Chan ran over. Mort stood in front of Roy. Chan pushed Vernon away from me. "Come on guys. Give him a break," Mort said.

Roy grinned. "Step aside, Mort. I don't care if your daddy's a deacon. I'd as soon knock you stupid as this prick."

Monkey Man Sims finally intervened. "That's all I want to hear. You boys hit the showers."

Vernon flicked his thumbnail under my chin. "Better watch yourself, boy."

I plopped down on the long wooden bench that divided the aisle of the locker room. I looked up at Ewing and Chan. "Thanks."

"Ah, it's nothing. Vernon and Roy are okay once you get to know them. They were hoping somebody would stop them. It's Ham and Tory you have to watch out for. Some guys here think you got a chip on your shoulder, think that you think you're better than the rest of them."

"Man, I've only been here a week. I'm just trying to get by."

"Sometimes the way to get along is to play along," Mort said.

"How do you mean?"

"Take your strokes from Sims if it means you make yourself part of the group."

"Have you ever been paddled?"

"Sure, for coming in late to class once too often from prayer meetings. But I took it as a joke and so it wasn't too bad."

Chan shrugged when I looked at him. "Not me, never felt the board. I've always been too polite and quiet. You know, too Chinese to draw their attention. It's too late for you though. They definitely know who you are."

"Sometimes the way to get along is to play along," Mort repeated.

"I don't think so. Not if it means letting someone beat me."

"Hang around us for a while until things cool down. You can come to our youth group meeting at my church on Wednesday. Maybe you'll be able to make peace with Roy there."

I cringed at the thought of stepping inside Mort Ewing's Holy Roller church. "Thanks Mort but I'll take my chances in a fight."

*

That evening while I lifted weights with Jeff on the back porch, I told him about my run-in. Jeff spotted me as I reclined on the bench. "I've got my own trouble with a couple of guys who hang around them. There are about eight fucks in total making life hell for the oddballs in school. Freaks, geeks, anyone who's different are targets."

"I don't get it, Jeff. I've seen you sitting with Tory at lunch. I thought you were tight with them."

"Not since they found out I'm Albert's friend. It's no sweat off my balls. Those guys are jerk-offs." Jeff helped me set the barbell on its posts. "There's this girl who's really something. She plays the guitar in the Gazebo in the shopping center across the street from MacArthur. She's a real peace and love type. If I want to get anywhere with her, I have to blow off the shit-kickers. Besides I like the people she hangs around with. They're kind of weird but they're nice."

"Jeff, we're going to find ourselves on the wrong side of the street."

Chapter 32

A month after moving to Texas Dad summoned Jeff and me to the garage. "Your sister is coming over this weekend. She'll be bringing your new nephew. I don't want you asking her any questions."

I'd overheard Dad's late-night telephone conversations with Jan. She was living in Farmer's Branch, a suburb an hour north of Irving, and worked for an insurance company. Fred was a manager trainee at Sears and Roebuck. Every discussion ended with Mother sobbing while Dad stood his ground.

"When you and Fred can demonstrate that you are sincere then you may come over, but not until then."

"Ernest, she's gone through enough."

"She's gone through enough! What the hell have I gone through with all your wailing and hand-wringing?"

I looked up at the ceiling when my mother entered the garage. Her face was wet. She lit a cigarette off a cigarette and tossed the half-finished one on the floor.

Dad crushed the hot smoke under his shoe. "Norma, think! There are all sorts of inflammable fluids in here."

Mom made a jerking motion with her arm like a marionette and brushed a twist of wayward hair off her forehead. "Did you tell them, Ernest?"

I said, "Mom I already know. You've been talking about it for days. Janet's coming over with her baby."

"Damn you! Show your mother respect." My father's cupped hand smashed across my right ear, leaving me with a ringing noise.

"When Janet gets here with Fred and Christopher you give them all a hug and pretend that everything is normal and you are glad to see them." Mom turned back into the house.

Dad slugged Jeff in the chest. Jeff's face remained impassive as Dad growled, "I saw you grinning at your mother, you little bastard." He shoved me against the workbench. "Get this straight. You had better shape up or I'll kick your ass until your nose bleeds. Now get out of my sight."

Jeff and I left through the side entrance of the garage. "What was that all about?" Jeff asked.

"I set him off I guess."

*

I was sweeping the garage in overlapping passes, as per the Colonel's directives, when I smelled burnt oil and gasoline. I popped my head out the door and saw a rusted Toyota Corolla. It grated to a halt at the curb and backfired. Fred threw his weight against his car door and popped it open.

With a cigarette dangling from his lips, he lopped around the front end of the Corolla and tugged on the passenger door. It groaned. Fred was a lot thinner than I remembered. His trademark swagger and loopy smirk were far less accented. He made eye contact with me and helped my sister out. Though only a year or so older than I was, Fred was haggard beyond his age. He had tallow skin and ringed eyes. In Lubbock, Fred had held down two jobs, delivering Pepsi and bussing tables. He managed to finish high school. Still, Fred looked in peak condition compared to Jan.

My sister had what was euphemistically referred to as a difficult pregnancy. In truth, Janet nearly died. Denied any financial assistance from our parents, she relied on an osteopath throughout her pregnancy for medical care. As for motherly advice, she depended on Fred's Grandma Jo, a spirited throwback to pioneer days. It was Jo who put the newlyweds up in her dustbowl shanty in Lubbock.

Fred helped Janet up the walkway. A baby dangled in a denim sling on her chest. They reached the house, but my father stepped outside and blocked them from entering. I passed into the kitchen from the garage. My mother was leaning over the counter jabbing a fork against its laminated surface; the prongs were all bent.

"This is my house, not yours. You will knock like any guest and wait for me to invite you in. The next time you and your husband arrive, ring the bell. Do I make myself clear?"

"Yes Sir, Colonel Brown."

On hearing Fred's voice Mom snapped to attention with so much fury that her neck cracked. She dashed through the house. I ran behind her. She screamed and hurled the misshapen fork at the front door.

Only when Jan pushed past Fred and Dad into the house was the spell broken. "Mom, this is Christopher." Janet lifted the baby boy out of the sling and presented him to my mother like an oblation. "I love him, and you will too. But if you refuse to treat my husband with respect, then you will never get to know how much you could have loved Chris because I'll never come to visit you again."

Mom looked at the baby and exhaled. "Has he eaten yet?"

My Dad extended his hand to Fred. "I hear you got your diploma. How do you like your new job?"

"Fine Sir. The Sears management trainee program is great. After I get my own department, I'll be eligible for their tuition refund plan."

So that cinched it. My parents welcomed Fred into the fold if not with open arms, then at least without baseball bats. Dad became unnaturally friendly with Fred. Mom, playing the role of the doting grandmother, gave Janet child-rearing tips.

Jeff and I came to dread my sister's visits, not because we didn't want to see her, but because of the aftermath of her appearances. My Mother would slink to the wingback chair and crawl into the pages of a book for hours. Dad, being a man of action, preferred to release his rage in a more aerobic manner, aiming straight-arm punches and verbal shots at Jeff and me. My five-year-old brother, for the most part untouched, cowered in front of the television, which was always left on whether anyone was watching or not.

After one of Jan's visits, my father stood up from the dinner table and hurled a plate at the wall. "How many years is it going to take you to learn, Norma!"

Jeff and I started to clean up the mess but stopped when Dad said, "Leave it there. Maybe it will help remind your mother that I don't eat cauliflower."

Chapter 33

Albert's yard became our island of escape. He was dribbling a soccer ball back and forth on his lawn and tripped over his feet when I walked past his house.

"Hey David, are you pumped for our project?"

"Yeah I'm pumped."

Although two grades behind me, Albert was in my sociology class. Determined to become a doctor he took all the science and math classes possible. Albert never gained entrance into any social circle he could call his own. On the periphery of even the outsiders' clique, he was a hanger-on, supplying weed and playing the buffoon. He went out of his way to suck up to our sociology teacher, waving his arms like an epileptic whenever Miss Kirsch asked a question.

Albert's idea, our joint project was about the effects of alcohol on mental acuity and motor skills. While I gathered information from the library, Albert contacted the police and spoke with a pharmacist.

*

Frau Angerman and my mother telephoned each other once a month. Even though my mother was in hysterics over the possibility that they would discover Janet's real reason for leaving Germany, she invited the Angermans to stay with us on their American tour.

In April the Angermans landed in Dallas. Mom made Janet promise not to come over during the two weeks they were visiting. Dad threatened to knock Jeff and me unconscious should we speak a word about our sister and her child. Mom and Dad played tour guides. They took their friends to Six Flags, Dealey Plaza, the Dallas Cowboys stadium, and a rodeo. On the Angermans' last weekend with us, my parents drove them to San Antonio along with Tommy to see the Alamo. There was not enough room in the car for everyone, so Jeff and I were left behind.

As soon as Dad drove away Jeff bolted to stay with Vince Crane, his dope-smoking partner and best friend. For the first time in my life, I had a house to myself. Albert came over after everyone left. Our report was due on Monday. Albert said he had put together a slide show of materials gathered from health agencies, the AA, and SMU's medical library along with enough notes to talk for a month. I hadn't even written an index card. He freaked.

"You're trying to make me look bad in front of Miss Kirsch!"

"Relax. I'll come up with something."

Albert's eyes bulged out of his pumpkin face while he paced the living room. He stopped in front of the china cabinet where Dad's collection of alcohol was visible through the glass.

"Your father sure has a lot of bottles."

"So?"

"So your father drinks a lot."

"He doesn't drink that much. He has one or two martinis when he gets home to unwind and a couple of drinks to relax before he goes to bed."

"He must really be tightly wound."

"Come on, Albert. Everybody's father does it."

"Not mine. He doesn't even touch beer."

'That's a crock.'

"Why do you say that, because I'm Mexican?"

Albert's heritage had never entered my mind. I just thought it was the norm for there to be more booze in a house than fruit.

"I'm American. My grandparents are from Mexico. But that doesn't mean my family sucks limes and shoots tequila. My parents don't drink or smoke. We're Mormons."

At the bookcase, he fiddled with the buttons of my father's reel-to-reel tape machine then stood back and smiled when Julie Andrews sang, "Just you wait Henry Higgins." He flipped the machine off and on a few times. "Does your dad have any blank tapes?"

"No, and don't mess with my Dad's machine."

Albert looked dejected. "That's too bad because I have a neat idea."

"I got a portable tape recorder, Albert. I use it with an ear jack to listen to music my father would kill me for playing."

"Great, we're going to get an A+! Instead of just copying down what somebody else has written on the effects of alcohol, you'll actually keep an oral log of the changes a person goes through over the course of four hours of drinking. Take a drink once every thirty minutes and then on the hour record how you're feeling. You know, the changes in your coordination, your speech, and your vision. I saw it done in a movie."

"Albert, where I am going to get the booze?"

He nodded at the china cabinet. We prepared a list of ten things that I was to do thirty minutes after every drink.

TASKS FOR TESTING MOTOR REFLEXES & MENTAL ACUITY

1. Touch toes.
2. Balance on one foot and count to twenty.
3. Walk a straight line from the living room to the front door with my eyes closed.
4. Do fifty jumping jacks.
5. Thread a needle.
6. Read out loud a chapter from our Sociology textbook.
7. Say, "Peter Piper picked a peck of pickled peppers" six times.
8. Construct a tower from playing cards.
9. Describe any physical or mental changes.
10. Dial Albert's house to report on the progress of the experiment.

It took over an hour to set up what Albert referred to as the control center. We put a fresh stack of sixty-minute reels on the dining room table next to my tape recorder along with several ballpoint pens, the list of tasks, and a spiral notebook to serve as a log. I used a six-ounce tumbler as my drinking glass.

"Don't you think that's too big?" Albert asked.

"Nah, my Dad downs two of these plus a beaker-sized Martini every evening."

"If you start feeling sick, quit the experiment."

*

After Albert went home, I poured a liberal amount of bourbon mixed with Pepsi. It didn't taste too bad, so I topped the glass with more Jack Daniels before finishing the drink. Thirty minutes passed and I recorded the data. Little if any decrease in mental alertness or coordination was noted. I was sober. I poured orange juice halfway up in an iced tea glass and filled the rest up with vodka. Tick-tock, thirty minutes passed, and I repeated the task list, adding another fifty jumping jacks to my routine.

"I feel fine, real fine," I muttered. Following my Mom's recipe for Dad's Sahara dry Martini, I poured a generous portion of vodka into my iced tea glass and added a drop of vermouth. Stumbling back into the kitchen I flung open the refrigerator door and rummaged through the shelves until I discovered Dad's precious stash of olives. I fished two out with my fingers. Back in the experiment room, I plunked them into the Martini.

"Somewhat woozy," I spoke into the microphone before turning on the recorder. "Ah fuck!" I laughed when I realized my mistake and activated the machine.

"Feeling a tad wobbly but this could be because of doing too many jumping jacks," I slurred.

Two hours later I was reeling around the house with the machine under one arm. In my free hand, brandy slopped over the rim of the iced tea glass.

"After many drinks, I am messed up," I spit into the mike. "Can't stand, jumping jacks are out." I snatched at the living room drapes as I tripped over my feet. The curtains came down. My stomach erupted, spewing out a mixture of Pepsi, booze, ice cream, cookies, and whatever else I had ingested over four hours.

I must have called Albert because he arrived at some point with my brother. Albert took one look and bee-tailed it to the bathroom. He slipped in a pool of vomit. "Sorry, I hear my parents calling me. Bye."

I threw my drinking glass at the picture of the mill house in France. "The son-of-a-bitch. I'd like to punch him in the nose," I screamed and raced through the house turning over furniture.

My only desire was to flee and never come back but I couldn't get past the couch without falling over. Jeff wrestled me to my room where I puked all over the rug and the bed.

Jeff worked like a dog to clean things up. He washed and re-hung the curtains, mopped the floors, scrubbed the bathroom until it sparkled, and washed my sheets, pajamas, and pillowcase over and over because I kept barfing on them. I was gone to the world.

It was dark, well into the evening when a car pulled into the driveway. Jeff sat in the chair next to my bed. He got up and peeked through the blinds. "Christ! They're not supposed to be back until tomorrow. Stay in bed. I'll tell him you're sick, that you ate something bad."

My brain felt like it was pushing its way out of my ears. Dad flipped on the light when he entered my bedroom with Jeff. My mother and the Angermans lingered outside the door.

I must have looked like five days of bad road because my father asked with genuine concern, "David, are you alright?"

I turned away from him. My throat was too dry to answer. "David, do you want to go to the doctor?"

My lips parted and the dried vomit that had cemented them together crackled. "No! I'm not sick. I am drunk, drunk enough to tell you to go to hell. I'm drunk, goddamn it! I wish you would go away and leave us alone."

"Well, at least you're honest. If there is anything I hate worse than a thief and drug addict it's a liar," he said and switched off the light.

The next day Dad woke me at six A.M. He handed me a pair of gloves a shovel and a paper bag. He told me to go around the neighborhood picking up dog shit. After I was finished, he wanted me to mow the lawn, wash the car, and do whatever else came to mind. At lunchtime he made me sit between him and Herr Angerman. He put a Bavarian mug with a pewter lid down in front of me then filled it with beer.

Hans lifted his stein and said "Prost."

"Drink up, big guy. A little hair of the dog is what you need to cure what is ailing you," Dad said.

When the Angermans were in the air on their way back to Germany Dad called Jeff and me into the living room. He made me watch while he flogged my brother with the buckle end of a belt. With every stroke, Dad said, "If there is anything I hate worse than a thief and drug addict, it's a liar."

*

At home, the line in the sand had been drawn between my generation and my father's. Mom fed Dad's increasing paranoia of the danger Jeff and I posed to his vision of America. She read him articles on drug abuse in high schools, the epidemic of teenage unwed mothers, the

211

politicization of youth, and the God is dead movement though Dad was convinced that God was an excuse, not a belief. When he had enough of Mom's editorials, he would throw open our bedroom doors and berate Jeff and me for imagined sexual, political, and drug-related indiscretions.

"If you two faggots don't get a haircut I'll scalp you myself. If I ever find out you're listening to that crap those hippie commie bastards call music, I'll drive an ice pick through your brains. Now get out of my sight."

At first, Jeff's reaction to the Colonel's attacks was to strike back at Tommy with equal ferocity. He scared Tom with tales of what he would do to him when he was asleep and would punch him lightly in the same spot until he cried. Tommy's tears incited a verbal barrage from Jeff reminiscent of Dad's finest moments. Then as suddenly as he had started abusing Tommy, Jeff stopped. Stopped not only the physical and verbal attacks but stopped talking or acknowledging him period. Jeff found solace in his music and in weed.

My survival tactic was somewhat different from my brother's. I studied and kept out of Dad's sight. The course material at MacArthur was two years behind what I had taken in Germany and Omaha, so I pulled down As and Bs without breaking a sweat. As far as Tommy was concerned, I was unaware of his existence.

Chapter 34

The small fringe group of leftists adopted me as one of their own when in Miss Kirsch's class I questioned if paddling students constituted cruel and unusual punishment.

Floe Walsh and her omnipresent friend, Hugh Swift, were genuine flesh-and-blood hippies. I knew Floe vaguely from Sociology and Latin. Her nose and sharp chin poked out from under her long lifeless hair like the snout of an Afghan hound. Her ears stuck out from the sides of her head like novelty store gags. She alternated wearing multi-colored feather earrings and peace symbol hoops. She owned a vast collection of Peruvian ponchos that hung limply on her coat-hanger body. Whenever Floe entered a room, she jangled. Dozens of silver, copper, and gold bracelets encircled her wrists and ankles. I was interested in Floe. Hippies were supposed to be into free love, but I was shy and felt that my neatly cropped hair and prep-school wardrobe would put her off. I tried to talk to her in class, but she would tuck her chin into the depression of her thin neck and avoid looking at me.

Floe and her friends hung out at the shopping center across from MacArthur. Several times after school I crossed the street to the Gazebo. I listened to the tie-dyed crowd play bad renditions of Simon and Garfunkel and Bob Dylan on their guitars and zithers.

Other congregants passed out leaflets against the Vietnam War, free copies of the Dallas Notes, and yellow leaflets quoting Karl Marx, Lenin, and Mao. Most of these kids were from El Centro Junior College and most were harmless.

I kept my distance from the hardcore activists even though I maintained a friendship with two genuine MacArthur left-wing firebrands, Johnny Jardin and Dan Somerset. Though shunned by the school at large for their pro-Weathermen views, they were begrudgingly respected because of their refusal to take crap from the school administration.

In early May, Hugh put up posters on telephone poles off campus encouraging students to emulate kids in New York who had worn black armbands to express their outrage at the Vietnam War. As the date for Hugh's protest approached, he, Floe, and Muffy, a chubby girl in braids whose wardrobe consisted of granny dresses, stood across the street from the school singing Blowing in the Wind. When students on their way to the shopping plaza stopped to listen, Hugh would break off singing and hand the person an armband with an explanation about the non-violent statement.

Lesman announced over the intercom that anyone caught wearing an armband on school property would be suspended. Hugh acknowledged the right of the school administration to make this threat. He said he would comply with Lesman's order and hold a peace-in at the Gazebo instead. He asked everyone to show up wearing their armbands and to bring donations for the Vietnamese orphan fund run by the Unitarian Church.

The protest never had a chance to get off the ground. Lesman contacted the police. He told them that the mall was being used as a gathering place for hippies and other unsavory characters. The mall owner, who believed in such quaint notions as the right of assembly and that kids were basically okay, caved when the authorities issued an ordinance that no more than ten students at a time were to be allowed in the courtyard. To ignore this ruling would result in a substantial fine.

Hugh refused to be cowed and showed up at school wearing his armband while his fellow flower children toed the line and kept theirs hidden. By midmorning, news had worked its way through the grapevine that Tory, Roy, Vernon, Ham, and two hangers-on were going to deal with Hugh. The gang snapped punches at Hugh as they strode by him all day long. Tory went so far as to knock off Hugh's Ben Franklin glasses. He feigned an apology when he ground them under the heel of his boot. By lunchtime, Hugh looked exhausted. A blue, egg-shaped bruise protruded over his eyebrow. His buckskin jacket pocket was torn, and its left sleeve was ripped. Still, he wore the offending ribbon and told everyone who listened that after school he was going to the park near the mall to continue his protest.

My opportunity to get on Floe's good side presented itself before the end of the day. She and Muffy were whispering outside our Latin class. I overheard Muffy say, "Go ahead and ask him." Floe moved away from the door and then walked toward me. She said straight out, "Hugh is in trouble."

"It's hard not to notice that," I said.

"Tory is telling everyone they're going to make Hugh eat his armband."

"Come on Floe, Swift is carrying this protest thing too far. He's already made his point. There's no reason to drag it out. He should just take off the ribbon and go home if it saves his ass."

"You would say that." Floe turned to Muffy. "See, I told you he's a jerk. All he's interested in is sucking up to the teachers and getting out of gym class."

I sought out my brother during lunch hour. "Have you heard what Tory and his pals have in store for Hugh?"

*

After school, Jeff and I headed to the park. Floe and Muffy were already there. They were crying and pleading with Tory and the other punks surrounding their friend to leave him alone. Hugh, though inches shorter, stood his ground. Vernon and another kid named Roddy who was in Jeff's grade stood behind Swift. They took turns slapping him across the back of his head. Roy was on Hugh's left side, dangling a black armband. On the other side stood Ham. He kept poking Hugh in the kidney with a sharpened pencil. "If the goddamn ribbon means so much to you, put it back on."

Hugh reached into the beaded spirit pouch he wore on his belt and pulled out another armband. Tory knocked him to the ground before Hugh tied on the ribbon. For a moment it looked like Tory was going to grind his boot heel into Swift's chest. Muffy shoved Tory and Floe slapped him.

"Fucking titless bitch!" Tory yelped.

Ham jerked Floe's poncho over her head exposing her naked stomach and small breasts nested inside a cotton training bra.

"Hey ya'll that's not right," Vernon said. He turned his back on his friends and walked away.

Before Ham could go any further, I hauled ass across the park and snatched the armband from Hugh, and tied it around my upper left arm. "Tory, I heard you're going to stomp anyone wearing one of these."

"I thought all you hippies are queers and pacifists," he said.

"I'm not a hippie."

Floe and Muffy led Hugh away and nursed his bruises. Hugh shook them off. He ran toward me. "Stop it! Peace," he said then got flattened by Roddy.

"Come on guys let's finish this pussy," Tory howled.

Once again Hugh jumped between us, this time his arms linked with Floe and Muffy. It looked like things were about to go from bad to worse when Johnny Jardin and Dan Somerset appeared. They gripped metal pipes wrapped with black electrical tape at the ends.

Johnny stared at Ham. Dan worked his way behind Tory. "Which one of you shitkickers wants to go at it first?" Johnny said and popped the pipe against his palm.

Tory spoke up. "This isn't your fight, Jardin."

"That's not what I heard."

"Keep his buddies out of it and I'll get it on with this redneck asshole right now," I shouted.

"You haven't got the balls," Tory said.

"Stop it," Hugh demanded. With the help of Floe and Muffy, he pulled me away from Tory.

"Take your friends and get out of here," Swift pleaded. Hugh didn't have to ask twice. Tory and his gang retreated from the park quickly but not so swiftly as to be accused of running away.

Hugh looked at me. He was shivering. "That goes for you too."

Johnny frowned. "Swift, you don't have to thank me, but the least you could do is show a little gratitude to David and Jeff."

"Nobody asked them to help me."

"All you did was make things worse," Muffy added.

Floe said, "If you bothered listening to us at the Gazebo instead of trying to figure a way into my panties, you'd know we don't believe in violence."

"What did you intend to do, kill them with kindness? Blind them with your goodness?" Johnny asked.

Hugh sucked back his tears. "Goodness is the one investment that never fails. That's from Henry David Thoreau. One day, you'll see, the majority will come around to our way of thinking."

"When were the good and the brave ever a majority? That's also from Thoreau," Johnny responded.

"You're twisting his words and you know it," Hugh said. "Thoreau was a pacifist. He knew you couldn't use violence as a means of forcing change."

"A revolution is not a dinner party. A revolution is an insurrection, an act of violence, Chairman Mao," Dan mumbled in what sounded like a bad imitation of Brando's Terry Malloy.

"Real change can only come through the barrel of a gun," Johnny said. "What do you think, David?"

"Think? What's to think?" I said and walked away, leaving Jeff to work out his innocence with his Gazebo friends.

Johnny and Dan caught up with me. They patted me on the back, talking up their radical beliefs. They invited me to a gathering of activists at a friend's pad. I was about to go off with them when Hugh called out, "Hey, David, it's cool. You were only trying to help. Floe wants you to go with us to her house."

"Later," Johnny said.

I nodded and ran back to where Hugh and the others stood. Floe gave me a hug and Muffy flashed me the two-finger salute of peace. Jeff grinned as if to say, "Brother, things have just started to get interesting."

Swift chattered about Gandhi and Thoreau and the anti-war, anti-materialism movement all the way to Floe's house. He was the genuine article, a 100% adherent to non-violence. Despite the abuse, he kept returning with bags of black ribbons. Martyrdom was a calling and not a sidebar of his incense-burning lifestyle.

On our way back from Floe's, Jeff remarked, "Anybody can be a hippie love freak in California. But hell, you gotta be tough, know how to fight to be a pacifist in Texas."

Chapter 35

I was marked as a troublemaker and radical. Monkey Man Sims barked at me for any infraction, for coming too late or too early for class, for running too fast and showing up the others, or too slow and holding them back.

During one gym class, Sims stood in the middle of the circle of a new wrestling mat.

"Boys, next year I'm gonna be the coach of MacArthur's first rasslin team. Today I aim to show you what I been studying in a book."

Monkey Man called each member of the class out to the mat. He demonstrated a very basic move, a one-legged takedown, on each one. He made some of the boys go into referee position on the bottom and drove their faces into the mat by jamming his head into their straightened elbows. When my turn came Sims didn't even wait for me to shake hands. He rocked me with a forearm push to my chest and kicked my feet out from under me.

"Brownie, you seem to have forgotten a lot since your varsity rasslin days," he laughed.

I kip-upped to my feet and said, "I wasn't sure of the rules but I'm ready now."

Sims's arm snaked forward so slowly that I had time to plan two moves. His fingers clamped around my wrist, and he jerked me toward him. He had no chance to tie up. I whipped behind him and took him down with a crotch lift, pancaking his face into the mat.

"Brown, get off me!"

I did and sidestepped his flying spittle. He screamed, "On the bottom, drop to all fours. I'm gonna put you down there and show these boys some mat moves."

"No Sir, you can get hurt if you don't know what you're doing."

"That does it. I'm gonna whup your sassy ass."

"I don't think so, Sir. You can't last more than a period with me."

"Here's how it's gonna be, Brownie. You're going to get into kneeling position or be expelled. If you do not pin me within three minutes, I will paddle you and you will say, thank you, Mr. Sims. If you win, I'll give you a pass and you won't have to take gym the rest of this year or next year."

Even if Monkey Man had not sweetened his offer, I really ached to pay him back. I dropped to my hands and knees and squared my position. Sims knew only one takedown from the mat and I let him try it. He pushed the top of his head against my elbow but was unable to flatten me. I raised the palm of my left arm off the mat just enough for him to slip a half-nelson on me.

"Now I got you," he hissed in my ear.

I shot my legs out in front of me, switched over him, and rolled him onto his back. Pressing my shoulder against his throat for leverage, I cut off his air supply and crushed his Adam's apple. I hooked his leg, pulled it up to his chest, and pinned him. I held the pin longer than I should have and released him only when I heard Coach Worell's hoarse voice from the front of the gym. "Let that man up, I ain't going to ask you twice."

Sims flip-flopped on the mat a little before struggling to his feet. He was gulping air, holding his hands around his throat. "You're expelled," he rasped.

"Mr. Sims, I heard you promise that boy an exemption from gym class if he beat you," Worell said. "That's what you said and that's what you're going to do."

Sims stuttered "Ya- ya te-te-telling me I got to let tha-that pissant go scot-free?"

"That's the sum of it." Worell looked at me. "Go clean out your locker. I don't wanna see you anywhere near here. That doesn't mean you're free. You still have to make up the credits for this class somehow. Starting Monday, you'll be in my driver's education course."

*

The first day of Driver's Ed., Worell chewed me out for a solid twenty minutes as he sat beside me in the car.

"That turn's too wide. You signaled too far in advance. Don't stop too long at stop signs. You drive as slow as my granny."

Once on the freeway, Worell became even more critical. "The way you drive you'll be lucky to get a bus ticket let alone a driver's license."

As we sped down the highway he shouted, "Don't be a pussy! Switch lanes and pass the car ahead of us."

"I don't think I can, Coach. That car's going too fast for me to overtake."

"Don't argue, just do it!"

I jerked the wheel and shot across three lanes of blacktop, jumping the median.

Worell covered his eyes. "Oh God! Get the car straight. Pull over. Give me the wheel. Oh God!"

I regained control of the car and coasted to a stop on the shoulder. Worell flung open his door and raced around to my side of the car.

Worell did not say anything to me either on the way back to school or after he let me out. When I returned to Driver's Education the following week, he handed me a slip of paper. It stated that I was removed from his class because of space constrictions and that I would have to arrange to take private lessons.

For the remainder of the school year, I moved between the peace and love hippies and Johnny Jardin's hard-core group of militant leftists and anarchists. At first, I spent a lot of time at the Gazebo with Floe's group. I soon tired of their flat renditions of Donovan songs and recitations of Kahlil Gibran poems. To top things off I was allergic to the incense Floe and her friends burned in a BBQ pit while enacting a Lone Star variation of Eastern meditation. Their chants in Texas drawls sounded a lot like "Ohm, ohm on the range".

My relationship with Floe was tepid. As it turned out she stood squarely against the free love movement. She saw it as another example of male dominance over women. But she and her friends invited Johnny, Dan, a girl named Nina Beaudry, and me to an evening campfire. Luckily Dad was out of state, so I went.

I vaguely knew Nina from my brother. She and Jeff had dated on a couple of occasions without anything serious developing. Floe set up the campfire next to the banks of the Trinity River, a muddy slip of water that meandered from North Texas to the Gulf of Mexico. The place was secluded, hidden behind a stand of cottonwoods and willows in the hollow of a gully and as close to a natural setting as existed in this Texas suburb.

Floe had organized the circle of fire pow-wow to get the radical leftists and peace movement people on the same side. She wanted the groups to join forces so they could mount an action against the school. Lesman and Mr. Berk had successfully lobbied the city council to institute bylaws against the assembly of kids in venues not sanctioned by the board of education. Clearly, the prohibition had been enacted to shut down student protests against the war.

Floe and Johnny hit it off. They agreed to develop a non-violent means of putting their views across to the community.

As the campfire crackled and the smell of incense and marijuana filled the ravine, Hugh sounded off on the superiority of Far Eastern religions over Western culture. Floe believed all the ills of the world could be laid at the feet of Western civilization. Dan kept quiet. He was remarkably restrained considering his hatred of anything that smacked of religion and mysticism. He passed me a joint without taking a hit. I passed it on the same way.

Hugh said, "The Judeo-Christian tradition has spawned more wars and injustice than any other force in history. We must look toward the Ganges for the path to enlightenment. Only by losing ourselves and becoming one with the cosmos will we ever find true happiness and joy."

"Fucking A! Don't you know man that happiness is a warm gun?" Dan sang out.

"What do you think, David?" Nina asked.

I froze when I looked at her. Her luminescent hair as thick and dark as a forest at midnight tumbled over her shoulders. The mounds of her breasts unencumbered by a bra rose above the plunging neckline of a pullover embroidered with coyotes and thunderbirds.

"I know what he's thinking," Floe snipped.

"No, you don't," I responded. "I think you guys are full of crap. Just because some guy in a diaper convinces George Harrison that the moon is made of blue cheese doesn't make it so." I dredged up something I remembered Kyle Bains saying back in Germany. "No culture has a monopoly on righteousness, evil, and stupidity."

Johnny yawned. "Give me a roomful of atheists anytime over devout God-fearing people. No atheist ever threatened to kill me for what I don't believe."

"Right on," Dan agreed. "We don't stand a chance of changing society until we wipe out all the priests, mullahs, preachers, and levitating dope-smoking gurus."

My attention was completely on Nina.

She said, "I don't think killing them all is the answer. I also don't think that blindly accepting Floe and Hugh's vision of Nirvana in Irving is a real option."

"Maybe all we can hope for is the freedom to believe what we want to believe without being strong-armed or strong-arming others," I said.

Hugh finished off his second joint and coughed up, "That's heavy, man. Maybe there's more to you than meets the eye."

The bulge in my pants was quite visible from where Floe sat across from me. "Not likely," she said and stood up.

"Can you guys get away on Sunday?" Johnny asked breaking my trance. "Some university students and union activists are getting together across town for a study session. We're going to discuss recent events and how to react to them."

Floe stared into the fire. "I don't think your friends will have much to say that will shed any light on peaceful protest."

"My father is going to speak," Johnny said. "He helped organize the autoworkers in Detroit. He knows something about non-violent confrontation tactics."

"Are you going, David?" Nina asked.

"I don't think so. I don't have a ride."

Floe reached down to help Hugh up. She said, "Don't count on me for a ride. There won't be room for you in my car. I'm going to take Muffy, Hugh, and maybe a couple of other people."

In a way I was relieved. It spared me the task of thinking up a credible excuse to leave the house on what Dad had recently designated as a family day.

He had declared, "Sundays belong to me. Our family needs to get closer, get back together. Friends come and go but you are blood. You boys must always be there for one another."

"That's okay. I'll pick you up. Maybe Jeff will want to come," Nina said.

At the mention of my brother, the campfire seemed to me suddenly cold and dull. I figured as usual that he had the inside track on the girl.

Floe's melancholy smile flipped into a wicked grin. "Yeah David, tell Jeff to come. Tell him we missed him here."

As Nina and the others climbed up the bank of the ravine Johnny and I lagged behind. "What's wrong, man?"

"What am I going to tell my Dad to get away?"

"Tell him you're meeting up with some guys to practice field goals."

Johnny's suggestion was fantastic. Dad had developed a distinct revulsion of my love of soccer. "You know only two types of sexes play fußball over here, girls and swishes." He harangued endlessly on how I should use my soccer skills to get a college football scholarship as a field goal kicker.

I used Johnny's suggestion on my Dad and embellished it. "Next year Sir, I'll try out for the varsity team. If everything works out maybe I can get a free ride to the University of Texas or Alabama. Place-kickers and field goal kickers are making a mint in the NFL."

"Son, it's not the money that counts. It's the love of the sport. Being good at something isn't enough. You have to be committed to it. Otherwise, it's not worth doing."

*

Later I took Dad's advice on doing something that I might love and tried my hand at journalism. I composed an article for the school paper questioning the right of school officials to beat their charges. My father walked onto the back porch as I showed the article to Jeff.

"What's that?" he asked.

"Nothing. It's just something I wrote for the school paper."

"Sports column?"

"No Sir."

Dad held out his hand. I gave him the article. He read it slowly, then gave his critique. "The piece is well written. You've demonstrated a good use of logic in equating the teachers' roles with prison guards rather than educators." He rolled up the paper into a tight cylinder. "I take exception with your statement that if we are old enough for killing, we are old enough to enjoy freedom from cruel and unusual punishment as guaranteed in the Constitution. What did you mean by that?"

"I'm making a case against paddling."

"Okay, that makes sense," he said and slapped the paper baton against his thigh. "But I don't agree with the statement if we do not enjoy this freedom then what are we doing in Vietnam."

"Sir, It's just a tagline, something to provoke emotion."

"Guess what, Tinker Bell?" Dad struck me across the face with the rolled-up paper then rammed the end of it into my stomach. "It worked!" He chased me out into the yard shouting, "Stick to sports. If you ever write vile shit like this again, I'll drag your ass down to the Marine recruiting station. I got a friend there who'll beat the reason we're in Vietnam into your head."

So there it is, the turning point. My Dad– not Bob Dylan, not a bunch of drugged out middle-class future Volvo drivers at Woodstock, not Tom and Dickey Smother's comedy routines, accelerated my conversion from an American teenager to the ultimate doubter of orthodoxy whether it be religious, political, social, artistic, or familial.

Chapter 36

On Sunday Nina waited for me in her lavender Pacer a block away from our house. Dad may not have been Sherlock Holmes, but he was certainly astute enough to know that a babe pulling into our driveway wasn't picking me up to launch a pigskin between goalposts.

Nina leaned across the seat and opened the passenger door. "Where's Jeff?" She tugged her tangerine tube top, revealing ample cleavage.

A fleeting, "I know what you're looking at" smile passed over her face. She tugged and stretched the tube top until it molded to the contours of her torso, her nipples ready to pop from the fabric.

"He's not around. He went to a friend's place."

I had never told Jeff of her invitation. My sin, one of omission, was minor. Given the choice, Jeff still would have opted to smoke weed and jam with Albert rather than sit around with a bunch of leftists droning on about the evils of the imperialistic military establishment.

"Too bad Jeff can't come," Nina said. "There's this girl I wanted to introduce to him."

Steering with one hand, she leaned over me and inserted a tape into an eight-track deck. Her free hand slid over my lap. The scent of her perfume lingered in the air.

"I dated Jeff a couple of times. Actually, it wasn't a date. It was an excuse for me to get to know something about you," she said.

"What did he tell you?" I willed my hard-on to shrink.

"Nothing. You're kind of scary."

"Why do you say that?"

"You never smile. You always walk around with your hands curled into fists." She took a sharp left onto a residential street, rounded a curve, and rolled into a driveway.

Standing on the front lawn of a suburban bungalow was a large white-haired woman. She beat the air with her floppy arms and yelled at a young man wearing a cleric's collar.

A few other people of various ages and dressed in every mode of fashion from retro fifties to mod squad, milled about the yard

Johnny walked out of the house with a woman dressed in jodhpurs and a turtleneck sweater. The woman's hair was pulled into a bun so tight that her eyebrows were raised to the center of her forehead.

She waved at Nina, rushed down to gather her in her arms, and kissed her on both cheeks. Her hand shot out to grab mine when she let go of Nina. "You must be David," she said and leaned forward aiming at my cheek.

"Yes Mam." I stepped back to stay out of kissing range.

The woman crossed her arms over her chest. "Mam? Do I look like your grandmother? Call me Ruth."

"Yes Mam."

"Don't hold it against him," Johnny punched me gently in the arm. "He's a military brat."

Ruth flashed a perfect set of natural teeth. "It is possible to overcome that stigma," she said and swooshed across the yard to speak with a guy who kept looking around furtively. Before she reached him, he quick-walked to the front of the driveway and looked right and left several times before withdrawing to the shadow of a bedraggled southern pine.

Ruth returned to us. She exhaled her sentences like an incantation, "Ever since Isaac got here, he's been a bundle of nerves. I don't blame him considering what he's facing should they ever catch him. Oh well, these are the times that... well you know."

Recalling Tom Paine's words, I hazarded completing her sentence, "...that try men's souls?"

"See, Ruth," Nina said, "he's not a jock."

"What do you think of what's going on in America right now, David?" Ruth asked.

"I don't know."

"Then you're no different from the majority of people. But you will learn."

Ruth slipped her arm through the crook of my elbow. She led me across the yard and through her house, pausing in the hallway to adjust an out-of-kilt picture of a woman waving a flag on a mound of rubble. Prints and posters hung on virtually every space of drywall. I recognized Lenin and Trotsky.

In the backyard people were sitting on anything available, folding chairs, a picnic table, the lawn, on the concrete edging of Ruth's raised vegetable garden bed. A man wearing a plaid cab driver's hat walked toward me with Johnny. He had the face of a bare-knuckle brawler and the body of a professional wrestling bad guy.

"David, this is my old man, Big John Jardin," Johnny said.

The man's lips parted in a crooked smile showing a row of broken teeth. His blue denim shirt stretched at the buttons each time he took a breath making the letters BAC and the trowel stencilled on his shirt pocket expand and contract. I jumped when Nina slid her hand into my back pocket.

Big John cocked his head to the side and winked at Nina. He pushed his tweed hat back to the middle of his bald dome. "What's your old man do, Davie?"

"He's in the Air Force, he's a hospital..."

Mr. Jardin wheezed. "Didn't ask for his resume, kid. Just give me his name, rank, and serial number."

"He's a Lieutenant Colonel."

"No shit, a brass-ass soldier. I was a ground pounder myself, never went above private for any long stretch of time," he said with a ring of pride. "Guess your old man never wore fatigues. He probably tip-toed his way through West Point or did the ROTC rumba."

"He was in the Aleutians in World War II." My face felt hot. "He started out as an enlisted man and then got recalled during Korea."

"Pulled himself up by his bootstraps, huh? Heil that means something. But then again some of the worst pricks I've dealt with in management labor negotiations were workers themselves at one time." Big John slapped me on the back. "Don't take offense kid. Johnny tells me that you got a hell-of-a temper. Learn to channel it and you might make a difference." He walked off lifting and dragging his stiff right leg.

Ruth joined Big John at a picnic table weighed down with pamphlets and buttons promoting every cause from the anti-war movement to a ban on non-union grapes. She rapped a wooden meat tenderizer on a book and said, "Please find a seat. Today we have three guest speakers. Jonathan Jardin will inform us of Texas' action to prevent the unionization of the construction industry. Our brothers and sisters in the valley are experiencing even worse harassment by goons hired by landowners to deny farm workers the right to unite. Pastor Evan Cook will talk about the role of religious groups in promoting social justice."

"What's he going to do, try to persuade us the Inquisition was an exercise to promote free thinking?" The large white-haired woman's gruff voice boomed across the lawn.

Ruth shot the woman a look. "And finally, Isaac is here to help us understand why the anti-war movement and SDS have fractured into several camps like the Revolutionary Youth Movement and Weathermen that advocate violence."

Big John's message was simple. Support unions and don't trust the bosses. The reverend's stance was to light a candle and pray for peace. Isaac interested me the most, not because of what he said, but because when he stepped up to the table he kept twitching and glancing over his shoulder.

"Go see if the two cars parked across the street are still there," he ordered no one in particular.

Johnny took leave and returned about five minutes later. "There's a van there now," he called out.

Isaac's gestures became agitated. He rapidly stumbled through an oral history of how the student and antiwar movement had fragmented after the Chicago Convention. "There are extremes on both sides," he said. "There are the before I raise my hand in violence I'll die for peace, pacifists, and there are the slash-and-burn anarchists and Maoists. Both camps are destroying the movement. We are our own worst enemies. All Nixon and Kissinger have to do is sit back and watch us devour our young. We must search for the higher ground, not the middle ground if we're to survive. Thank you." He scooped up his papers and dumped them into a backpack at his feet.

Ruth told him to calm down and that there was a car waiting for him on the next street. Isaac dashed across the backyard flanked by two guys who acted like backfield blockers protecting a quarterback.

When Isaac was gone Ruth addressed the gathering. "Next meeting will be at the Unitarian Church. Our speaker will demonstrate passive resistance techniques."

A man sitting on the ground in front of me said, "What bullshit." His red Afro spread out like a wild shrub. When he stood up, he looked as substantial as a scarecrow. He pointed at Johnny. His bony arm extended beyond the cuff of his bumblebee-striped jersey. "I bet your old man didn't go to any peaceful resistance training sessions when he was knocking heads with the company stooges and pigs back in Detroit."

"My pop left his front teeth in some limp dick's nightstick because he wouldn't fight. Staging punch-ups with the blues just turns the public against you, just brings down more heat."

The scarecrow's long fingers spread out in an enormous fan as he waved off Johnny's comment. "Right, I'm sure Big John never beaned a scab when the jackboots weren't around."

Johnny did not reply. The scarecrow ran his eyes up and down Nina's body then looked at me like I was a Martian. "Who's the narc?" He wiped his hands on the front of my shirt.

"He's not a narc," Johnny said.

"Then he's an establishment plant." He started to wipe his hands on my shirt again.

I dropped back and raised my clenched fists. "Don't do that again. I'm not a narc, a plant, or a wimp. I'm here because I was invited."

"Whoa, back off little man," the scarecrow said. "I'm just doing my job."

"Your job's to hassle people?"

"Right. I'm Stoney Burns the publisher of the Dallas Notes." He waited for me to say something. He looked disappointed when he saw that his statement didn't register. "The Dallas Notes, Texas's largest counterculture newspaper."

"Never read it."

"You're not the only one," Johnny broke in. "It's a rag. It has more want ads for kinky sex than a bus station men's room has graffiti."

"We do radical political stuff but we gotta get advertising to pay the bills, comrade," Stoney protested. "If you're not a narc or informer, kid, what's your bag? Doper, roper, Bircher, searcher, hippie, or commie?"

"I'm just a guy who doesn't like being picked on or seeing others picked on."

"What about the war, for it or against it?"

Stoney's questions were getting on my nerves. "Against it but probably not for your reasons. It's a mess. Ho Chi Minh is a hero in Vietnam. Nobody wants us there. All we're doing is cleaning up the shit the French left behind."

"That's heavy, man," the aging yippee said in a mock-serious tone.

Chapter 37

My father was gone during most of May and June. His absences gave me ample freedom to attend the lectures and workshops held by the scattered left-leaning groups in the Dallas/Fort Worth area. Initially, I restricted my outings with Nina and Johnny to tame gatherings of Unitarians, Reform Jews, and Quakers. I listened to speeches about love, peace, and people power until my eyes went glassy. They taught me how to go limp so cops clearing out protesters would have to drag dead weight and would not have an excuse to use their clubs. Good in theory but not very realistic; I knew from Chief Brown a cop would beat you senseless for making his job more difficult.

The first teach-in I attended with Nina inspired me. The host was the direct opposite of the touchy-feely crowd I'd been associating with. "Hey there, I'm Farron," he said in the pinched-nose accent of a New Englander. "Welcome to the revolution."

Farron was not his real name. None of the people who traveled across the country giving talks and recruiting fresh members used their actual birth names. Farron was a caricature of a revolutionist.

His curly hair stuck out from under a black beret like a fright wig. His body was as wide and solid as a Maytag washing machine. His jaw was buried in a Walt Whitman beard, which fell over a red-and-white checkered bandana tied around his neck. Renegade neck hair crept out of the open collar of his Fidel Castro fatigues.

Farron said, "I hear your old man is a stooge of the military establishment. Don't sweat it, so is my old man. He's a full-bird colonel in the Marines. You know what takes real balls?" He shook my hand. "Going against the things you were taught to believe your whole fucking life takes courage, man. Any half-wit coward can be a jarhead." Farron's eyes moistened. "It isn't easy Dave when you realize that everything you've come to accept as the truth is a lie."

Farron talked in sports metaphors. "The best defense is a good offense" was the subject of the lecture. He and two other guys cleared away the furniture and showed us not-so-passive resistance techniques. Some of the moves I knew from Judo and wrestling. Other tactics were right out of a hand-to-hand combat manual. I loved the physical action. It reminded me of being part of a team again.

I came to the next sessions willingly. The class grew until it could no longer be contained in the apartment. Farron shaved his beard, cut his hair, and approached a local community center equipped with a weight room and floor mats for the use of their facility.

"We're in," he announced at the last teach-in held at his place. "The manager believes we're running a free marital arts program to keep wayward youths on the straight and narrow. When I explained, our program is designed to make teenagers less susceptible to the temptation of drugs, sex, and wrong thinking that permeates America, the bourgeois pig nearly came in his shorts."

The con worked. Not only did the center's manager buy it, my Dad endorsed it as well.

"That's good, David. I was beginning to worry about the gang you've been hanging around with. That girl, what's her name?"

"Nina, Sir."

"She's very attractive, so attractive that her father called me. He thinks you are seeing too much of her. He said that if she sees any more of you, he'll send your prick to me in a box. You know what I told him?"

I knew better than to step on a punchline.

"I said I'd pay for the postage. Do you believe me? Do you believe I'd honor my promise?"

"Yes Sir."

"Good. Need any money for the lessons?"

"No Sir." I had my own cash from a part-time job as a soda jerk at the Polar Bear Ice Cream Shop.

Although Nina quit attending Farron's sessions she still drove me and picked me up. She couldn't stand the way the other guys groped her as part of their training.

I felt the same way.

Securely ensconced in the center, Farron's lessons moved from learning how to break the bridge of a guy's nose with the heel of your palm to talking about how only those individuals with the courage to engage in guerrilla actions would succeed in making the establishment change. Farron invited a group of us to his apartment. Normally I would have begged off. Dad expected me home immediately after my workout, but he was in Washington D.C.

When we got to Farron's apartment he went into the kitchen. He returned with an open beer. He ordered us to sit down without offering us even a drink of water. "You guys are my best listeners," he said. "But listening isn't the same as doing, is it?"

"What's on your mind?" Johnny asked.

Sloshing his beer on the carpet, Farron motioned us to follow him into the bedroom. On his dresser was a box holding several bottles filled with a thick brown liquid. He picked a bottle and pulled out the cork. He sniffed the opening before handing it to me.

I took a whiff and gagged at the stench. "Damn! It smells like something crawled in there and died."

Farron took my remark as a compliment. "It's better. I paid good money for it. It's a mixture of cow blood, piss, and shit."

"That's cool man, but I doubt if it's going to replace Dr. Pepper," Dan said.

"Grab the box and come with me," Farron said without cracking a smile. We went outside to his Dodge Dart. Dan placed the box on my lap. Farron sped down the street and entered the freeway that led to downtown Dallas. Once in the city Farron tossed three bandanas like the one he wore around his neck behind the front seat. "Put them on," he said.

Making a series of lefts then rights and lefts again we ended up across the street from a drab three section office building. Even in the dark I recognized the structure as the Federal Building. The upper floors housed the FBI, the Treasury Department, and my father's office. At street level a series of recruiting posters called on passersby to "Join the Navy and see the world" and "Be the best you can be. Be a Marine!"

"Let's do it," Farron shouted. He leaned over the seat and snatched a bottle. He was out of the car before I knew what was happening. He hurled the bottle at the lintel above the main entrance. An old man in a baggy security guard uniform sat inside the building in front of the revolving doors. He fumbled with his keys.

Bottles flew through the air, splattering the recruiting posters. The slaughterhouse sludge ran down the walls and windows of the building and puddled on the pavement. The night watchman finally managed to open the door. Farron laughed at the sight of the unarmed guard shining his flashlight at us while he squeaked, "Freeze!"

Farron pitched the last bottle at a space of brickwork next to the old man's head, showering the watchman in liquid filth.

We piled into the car and peeled rubber, leaving a trail of black smoke. The leaflets Farron had tossed out the window floated in the air. Farron dropped us off at the center. "Not bad guys. Next time let's see if we can burn it down. A couple of Molotov cocktails should do the trick. Maybe these pigs will know that Revolutionary Youth Movement means business."

The next day I leaned into the television tube to see if our act of vandalism had made the evening news. With the Weathermen lobbing real bombs and the Black Panthers engaging in urban combat, our stunt didn't even draw a yawn. Still, I was on edge for the rest of the week. Johnny and Dan told me that they were dropping out of the Revolutionary Youth Movement.

Johnny summed it up succinctly. "Farron and his crew are fucking nuts."

"Completely out of their minds," I agreed.

I missed the next two meetings at the civic center and experienced my father's wrath when he returned home. "If you are going to sign up for something, stick to it. People are counting on you." He forced me out of the front door with my gym bag. "If the parents of those silver spoon socialists who smeared shit all over the Federal Building had gotten their boys into activities like this, they wouldn't be doing what they're doing today."

"You can't put all the blame on the parents," Mom chimed in. "The movies and television share a lot of the responsibility. As for the boys who did this, flogging is too good for them."

I did as instructed and returned to the civic center for my very anti-civic lessons. When I walked through the steel doors of the gym, Farron was yelling at some high school boy. "How many grams of grey matter does it take to pass out a few leaflets?"

The kid broke into tears. "I wanted to pass them out but the cops threatened to arrest for me for not having a permit."

"Don't give me any excuses. There's no room for excuses in the movement."

Farron stepped away then feigned a kick that went past the boy's head. His eyes lit on me. I wasn't sure whether I should take his frozen smile as a threat or a greeting. His mouth relaxed. "Thought you'd taken off for good like your friends. Those guys talk a good show but when it comes to

putting their ass on the line for the cause they flake off."
Farron was talking too fast for me. Every sentence had the
words infiltrator, capitalist pigs, revolution, and death to
reactionaries twisting through a maze of Marxist drivel.

"Maybe now that you're back Johnny and Dan will change
their minds. I don't know if I'll accept Johnny. That prick
said he didn't reject one corrupt ideology to join another."
He gulped a lung-full of air after his breathless rant and
said, "Well, what do you think?"

"Farron, I don't swallow your bullshit and I don't want to
go to jail or worse for carrying off your half-cocked
schemes."

I danced away and headed for the doors. "Brown, I'll
come after you if you rat on me."

Word got around that Farron split when he was dimed
him out to the police for copping more than a feel with jail
bait girls. When my father returned, he asked me why I no
longer attended the martial arts class, I told him that the
instructor had moved.

"At any rate, Sir. I don't have the time. I got a job as a
waiter at El Chico."

"Between studying and working at Polar Bear and El
Chico your plate is full."

"Yes Sir, but I should be able to put away some money for
college."

"Is that all you want to tell me?"

"Yes Sir," I was pretty sure he had bought the story. Most
of it was true. Albert was working at El Chico as a busboy
and had told me that they were looking for waiters.

The back of my father's hand whizzed through the space separating us. I felt the steel of his wristwatch wrapped around his hand like brass knuckles, slicing into my gums.

"How many times do I have to tell you that I loathe a liar worse than some vile creature that squats in the muck licking its own ass?" Dad's green eyes were as dull as the eyes of a perch left in the sun all day.

I wasn't aware of the stream of blood that poured out of my mouth and down my chin. Stuffing his hand in his back pocket he pulled out a handkerchief yellow with age that bore his monogram, E.H.B., and threw it in my face. "Get yourself cleaned up and stop your pouting. I'm the one who should be upset. Do you have any idea who called me today? Mr. Beaudry, that's who. Do you know what he told me?"

I figured the safest course of action was to bleed and keep my mouth shut.

"Mr. Beaudry told me that every Tuesday and Thursday for the past few weeks when Nina was supposed to be at the library, she was actually picking you up at that civic center."

I struggled to keep my face impassive. If Nina told her father about Farron and his political leanings I was in for more than a split lip.

"Nina is also coming home entirely too late on the weekends."

Dad hit me in the upper arm. His extended middle knuckle paralyzed my muscle. I did not flinch.

"Well, what have you got to say for yourself? I warn you before you open that cesspool you call a mouth that it had better be the truth."

I breathed slowly and delivered what would either be my salvation or my final lie. "Nina has been picking me up and taking me home after my class. It's on the other end of town. Sometimes we see each other after I finish my shift at the Polar Bear. She works as a cashier at the pharmacy. If you've been speaking to Mr. Beaudry, you know that she comes right home after dropping me off. She is always home by 11:30 on the weekends. You know it's true Dad because I have to be home by 11:00. If I wasn't I'd be grounded for a year."

The Colonel relaxed, sliding down into his chair as he sipped his Bourbon. "So nothing's happened between you and the girl that I should worry about?"

"No Sir." The place and opportunity had not yet presented itself.

"I'm not here all the time. How do I know what you're up to when I'm gone?"

My answer came out slowly. I could not afford a misspeak. "Sir, I'm doing what I am certain you would expect me to do."

He stuck his long middle finger in his tumbler and swirled the solitary ice cube floating in it. He stood up, placed a hand on my shoulder, and dug his nails into my collarbone. "I expect you to do as you've been brought up to do."

Chapter 38

Eliot thought he was the coolest guy in Texas. In his El Chico red waistcoat and cummerbund, slick black pants, white shirt with a frilly bib and cuffs, he looked like Disney''s gringo Zorro.

Albert introduced us within my first five minutes working at the restaurant. As if something was caught in his eye, he gave me an exaggerated wink. "I'm sure I told you about Eliot. Miss Kirsch gave him special attention." Albert punched him lightly on the arm.

Eliot shoved him away.

"What class did you have with Miss Kirsch?" I asked.

"I wasn't in her class officially." Eliot pulled up his shoulders and dropped them in a manner reminiscent of James Dean. "You might say, Tracey was my private tutor."

"Tracey?"

"Miss Kirsch."

Albert followed Eliot around making sure his tables were bussed before anyone else's. Every once in a while, Eliot threw him a crumb. "Way to go, keep my tables spic and span and I'll make sure you get a shot at waiter."

After work in the locker room Eliot said, "Brown, you don't look like the hard ass commie Albert's been chewing my ear off about. You look like Wally Cleaver out on a date. You hang with Jardin and Somerset, right?"

"They're friends of mine."

"I've seen your girlfriend waiting for you at the Polar Bear. Man, that's fucked up. Not the girl. The job. Your chick has a body that won't quit. You popped her yet? Don't know about her but you've got virgin written all over your face."

"Fuck off." I removed my waistcoat and cummerbund and threw them on a chair. Eliot handed them to Albert who put them in a paper bag. I took hold of Albert's sleeve as he walked off with the sack stuffed under his arm.

"Don't worry, man. He's just bringing them home to wash. He does it for me. See, the waiters who get the biggest tips are the ones who dress the part. You know, look like a slob and you serve the slobs. Slobs don't tip."

"That's your secret to getting big tips?"

"Part of it but I don't know you well enough to share the other tricks. Tell you what. Come over to my place tonight and I'll share a zombie joint with you."

"I don't think so. I don't know you well enough to get busted with you."

"Come on, man. Cheryl won't mind."

"Who's Cheryl?"

"The woman I'm living with," Eliot smiled. "She's twenty-five."

Eliot slipped his hand into his back pocket as we left El Chico's. "I thought all you revolutionary hippie types wore your hair past your ass." He pulled out a rat-tail comb, swept the chestnut hair off his forehead and handed it to me.

The next night I found myself at Eliot's pay-by-the-week furnished apartment downing a Mason jar of Boone's Farm Apple wine. He and his woman friend sat on a sagging twill sofa in their underwear sharing a joint. I used a cold as an excuse to beg off a toke when the number was passed to me.

Cheryl grinned lopsidedly. She pushed her bleached blonde hair behind her ears accentuating her square, almost masculine features. She teetered as she stood up and walked to the bedroom. "Don't go nowhere. I'll be right back. I gotta check on my angel. She's only three but she's already a charmer."

Eliot shattered the couple of seconds of silence that to a guy stoned out of his gourd dragged on for an eternity. "The kid's not mine but I'm here for Cheryl and she's here for the baby. Guess that makes us a family."

"I got to get going," I said.

"Okay, okay, don't freak out, I'll drive you."

"That's okay, next time."

"Cool. Next time, next time I'll be straight and say hello to your old man. He's an admiral in the army, right?"

*

Out of self-survival during subsequent visits I increased my consumption of cigarettes and even faked a couple of hits off a joint as it passed around the ever-growing circle of dopers partying at Eliot's apartment.

I did not like the sensation of being stoned, did not enjoy the feeling that my head was trapped in a garbage can from under which I occasionally caught echoes of conversations. Because of my uptight nature, inability to relax, and complete lack of humor when toking, a few of Eliot's acquaintances took me for a speed freak. I let the myth stand.

Being a speed freak gave me a certain cachet and the latitude to be cruelly mocking and anti-social when some yokel started pontificating on the meaning of life while licking the icing off an Oreo cookie. The pot smokers were marginally tolerable. The people who came over to drop acid or mescaline annoyed me the most.

One guy was a nature lover. He never ingested processed foods or chemicals. His preferred mind-bending substance were peyote buttons pulverized into a mash that he ran through a blender with ice cream and bananas. Five or six deep swallows of the concoction he would vomit then recite passages from "Lord of the Rings" and insist everyone call him Frodo. To make things worse he called me Bilbo. After a string of nights of this nonsense I longed for the company of Johnny, Dan, and even Farron. Slinging bottles filled with blood and shit was more enlightening than listening to a roomful of stoners slinging clichés and exclaiming, "Wow!" while watching a television test pattern.

Albert became one of the regulars. Eliot called him Chubby Gonzalez and never tired of hearing him do horrid renditions of Purple Haze and Foxy Lady. He used Albert as a runner to transport tabs of acid and mescaline around Irving, paying him in dime bags of grass. Eliot detested the term pusher. He said, "I am a supplier of fantasy. I don't force anyone to take what I wouldn't take myself."

Eliot volunteered to pay for my hits and said I could invite Nina to join us. I declined the offer so many times that the rumor that I was a narc started being taken seriously. The worst repeater of this line was B. B. Oakley. This Easy Rider wannabe fashioned his wardrobe after Denis Hopper.

Oakley wore mirrored sunglasses to shield his pink eyes from even the weakest light. He smelled like a toxic mixture of cigarettes, weed, fried food, bad hygiene and Jade East cologne. Because I hardly took more than a few weak inhalations of the joints that were passed around Eliot's apartment and never acid, Oakley genuinely thought I was an undercover narcotics officer. He hit on Nina without any luck and made a crack about how her nipples always grew hard and pointy whenever she walked by him just like his dick did. I told Nina I'd take care of B.B. but she said he wasn't worth it. She wanted me to adopt her pacifist outlook.

My feud with Oakley came to a head one day when he was revving his chopped hog in front of a 7-11. He crooked his finger at Jeff as we walked home from school. Jeff crossed the street. Still seated on his motorcycle he shoved Jeff to the ground. Jeff stood up, dipped into his pocket and handed him a wad of bills. I stormed across the street and jerked Oakley off the back of his bike by his helmet. He landed on his feet. Jeff grabbed me and pulled me away.

"What are you doing?" Jeff yelled and scanned the street. "You're going to get me busted. B.B. and I are friends, partners."

As Jeff and I walked home he asked, "You think you saved my ass? Oakley is my donkey not the other way around. The truth is, it's because B.B. and I are tight that he didn't kill you. You know what B.B. stands for?"

"Brainless baboon?"

"Get real, David."

While I played at being a hard ass, Jeff was the real thing. He sold grass and acid in more than just a little extra stuff to spare sort of way. He always had money even though he rarely worked except on Saturdays at a local garage that specialized in repairing European cars. Dad had been elated by Jeff's interest in automobiles and wanted me to quit prancing around a restaurant dressed like Rudolph Valentino and follow Jeff's lead. The car repair shop was where Jeff met Oakley.

*

As Eliot's habit grew, so did his paranoia. "Man you gotta join in," he demanded. "People are wondering about you."

Oakley backed him up. "Hey Brown, are you a narc or just a pussy?"

"The Yaqui ate mushrooms and peyote to communicate with the spirits," Nina said. "Forget about acid and all those chemical hallucinogens. They distort reality. What we need is something that will make us more aware of the nature of the world around us."

"I got no idea what you're talking about but I know where I can score some pure stuff," Eliot said.

Eliot arranged a party to coincide with the Colonel's absence. He displayed eight hits of mescaline on a paper plate. "We are going to fly sky high."

The television was blaring full volume. In rapture with a CBS special on the Apollo 13 mission, B.B. squatted in front of the tube with his lips almost pressed against the glass. He bypassed the hit of mescaline but made up for it by smoking three pipes of hash. "Man, it looks bad. We gotta send a rocket up there to get those guys."

I stopped myself from telling B.B. that James Lovell and his crew had come back safely two months earlier.

"Jesus, look how many showed up," Eliot said, waving his arm at the people seated on the couch, bar stools, kitchen chairs, in the corners, anywhere there was free space. "I don't know if I have enough to go around. Do you think Nina would mind if you split a hit between you?"

I dropped my eyes, masking my relief. Nina's doe eyes indicated her letdown. She claimed to be a mixture of French, Spanish, Irish, and Arapaho with perhaps some spirit trace of Aztec or Inca and had tenaciously latched on to native southwestern spirit worship. She consented to the half ration, and we sat down and dropped.

The effects of the hallucinogen were negligible. I had no heightened sense of either my surroundings or of my body apart from an irritating bout of tinnitus. In fact, I got more of a buzz from a shot of Jack Daniels while hot boxing a cigarette.

Nina rambled on about how she could see the blood coursing through her fingernails when she held them over the lens of a flashlight. She lifted her blouse and slipped it over my head. My lips were pressed between her cleavage as she shone the light down the neck opening of her blouse.

"What color are my breasts?" She asked, oblivious to the crowd in Eliot's living room. It wouldn't have mattered anyway. Half of his guests were in various stages of undress and locked in sexual positions of their own.

"They're wonderful," I gasped from under the shirt. I circled her nipples with my tongue through her sheer bra.

"I know that. But what color are they?" Nina squeezed me against her flesh until I couldn't breathe then pushed me out from under her shirt and stood up. "Come with me. It is only through two becoming one that one becomes many." She pulled me toward the open door of the bedroom.

"I don't know if we should. I want to but I don't want to do anything that will cause you to lose your respect for me." My voice cracked.

"Fuck respect, that's what she wants to lose," Eliot said. I turned to see his hand pushed down the front of Cheryl's jeans.

"For Pete's sake go with her," Cheryl panted while she squirmed under Eliot's touch, thrusting herself into the heel of his hand. Cheryl's glassy eyes and yellow complexion gave away her age. The fat between her thighs were squeezed into dimples that filled out the creases of her jeans. Her breasts were succumbing to the force of gravity.

I was petrified. Nina shut the door and pulled me toward her so swiftly, our lips met in a bruise rather than a kiss. We remained standing, lips swollen and hurting before I slipped my hand under her shirt.

With beginner's luck I unfastened the clip of her bra. Nina didn't give me time to marvel at my dexterity. She moved away just enough to pull her shirt over her head leaving me to gawk at her thin arms and full breasts. She lifted my left hand and placed it over one breast. Placing an arm behind my neck she drew my mouth to the areola of her other breast.

"Suck my nipples," she said.

I obliged even though my back was killing me from bending over straight-legged, knees locked.

When she finally lowered herself onto the mattress, dragging me to the floor with her, I "oohed" with relief. She unhitched my belt and unzipped my pants. Thrusting her hand down my underwear, she wrapped her fingers around my engorged penis.

She arched her back, undid her denim skirt and guided my right hand under the waistband of her panties. My fingertips combed through the dense bush of her pubic area. Gradually she moved herself up my hand until my fingers touched the thick wetness of her clitoris.

Nina laughed. She raised a leg and placed its firm calf on my shoulder. She smiled coyly as she slipped her panties down her smooth legs. Suspended from a garter belt was a device that resembled a hammock. Inside the hammock was a sanitary napkin. "It's okay, baby." Nina pulled me on top of her. "Don't be worried. I'm on my cycle," she said as she guided me inside her. At that moment Planned Parenthood was not on my list of things to contemplate.

*

With the exception of Eliot and Cheryl asleep on the couch, the apartment was vacant when Nina and I came out of the bedroom. A cuckoo popped out of its plastic alpine coop. Nina glanced up at the clock. It was midnight.

"My father is going to kill me!" Nina raced frantically around the apartment hunting for her purse and car keys.

"What time did you say you'd be home?" I heard my words bounce around my head like a marble in a bucket.

"I told him we were going to a movie and dinner and I'd be back by ten. What I am going to tell him?"

"Anything but the truth," I thought as she gathered up her stuff and headed out the door. "Tell him we went in my car, and it broke down."

For a couple of hours, I dozed on the sofa, snapping my eyelids open like a window blind every few minutes. Somewhere in the middle of that sleep a thunderous pounding jerked me up.

Eliot dashed out of his bedroom wielding a tennis shoe. He pressed himself against the wall and motioned me to open the front door. I barely cracked it when a hand pushed it so hard that the door hit Eliot and sprang back with a bang. Eliot emerged from his hiding place with his hand cupped over his eye. The pounding commenced again. This time I held onto the knob when I opened the door. A fist slammed into my chest and my glasses went flying.

"Which one of youse dinks is David Brown?" The man's head filled the space in front of me like a medicine ball.

Eliot sat at the breakfast bar holding a dishcloth wrapped around an ice cube on the lump above his eyebrow. "He is."

"You're Brown? You sure don't look like what I expected."

The man's head moved within a foot of my face. He bent down, reappeared with my glasses, and adjusted them on the bridge of my nose. The hard wedge of a lacquered pompadour extended beyond the man's square forehead.

"You know who I am, David?"

"Yes Sir."

"You getting smart with me?"

"No Sir."

"Don't call me Sir. The name's Roger." His fingers crushed my knee like a vise.

"Sorry, sorry," I stammered imagining the beating he was going to inflict on me. "I was brought up to say yes Sir and no Sir as a matter of respect, Sir."

"Yeah, Nina told me your pop is a lifer."

His eyes drooped and a smile crept across his beefy face. "Tough being a military brat isn't it. I did my time, four years and was done with it. Tough luck for you, the government owns your ass for as long as your dad's in plus more if you're drafted, huh?"

"I guess so, Sir."

"In the real world you don't go around calling every one you meet, Sir. It's not a mark of respect. It marks you as a wimp, a pushover."

"You're right," I agreed.

"Let's get back to the reason I'm here. Nina was supposed to be home at ten. She didn't show up until after one in the morning. What you got to say about that Dave?"

"It's not her fault, Roger. It's mine. We were going to go to the drive-in in Nina's car, but I persuaded her to go in my car when she came over here to pick me up."

"Nina told me that you don't drive."

259

"Only because I didn't have wheels. I feel like an idiot, but I spent 150 bucks for a 1960 Ford Falcon. I wanted to drive her for a change because she's always taking me places. You know how embarrassing it is to always have your girlfriend drive?"

"No, my old man owned a used car lot in Newark and gave me my first set of wheels when I turned sixteen."

Roger chuckled. "Guess it would be a real ball breaker though to be chauffeured around by your date, especially in the Wild West."

"My car broke down as we pulled into the drive-in. Pieces of metal and other stuff were falling off. I didn't want Nina to take a chance going back with me, so I called Eliot to come pick her up and follow me back to his place. I was lucky, Mr. Beaudry that we made it. Smoke was pouring out from the tailpipe and from under the hood."

"Why didn't you call me or your old man to get you?"

"I felt like a big enough pansy as it was without calling you to help me. And I couldn't call my dad. He's out of town. I wouldn't have asked him to come anyway. He advised me against buying that junk car. Also, he's against my dating Nina." I let the last sentence hang without explanation.

"Let me get this straight. Your old man is against my girl seeing you? I think he's got that ass backwards. It's me who has reason to worry."

"You have nothing to worry about. Nina is a good girl. It's my fault she came home late."

"Forget about it," Mr. Beaudry thrust out his chest as he stood up. He encircled my shoulders with his massive arm and made me accompany him to the front door. Once outside he pointed at a blue Ford Falcon with its hood held down by picture wire. "Is that your car?"

I nodded, startled and grateful. I leaned against the front end of the Ford. "I should have listened to Nina and gone to the movie in her car. I should have listened to my dad and not bought this piece of crap."

"Things happen, Dave." Roger pulled out a Lucky Strike from its pack and tapped both ends of it on the hood of the Falcon. "Just don't let them happen too often. You seem like a straight enough guy. You could have whined about my coming over here or played like a hard ass. It wouldn't have been a good idea. It would have given me an excuse to mop the parking lot with you."

We were silent as Roger lit his cigarette and sucked in a lungful.

"Your old man is a prick, huh? Nina tells me he runs your house like bleeping Paris Island."

I shrugged preferring to keep what went inside the Brown's camp private.

"So, your old man doesn't want you to date my girl? Well, Dave, you seem okay by me. Tell you what. You can continue to see Nina provided you get her home on time and that you visit our place so we can get to know you better." He flicked the remainder of his smoke to the pavement and gave me a not so playful shot in the arm before walking away.

Chapter 39

One evening after work at El Chico I stepped into a right-cross when I entered the house. I didn't have time to backpedal from the second punch that caught me in the stomach. Christ, Dad was supposed to be out of town.

I propped myself against the wall and shielded my face with my forearms. The days of my standing still and taking it "like a man" were long gone. I slipped the Colonel's third punch aimed at the top of my head and ran into the dining room, keeping the table between us.

"You worthless piece of shit!" Dad tore off into his bedroom and returned clutching a government green file folder. He threw it on the table sending its contents spilling out. I glanced down at a photograph and recognized Ruth's house. Groups of people were milling about her front yard. Another photograph was of Johnny Jardin and me talking to the nervous speaker who had hopped Ruth's back fence. The last picture caught me leaving the community center where I'd listened to Farron's revolutionary rants.

"If the government thinks for one instant that you are affiliated with these cock-sucking commie queers my career is over! It's goddamned lucky that I got friends in the Bureau who brought these to me before showing them to my superiors. I'm going to ask you one question and one question only. Do you know these people?"

"Yes Sir."

He flung a chair out of his way and tried to grab me from across the table. I sidestepped his reach.

"Dad, I dropped these people when I found out what they are about."

"What are they about?"

"They're against the war, against the military and the government."

He sighed. "Who the hell isn't these days? What are they for?"

"Free medical care and education, and equal rights."

Dad sat down in a chair and wiped his palms on his pants. "I see, motherhood and apple pie stuff."

"Sir?"

"You can't argue against someone feeding you motherhood and apple pie," he said. "But you know what? After you've filled yourself up on breast milk and pie, you're too full to catch the rest of their line."

"Dad, I stopped going over there. It was all I could do to stay awake when they talked."

"You should have gone and listened. You need to know both sides before you can come to your own decision."

"Yes Sir."

"This place. What do you know about this place?" He pointed at the picture of the community center.

Feeling the crisis had passed I walked around the table to stand next to Dad. "That's where I told you I was taking martial arts lessons."

"You lied to me!" Dad used his fist like a mallet on the dome of my head. The sound of my front teeth being driven into my lower ones was like a rifle crack. "I have more respect for a bomb tossing nutcase than I do a liar." He slapped me across the face then stomped out of the house into the garage.

When the coast was clear my mother came in from the backyard carrying a basket of tomatoes picked from the garden. Tommy trailed behind her with a plastic garden trowel in his fist and a scared shitless expression on his face. I expected Jeff to appear but then remembered that he was staying at Vince's, restoring an old MG Midget they had picked up at a scrap yard.

"I didn't know you were home," Mom lied.

I spit out the tooth chips that clung to the inside of my lips like bits of eggshell. "Dad's home too."

"He thinks you boys don't respect him or the uniform he wears."

I went to the bathroom and rinsed my mouth, wincing as cold water washed over the raw pulp.

The Colonel stayed close to home for a few days probing me for names and dates related to my spring fling with the antiwar movement. He told me that agents from the Treasury Department and FBI wanted to talk to me. I wandered around the house neither smiling nor frowning. The Colonel announced that he was going to D.C. to meet with his boss. He asked me what I wanted him to bring back.

"Nothing, Sir."

He reminded me to send out my applications to the Air Force Academy and West Point. My expression did not alter when I told him that I had no intention of applying to either school.

He looked at his watch. "I don't have time to deal with you now but believe me, you'll change your tune when I get back."

I swallowed the venom he was waiting for. "Yes Sir."

Later on that evening I got three phone calls that shook my world for good. The first one was from Johnny Jardin.

He said, "The Feds came by my place. They showed Big John pictures. You better lie low. They asked me your role in starting a radical student group in Irving. My pop brushed them off. It was rich. He told them they were barking up the wrong tree and that if they really wanted to find out who's fucking over America they should talk to Tricky Dick."

Phone call two was from Nina. Her mother had discovered a thirty-day supply of birth control pills stuffed in the toe of her dress shoes.

"What did you tell her?" I envisioned Roger and my father taking turns beating me.

"I said my gynecologist prescribed them for menstrual cramps."

"Do you think she bought it?"

"For now, but she's going to talk to my doctor."

That evening gave credence to the saying, bad news comes in threes. I sweated bullets in the monstrous Texas heat while lifting weights on the patio to work off my anxiety. My mother poked her head out of the air-conditioning long enough to tell me, "That nice boy Eliot is on the phone for you."

When I picked up the phone Mom retreated into her novel, zoning out and giving me privacy in her presence.

"We gotta get out of town," Eliot said. "Christ, get over here!"

"Eliot, this is the wrong day to be hassling me."

"Albert stooled on us."

"I have no idea what you're talking about."

"Albert's sister called me. Her parents called the cops on us. You remember last month when we dropped mescaline together?"

"Uh-huh," I said, remembering an evening I wanted to forget.

"Well, I used Albert as a gofer to pick up the stuff then I told him he couldn't trip with us because there wasn't enough. He was a little pissed but calmed down when I promised to score him two hits of acid."

"I don't see what all this has to do with me."

"The little tamale kept ragging me on when he was going to get his tabs. 'Is it in yet? How good is it? Where's it coming from? Have you tried it? His questions were driving me squirrelly."

"Albert's got that routine down pat."

"He was at me non-stop for six days. I do it. I get him what he wants. I give him three tabs of orange paradise. He says he'll drop them later with two friends. Fine, well enough. But then he calls today and tells me he's freaking out, screaming on the line about seeing things and laying out weird stuff like if your right eye offends you then pluck it out."

"It's been a bad day, Eliot. Get to the point or I'm hanging up."

My mother shifted in her chair and raised an eyebrow before going back to her book.

"The point is he tried to gouge out his eye with a spoon. We gotta get out of town!"

"Eliot, what do you mean 'we'? You sold the shit to him. I'll front you some bread, but I don't see what it has to do with me."

"Listen, man, Albert doesn't. trust me so when I gave him the tabs, I told him I got them from you."

I could not speak.

"It's a bitch, David. The stuff I sold him, the orange paradise, was fake, St. Joseph baby aspirin. I dabbed a blue dot of food coloring on the pills and told him it was acid."

Again, I said nothing, waiting for Eliot to fill in the blanks.

"How much money do you have?"

"Five-hundred or so."

"Pack up and bring it. Cheryl took her car to the garage to put on some retreads. It should get us where we're going."

"And that would be where?" I closed my eyes and pictured Cheryl's corpse white Impala. The machine hardly managed to grind its way out of the apartment's parking lot without depositing bits of metal and oil on the asphalt.

"If you're going to San Francisco, you better put some flowers in your hair," Eliot sang off key.

I held onto the phone listening to the buzz after he hung up. If I stuck around waiting for the Feds to grill me, Nina might show up with Roger. Or the cops would haul me in for supplying Albert with a headache remedy. Given Texas jurisprudence I could end up in the joint for thirty years. I'd become the queen of hemorrhoids before I turned eighteen.

Retreating into my room I catalogued the items I could stuff into Dad's duffel bag. I wished Jeff was home to help me decide what to pack. Always oblivious during her zombie hours of reading, Mom lifted her head once as I came out of the garage. "Isn't that your sleeping bag?"

"Yeah, I'm going camping and fishing with some guys in the morning."

"That's good. Isn't that your shotgun?"

"We may go skeet shooting at a range near the campground."

In my bedroom I broke down the shotgun into three separate pieces. I wrapped them in my sleeping bag and stuffed them into the duffel bag. The rhino blue barrel of the shotgun protruded slightly from its hiding place. I glanced around the room for something to conceal the bore of the shotgun and settled on two books I had bought at a garage sale, Walden and Civil Disobedience and The Revolutionist Handbook.

When I heard Mom's slippers shuffle across the shag carpet to her bedroom, I raided the kitchen. I crammed crackers, ding-dongs, half a block of cheddar cheese, salami, Mountain Dew, tomatoes, apples, a cucumber, a tin of kippered herrings, a jar of horseradish and a cauliflower into a knapsack. Obsessive about hygiene, I pilfered the bathroom, grabbing a new tube of toothpaste, dental floss, my toothbrush, and three bars of Ivory soap still in their wrappers.

Around three in the morning Eliot scratched on my window's screen. In the driveway was Cheryl's Impala. No words were exchanged. Eliot popped the trunk and threw my stuff in alongside two ratty vinyl-covered suitcases, a metal ice chest, a portable 14" color TV, and a box containing plastic barnyard animals, coloring books, crayons, and other kiddy junk. Cheryl was curled up on the backseat of the car with her daughter tucked closely to her. She lifted her head a few inches when I slid into the front seat. The dark circles under her eyes made her smile seem hopeless. Eliot started the engine and the car lurched forward. "How much money you got on you?" Eliot asked as he rolled through a stop sign.

"Over five-hundred bucks, you?"

"Less, food's no problem. Cheryl ripped off her restaurant. We got cold cuts, bread, drinks and some pies. Besides we got some stuff to pawn if it comes to that."

"Me too. I brought my shotgun."

"Who knows, we might do a little Bonnie and Clyde if things get too tough."

I assumed Eliot was joking.

By dawn we had left Fort Worth in our rear-view mirror and were rolling west to California, a journey of some 1,400 miles. The first stop was in Abilene, a central west Texas town midway between anywhere you were going or getting away from.

When Eliot pulled up to a gas pump at a no-name filling station, he asked me if I wanted to drive then recanted when I told him about my driver's education experience.

I threw my shoulder against the door and stepped out into the full sunlight of a hot morning promising to get hotter and walked toward a phone booth at the edge of the road.

"What do you think you're doing?" Eliot asked. "The police might have the line tapped."

"Did you call the police to let them know that we would be stopping at a gas station in Abilene to use a pay phone?"

"No."

"Then relax, I'm just calling my brother to see what's going on."

"And if your mother answers?"

I fished a dime out of the watch pocket of my jeans.

"My brother's at Vince's house."

"Vince sold me some good stuff. He's alright."

I wanted to scream, "Don't you ever think about anything else except dope?" But this was not a filling station just anywhere. This was a gas station in the Lone Star State. A state where the smell of gunpowder on your clothing at a shooting scene barely got you a nod while a whiff of hash and 2 ounces of tea could see you do life next to guys who had chopped up entire families and fed them to livestock.

The sound of the phone swallowing my coin and the operator's good day, was the most encouraging thing I had heard in two days. I gave her the number to Vince's private line. The phone rang several times before a sleepy voice said, "Wrong number, man," and slammed down the receiver.

I dialled again and this time shouted, "Don't hang up Vince."

"This is a collect call do you accept the charges," the operator spoke over me.

"Whoa! What charges? I didn't do anything, here you take it." I heard the thud of the phone on something soft and then Jeff said, "Hello."

"I have a collect call here, y'all. Do you want to take it or not?"

"Jeff, Jeff it's me David."

"Sure," Jeff said.

The hum of ten cents of dead air lingered between us. "Oh, man, are you ever in trouble," Jeff said at last.

"No shit, man. That friggin' moron, Eliot, told Albert I supplied the shit. So now I'm on the lam with him and his make-believe family." As I related the story, I heard voices in the background twittering.

"David, let me get this straight, Albert's sister called to warn Eliot?"

"What is this, To Tell the Truth?"

"Listen, blood, you've known Albert for what, about eight months? During this time did you ever meet his sister? No, you didn't, and you know why? Because Albert is an only child."

Away from the speaker I heard him say, "Big Brother wants to know if he's been had."

Albert's unmistakable accent came through the phone line. "Not on purpose. He's an added bonus."

Vince's voice, hoarse and shrill from toking too many joints, chimed in. "Tell him I don't know who's a bigger turkey, him or his dumb ass friend."

"What's going on?" I asked.

"You might say it's payback for Eliot trying to pass off baby aspirin as acid and for screwing Albert's dream teacher last year. Vince and I came up with the idea. Not bad, huh?"

"The cops aren't after us? We're not in trouble?"

"Can't say for Eliot, man, but you're in deep shit. Dad's going to cripple you when he gets home and finds out you've taken off. If I were you, I'd keep on heading west. It might be the only chance you have to see the coast in the lifetime left to you."

"Funny, Jeff, real funny."

"Albert wants you to tell Eliot that because he took off without giving notice he's been fired and Albert's been promoted to waiter."

"You're just full of good news."

"Seriously David, keep cool and ditch that turkey before you get into real trouble."

When I repeated what Jeff had told me, Eliot's face turned as white and soft as a slice of Wonder Bread.

"Jesus! Don't tell Cheryl."

"Come on man, you gotta tell her so she doesn't go driving across the fucking country with a kid. She can go back to her place and be at work by Tuesday."

"Not that simple. We split without paying the rent. She's also skipping out on a custody hearing that was scheduled for Friday. Her parents are trying to get Cotton. Do you fucking believe it? They claim Cheryl's a bad influence and isn't caring for her kid properly."

"How the hell did I get myself involved with you?"

"Even if the cops aren't after us for the dope thing they got people looking for us because of jumping the hearing. I know it's a lot to ask but come with us. We're close to broke, and we were counting on you. When we get to LA I'll call my brother and he'll front us enough bread to pay you back and get us to San Francisco."

Chapter 40

There is not a lot to recommend on the drive from Abilene to El Paso. Topography along the way is flat and the coloring of the scraggly vegetation drifts through a range of sandstone to taupe.

Cotton whimpered in the back seat. Suddenly she screeched, "No Mommy, burns! It burns!"

Cheryl had been sponging Cotton's face with a damp cloth to cool her down. Without realizing it she'd been. basting the little girl's exposed skin, roasting her like a turkey. By the time we pulled over at a rest stop outside El Paso, Cotton was a red as a beet and covered with water blisters.

"Eliot, we got to find a doctor," I said.

Cotton screeched, her blisters bursting open with every movement. Unable to pick up her baby to comfort her, Cheryl still refused to seek medical help.

"We ain't going. All I need is for some nosy nurse to wonder why a mama is traveling with two boys and a sick child. Next thing you know they'll take Cotton away from me. She'll be okay as soon we get clear of this desert."

"The desert is ahead of us, not behind us," I said.

"You keep quiet. She's my child. You'll see, she'll be better once she gets some shade."

"Do you think that when we cross the Texas-New Mexico border all of a sudden there's bunch of oak trees lining both sides of the road?"

From El Paso to Tucson, Arizona not a word slipped through our chapped lips. Eliot still managed to convey his need for me to open my wallet and pay the attendant at each stop.

As we drove into Tucson the car belched black smoke and the brakes screeched. Eliot rolled into a garage. A man wearing a railroad engineer's cap and a pair of bib overalls over a white dress shirt jumped down from an old Coca Cola ice chest. His face was gullied with creases as deep and discolored as the exposed rock formations.

"Looks like you have a problem there, boys." He looked into the back seat. "Bit hot in there for that little girl." He opened the door for Cheryl the creases around his eyes growing more pronounced as she got out with Cotton in her arms. "For the love of our savior, lady, that child's cooked something bad."

"She'll be okay," Cheryl said.

"Don't think so, Miss. Not unless you put something on those blisters. They're liable to get all pussy." He reached into the wide pocket at the front of his bib, took out an unwrapped stick of gum, tore off a corner and pushed it into Cotton's mouth with his thumb. "Miss, across the street my church is throwing a fellowship picnic. You go over there with your little girl and tell 'em Joshua sent you and they'll fix you something to eat and put healing lotion on her sores."

Cheryl gave him a warm smile and crossed to the park. A woman wearing a straw sombrero and faded floral print sundress spoke with Cheryl a moment then took Cotton from her. They walked to a large canopy and sat down at a table shielded from the white blaze of the sun.

"Now let's take a look at this thing," Joshua said. He knelt at the front of the car and dipped his fingertip into a black puddle of liquid that was too watery to be oil and held it up to his nostrils. "How far you boys planning to go?"

"California," Eliot said. "Is that a problem?"

"Only if you intend to get there." Joshua sucked his teeth. "No worry boys, it's the Lord's problem. And you have come to the right place to take care of it." He tilted back his head and looked up at the hand-lettered Good Samaritan Garage sign. "You boys go join your girlfriend. While you're chowing down I'll fix this buggy."

Eliot closed his fingers over the car keys. He shook his fist like he was going to roll dice then handed them over to Joshua.

"The fried chicken's mighty good," Joshua said as he popped the hood, "but a tad too greasy for me."

The chicken was great. The skin crackled as I bit into a drumstick. I avoided the potato salad that sat in the Arizona heat. Cheryl caught me looking at her and wiped away the tears trickling down her cheeks. She marched over to Eliot and said, "Let's get out of here."

Eliot held up his plate. "I'm not through eating, baby."

Cheryl swiped at the plate with her free hand. Macaroni, potato salad, a half-eaten chicken wing, and a glob of lime Jell-O flew into the air. Eliot jumped up and sped across the road to the garage. When I caught up with him, he was shouting at Joshua. "Ninety-five dollars?"

"It would've cost a sight more if I hadn't pulled out some old parts from a car I got in the garage," Joshua lathered his hands with gunk. "It wasn't worth putting on new parts. This car is long overdue for the scrap yard. Four new seals should take care of the leak but the drums are shot and the linkage is about to go." He spread an oil-stained blanket at the front end of the 1960 Impala, lay on his back and scooted his head under the car body. "Boys, come on here and look for yourself."

Eliot cursed, "Shit, go ahead and pay him."

I counted out five twenties and waited for him to fish a fiver out from his bib. Cheryl stepped back when Joshua extended an arm and opened her door. She tried to close it but he held onto the handle when the sombrero woman appeared with a cardboard box. The woman thrust the box containing a half-eaten pie, some burned weenies, fried chicken legs, a pack of rolls, a tub of fruit salad, and some soft drinks into the car.

"Remember, the Lord will show you the way if you know the destination." The woman charged across the road back to the church social.

Eliot jammed the car into drive. He peeled rubber, leaving Joshua to wave at us in the rear-view mirror.

If the Lord guided Joshua's hand, then God is a pitiful excuse for a mechanic. A hundred plus miles away from Tucson the car belched smudge into the clear desert sky. Eliot topped a hill and depressed the brake pedal. The car did not slow down. It picked up speed on its forward momentum. "Son of a bitch," he exclaimed and downshifted. The sound of metal eating metal deafened me.

"We have to stop," Cheryl pleaded.

"We're in the middle of the fucking desert," Eliot said.

"She's right, Eliot. Without brakes, we'll never make it over the mountains."

"Fine, fine, just keep the brat quiet."

To conserve the brakes Eliot low geared the car on the downside of every hill then let it coast almost to a stop before shifting back into drive and accelerating. It took us two hours to travel fifty miles. Just as I had given up hope, I saw a bald dome rock rising out of the arid landscape like a wart. A sparse garden of creosote bushes, sagebrush, mesquite trees, and dwarf spiny cacti competed at its base for what little moisture existed. A sign proclaimed, Tacna, Arizona (Gas, Water, Food) ½ mile. Eliot gave the car just enough gas to keep it moving and coasted to a stop.

Tacna Arizona consisted of three saloons, a garage, a diner, and some slat board buildings that had lost their paint to the elements. Eliot rolled into the lot of the garage. After a few minutes it became clear that no one was in a hurry to see what we wanted. We got out of the car.

As Eliot returned to the car a guy from across the road hollered, "Hang on there, hombre. Be right over." He wore a straw cowboy hat, a denim shirt, and blue jeans tucked into a pair of snakeskin boots. "Christ almighty it's been a busy day."

"Got many customers today?" Eliot asked.

"Just you guys, but that's enough." A hint of a Yankee accent slipped out. "Came here to get away from it all and found out that it comes with you." He smiled widely at

Cheryl. Her blouse had come undone to the third button. His smile faded when Cotton stepped out from behind her.

"So what gives with this old bucket?"

"The brakes are shot and the car is burning oil like a smudge pot," Eliot said.

"One of you back the car into the bay and the rest of you come with me across the road. I got a beer waiting for me. You guys look like you could do with a cold soda."

Eliot tossed the car keys at me. He hooked his arm through Cheryl's and took hold of Cotton's hand and walked to the road.

"Eliot, where are you going?"

"Where's it look like? I've been driving since Dallas. The least you could fuckin' do is back the car into the garage."

"No way," I said, pointing at a sign over the garage entrance that read, "Allow attendant to move vehicle."

"Kid," the man growled. "It's too damn hot for me to stand here waiting for you guys to argue about who's going to move the damn car. Either get it in the garage or get the hell off of my property."

What I failed to remember as I stomped on the accelerator was that the car had no brakes. Despite my efforts to steer, three thousand pounds of metal, rubber and glass leapt backwards and veered off the Tacna garage's lot. The twang of sprung wire and the bone crunching sound of wooden posts breaking, drowned out the squish of chickens flattened by the Impala. A two-foot-wide dry creek bed halted the car's momentum.

The man flung open the car door and tossed me into the ditch. "God damn, my God damn chickens, you killed my God damn chickens!"

I jumped to my feet and squared off even though I was pretty sure the garage owner could kick my ass. He doubled over, let out a huge hoot and laughed until his face was wet with sweat.

"Nobody is going to believe it when I tell 'em what happened," he wheezed.

He got into the car and slowly rocked it back and forth between drive and reverse until it rolled out of the ditch then drove it into the garage bay. Without talking he jacked up the lift and looked at the underside of the Impala. "You're missing two brake seals and your oil pan's sprung a leak. No telling what else is wrong."

Eliot looked like he was going to burst into tears. "How much is that gonna cost?"

"Depends if you want new parts or will settle for scrap ones."

"We already got taken once. We want new parts."

"It's your money and time. I got to order the parts from Phoenix, so you'll have to pay for the transportation too."

"How much and how long?"

"More than you've got from the looks of it. Tell you what, I got to go out this afternoon to the junkyard and pick up some bumpers and doors for a station wagon I'm reconditioning. One of you boys come with me and I'll pull what I need to fix your piece of crap. I'll charge you half what I generally do for the labor."

Eliot put his arm around Cheryl's waist. Cotton leaned against her mother's hip and sucked her thumb. Her eyes flickered with exhaustion. The verdict was clear. I was elected by silent acclamation to accompany the garage owner.

"Give me a hand with this," the man said and nodded at a plank of plywood leaning against the side of the building. I helped carry it to a pickup truck that came out of the 1950s. The sun had faded the paint job to the shade of a rock lizard. Holes of various dimensions peppered the body of the truck, the largest ones being patched over with auto putty and fiberglass tape. The bull nose cab had dark gaps like absent teeth where once shiny grillwork and letters spelling Ford had been. The front chrome bumper had been replaced with a black piece of metal secured to two brackets extending from the bottom of the cab by baling wire.

"Quit admiring my ride and help me lay this thing down." The man threw his end of the plank into the rusted-out bed of the truck.

I climbed into the cab. The man tucked his hand under the seat and pulled out a pint of Wild Rose fortified wine. He took a gulp then handed it to me. I screwed back on the cap and said, "No thanks. What I could really go for is a tall glass of water."

"Christ, kid, water is 'bout the only thing people don't give away out here." He worked the clutch as he shifted from neutral to drive. "I know guys that would sooner let you poke their old ladies than hand out H20."

"Is that so?"

"You must think that because I live in the middle of nowhere, I'm an ignorant hick."

"No Sir."

"What did you call me? I fucking hate being called sir. Had enough of that shit. Served four years as an officer in the Army Corp of Engineers to pay back Uncle Sam for sending me through college. When I got out, I swore I'd never build another pontoon bridge or tramp through a fucking mud hole or rice paddy. Don't see a lot of water out here and that's okay with me." He snatched the bottle and took another swig.

"You guys go in for threesomes?" He asked. "Your doll is really sweet. Too bad she has a kid. That must put a damper on things. I had a couple of women break down out this way about a month ago. One was a bony white girl with bigger kneecaps than tits but the other one, a black honey, was built like a brick shithouse. Turned out they didn't have enough cash between them to cover the repairs. I'm a fair guy but business is business. I told 'em I was going to take back my parts and call the sheriff. The white girl asked me if I would consider taking something in trade. The black girl stuck her hand between my legs and squeezed my balls. Well, things being the way they are out here I don't get a lot of strange, so I told them to hop in the truck and drive out this way with me. Couldn't very well do it in the garage. Maria stays in the trailer until sundown, but you never know, she might decide to pay me a visit." The man squinted as the sun drilled through the windshield. "That bony kneed red head fucked and sucked me drier than is decent, leaving me a spent force for more than a week." He paused and finished off the bottle. "Think your girlfriend

283

might be interested in making up part of the repair cost in trade?"

"How far is the junk yard?"

When we got back, a plump, black-haired woman with the high cheekbones and broad face of a native sat on a lawn chair under a beach umbrella. Cheryl and Eliot sat next to her. Cotton was curled up on the woman's lap.

"Shush, Gill, she's sleeping," the woman said and stroked Cotton's hair. "Looks like we got plenty of chicken." The woman tilted her head at a bucket with two of the birds I had killed inside it. "I invited these kids for dinner. From the state of their car, I don't think it will be ready before dark unless you get to work on it now."

Gill's shoulders slumped as he tramped off into the garage. He came out about three hours later immaculate except for a spot of motor oil on his shirt pocket.

"Wasn't as bad as I thought it would be." He handed Eliot a bill.

"Two-hundred and twenty bucks. I asked you to fix my car not gild it."

"Actually the car part is only about sixty bucks. The other hundred and forty are for the damage to my pen and for killing a cock and two hens."

"I'll pay for the car but the chickens are his fault." Eliot glared at me.

"Eliot's right," Cheryl said.

"The money is coming out of my pocket so it comes to the same thing," I said. "But it doesn't matter because I'm not paying for his chickens." I passed Gill sixty bucks.

Gill stuffed the money in his shirt pocket and extended his empty palm again. "Still a hundred and forty bills short."

"See that sign over your garage? Allow attendant to move vehicle. I'm not responsible under the law."

Gill strode past me into the garage. He picked up the telephone and dialled. He stayed inside for a half-hour then walked out when a police car skidded to a stop on the dirt lot.

Maria stood up and gently placed Cotton in Cheryl's arms. A short man wearing a tan uniform with a star pinned to his Stetson got out of the cruiser. A long barrelled 38 in a red hand tooled holster rode high on his hip.

"Frank, you come for dinner? We got plenty of chicken so no sense in you going back to an empty trailer."

"Sounds good to me, Sis, but that's not the reason I'm here. Gill called to say he has trouble." Frank licked the tip of his finger and used it to smooth his pencil line moustache.

Gill slapped his brother-in-law on the back. "You must have set fire to the highway getting here as fast as you did."

"What's the deal, Gill?"

"See these kids, they had me work on their car then don't want to pay."

"That's not true." I advanced from under the umbrella. "I paid him for the repairs."

"That's right Frank. He did," Maria said.

Gill twisted his face as he addressed her in clipped words, "Did he ask you?"

"Easy Gill." Frank stepped between Gil and Maria.

"I paid him for the work," I repeated.

Eliot lifted his eyes, roused himself from his lawn chair and yawned. "It's not the car work that's the sticking point," he said. "My friend ran through a fence and killed a couple of the owner's chickens."

I wished I'd run Eliot over with the Impala.

"That true kid?" Frank asked.

"Only partially." I recited from memory the words that hung above the auto bay's door.

"What do you think you are, a lawyer?" the deputy said.

"No, but I can read..."

"Don't say another word," Frank said. "Gill, how much is the damage?"

"About 140 bucks worth."

"Pay him," Frank told me.

"No way."

Cheryl shifted Cotton off her lap and handed her to Eliot. She stood up and shook her head. "Quit acting stupid, David. It's only money."

"If I pay him what he wants we'll have less than forty bucks to make it to San Francisco."

The smirk on Gill's face conjured up a picture for me of how he must have looked when he was screwing the two girls.

"You know," I said and faced the woman. "Your husband told me how once he helped out two girls awhile back who didn't have enough money to pay for their car repairs."

Maria smiled benevolently. "Very nice girls. Gill fixed their car and I invited them to dinner, but they were in a real hurry and left without eating."

Gill's eyes burrowed into my neck.

"What did you tell me, Gill? Something about how you were willing to take something in trade for the work?"

"That was really nice of you," Maria said. "You never told me."

"It was nothing, nothing worth talking about."

"Sure it is," I said. "A good deed like yours should be shared. What was it they gave you in trade?"

"I forgot. It doesn't matter anyway I just did it to help the kids out of a jam."

Maria waddled over to Gill. "I know you raised them chickens from eggs, baby, but really they were too scrawny and tough to be worth more than about three bucks for the both of them."

"What about the pen? I put a lot of work into it."

"You did darling, but it's nowhere near $140 worth."

"Okay, okay, give me another sixty-eight bucks and we're square."

Cheryl broke in. "You said you'd take something in trade. I got a 14" color TV in my trunk."

Gill bit his lip a moment then said, "Fine, fine I'll take the damn set."

Maria hugged Gill. "Now that that's settled, how 'bout dinner? There's enough chicken for everyone." She beckoned us to a doublewide trailer sitting on top of cinder blocks behind the garage.

Frank hooked me by my belt loop and tugged me back to him. "Not so fast Perry Mason. Let me see your license."

"My what?"

"Your driver's license."

"I don't have one."

"Well, I guess you're in deep shit, kid. I'm fining you twenty-five dollars or a night in jail. It's your call."

The others disappeared into the trailer. "It's not fair. I didn't want to drive the car. Gill made me. I'm not paying."

"Have it your way." With the heel of his palm against my back, Frank pushed me across the road. We stopped at a metal tool shed. He disengaged the padlock and slid the shed's door open. "There's a light switch over there in the corner. Best leave it on tonight. The scorpions come out when it gets dark."

I ran to flick on the switch. The metal door clanged shut. I sat in the sweatbox for about an hour and half before the door slid open. The deputy shoved another man in. A combination of body odor, dirt, stale tobacco, and mescal seeped out of my tottering shed mate. He sat down beside me. Patches of reddish skin broke through the crust and grime covering his torso, bare except for a Polo shirt that had more holes than it did fabric. The man reached up to his ear and fumbled before pulling out a half-smoked cigarette. He inserted his fingers into the pocket of a pair of remarkably white bell-bottom trousers. A moan escaped his cracked lips. He withdrew his fingers and slipped the dead cigarette behind his ear.

He raised his head. "Mister, mister, what time is dinner mister? No drink, I don't drink, just water. Booze ruined my family. Mister, mister, I'm hungry. What time is dinner?"

I scooted to the far side of the shed and avoided looking at him, wondering what the hell I was trying to prove. Once more the door slid open. Frank and Maria were outside bearing two large bowls. Red beans and pieces of orange chicken were plopped on mounds of yellow rice. They placed them inside the shed then stood a couple of bottles of Pepsi beside them and waited for us to eat. My companion dove for a bowl. He scooped out gobs of wet rice and chicken with his fingers, stuffed them inside his mouth and swallowed without chewing. I pecked daintily at my food barely able to tolerate the five-alarm seasoning. When I put my bowl down to take a sip of Pepsi the man snatched it up and devoured it.

Frank retrieved the empty bowls. "Hard to believe his people once stood off the whole US Calvary," he said.

"Frank, come on you had your fun, let the boy out."

"No way, he still has the night to finish and we'll be square. By the way, kid, your friends are bedded down over at my place. Pleasant dreams. Remember to keep the lights on if you don't want to wake up with a scorpion down your shorts."

As the door scraped across its tracks the Apache curled up in a ball and fell into a loud sleep. I did not sleep. Even if I had not been on watch all night for scorpions, I would have remained awake. My companion screamed off and on until dawn as he twitched and engaged in hand-to-hand combat with his nightmare demons. Frank let me out in the morning.

Eliot and Cheryl were waiting by the car with steaming cups of coffee. They had showered and changed their clothes. I got into the front passenger side and slammed the door. Maria rapped on my window. I rolled it down a couple of inches.

"What kind of trade did my husband take for his work with those girls?" She asked.

"Guess," I said and rolled up the window.

Chapter 41

The 325-mile road trip from Tacna to LA takes about six hours. The scenery changes from sandstone brown to verdant green as the desert gives way to the artificially fertile landscape of Southern California. Orange groves appear where only sixty years before nothing existed but sidewinders and scrub.

Not a single word passed through my lips on the journey. My face remained turned to the window. When we got to San Diego I gazed out at the Pacific and fell asleep.

Eliot woke me. "There it is, man. I never thought we'd make it the way things have been going."

I saw the wooden letters spelling out HOLLYWOOD on the side of a hill. Cheryl leaned over my seat and touched my arm. "Thanks, David. We wouldn't have made it without your help."

"What help?" Eliot asked. "If he didn't kill those chickens we'd have a TV to pawn and more money."

"His money, prick. It was his money that got us here. He paid for the gas, all the repairs, and most of the food."

"Yeah, yeah, don't worry about it. After I visit my brother, I'll pay him back."

Frowning, Eliot took his eyes off the road and looked at me. "Come on, man. Don't just sit there, spit it out. You've been playing deaf and dumb since we left Tacna.

"Is your brother expecting us?" I asked.

291

"Of course. Maybe. For sure. Well, maybe not right now."

"Either he is or he isn't."

Eliot turned his face toward his window. "Well, he knows I planned to come out this way one day. I'm sure he won't mind having us drop in but it might not be such a great idea for all of us to land on his doorstep at once."

Silence lingered inside the car like a bad smell.

"Drop me off at a freeway entrance heading north," I said.

"No way, man. I can let you off at a YMCA. After I've talked to my brother, I'll come get you."

"What about us?" Cheryl said. "Are you going to let us off too?"

"No sugar, we're together. Cotton might be a shock, but he can't very well put us on the curb."

"Don't call me sugar," Cheryl slumped back on the seat.

"Like I said, drop me off at an entrance ramp and I'll start hitchhiking."

"Okay man, we'll hook up in San Francisco then."

Eliot let me off at a service station near the Santa Monica Freeway. We did a lame imitation of a brother's handshake. Cheryl crawled over the seat and took my place without saying goodbye.

*

After two hours of thumbing a ride, I had had no luck. I sprinted across the freeway with my duffel bag hanging off one shoulder. I felt safer walking in the center of the wide grass, covered median than tramping along the side of the road with cars whizzing past at seventy miles per hour. I planned to walk north until I found a better location to hitch a ride to the Bay City. Within fifteen minutes a cruiser roared up with its cherry dome lights spinning. Two Highway Patrol men who looked like they had stepped out of a Muscle Beach poster got out of the squad car.

"Assume the position," one of the cops said. He placed me with my palms flat on the car roof, arms stiff and legs spread apart. He went from the outside to the inside patting me down for a concealed weapon. I couldn't really blame him seeing how his partner came eyeball to barrel with the shotgun in my bag when he lifted up my books.

The CHIP politely told me to put my hands behind my back. He cuffed me, smiled with his Chiclet white teeth, and said, "Welcome to California, the Golden State, land of movie stars. We got plenty of mountains, lakes, and an ocean playground. None of which you'll see on this visit."

*

They radioed several juvie halls before finding one in East LA with enough room to take me. The patrol car sped down the freeway with its dome lights flashing and its siren off. It passed under green exit signs with white letters pointing the way to beach after beach. The exit we took held out no promise of water and waves. Directly off the freeway ramp we entered a war zone not found on any tourist brochure. Pawnshops, all night greasy spoons, convenience stores, liquor stores, X-rated bookstores, and bus stops with derelicts asleep on benches defined the neighborhood. On every wall, graffiti alerted the unalert that they had wandered onto the turf of some gang that defended its broken sidewalks and bottle strewn lots with as much ferocity as the Vietcong. The cops stopped at a Dunkin'

Donut and bought two cups of coffee and a dozen assorted donuts.

"Kid, you want chocolate glazed with sprinkles?" the cop who had frisked me asked.

"No thanks, it's hard to eat with my hands cuffed behind my back."

"Tell me your name and where you're from and I'll take those off. Then you can pick your own donut."

"I'm not hungry."

"How's your Spanish," the other CHIP asked.

"I don't speak Spanish."

"Where you're going you better learn quick."

"My partner's right. Give us your name and where you're from and we'll drop you off at a place in the valley. A place with horses. It'll be like a dude ranch compared to the hole we're taking you to. So go on give us your name."

"I don't like horses," I said and closed my eyes for the rest of the ride.

The patrol car pulled up in front of what looked like a tollbooth covered by a concrete awning. The booth was affixed to an institutional monochromatic grey building. On either side of the booth were electric sliding doors with signs instructing those passing through to STAND BEHIND YELLOW LINE UNTIL BUZZER SOUNDS.

The cop riding shotgun opened my door while his partner walked to the booth. "Watch your head," he said and helped me out. He took my bag with one hand and frog marched me to the entrance. I was too tired to be scared when the cop prodded me into the booking room of the

Juvenile Detention Center. The duty officer was in no hurry to process my paperwork, preferring instead to shoot the shit with one of his buddies on the telephone. The handcuffs bit into my wrists. Finally the CHIP who had brought me in barked out a command to the knob-headed pencil pusher.

"Here, fill in the blanks," the man said as he slid a paper across his desktop toward me. He smiled broadly at the joke he must have played on every kid who came through the electric doors wearing handcuffs behind his back.

The pencil pusher rattled off a series of questions all of which I answered except for my parent's name and address. "You're arresting me, not them," I said.

"Tough one, huh?"

"If you had seen the shotgun he had with him and his goddamn books, you wouldn't say that."

"Uncuff him. We'll see what goodies are in his system."

The officer removed my cuffs and waited for the pencil pusher to buzz open a sliding door that sealed off a long corridor from the booking room. At the second door a man wearing an olive T-shirt and surgeon's pants replaced the cop.

"Okay I'll take it from it here." He pushed me into a room no larger than a broom closet. Shelves hanging on three of the four walls held tongue depressors, Band-Aids, iodine, ace bandages. A rack of empty test tubes stood next to a jar filled with syringes and alcohol.

Ben Casey stretched a brown length of surgical tubing. "Roll up your sleeve."

"Why?" I crossed my arms over my chest.

"Because I'm going to take blood."

"No you're not."

His resemblance to Eugene Lesman made me determined to stand my ground.

"Who told you, you have a choice?" He grabbed my wrist and tried to pull my arms apart. Like Lesman, the medic was too weak to pull apart a Tootsie Roll without assistance.

He pushed a blue button on the wall. Within a few seconds a scrawny white guy and a George Foreman look alike marched down the corridor wielding nightsticks. Despite the tags attached to their starched khaki shirts that identified them as counselors, they were prison guards.

"The prick won't roll up his sleeve."

The black guard moved in front of me and bent over so that his eyes came even with my hairline. "Why not?"

"Taking blood without my consent is against..."

"Shut up," the white guard said. He spun me toward the corridor. "Come on let's get moving."

"Hang on there, he still owes me blood."

The black guard pushed me down the hall. "Forget it. You can tell he's clean."

I passed through another set of mesh doors. The white guard disappeared into an office and closed the door behind him.

"Strip down," the black guard growled. When I hesitated, he said, "Take off your clothes or I'll do it for you."

He handed me an orange jumpsuit and a pair of slippers. I got dressed and gave him my clothes. He stuffed them into a paper bag on which he scrawled a file number in black magic marker.

"Sit down." He pointed at a row of molded tangerine-colored chairs along one wall, the only spot of brightness in the corridor of cinder blocks and beige floor tiles. "Make yourself comfortable. That's where you're sleeping until a bed opens up."

I collapsed on a chair and dozed, awakened every time my chin fell into my neck. Sometime around two A.M. a tidal wave of voices cursing and laughing in Spanish startled me. I looked up and saw a gang of five Chicanos boxed in by three very mean looking street cops. The kids varied in age and size from grade school adolescents to high school toughs. They wore the same tight black pants, white dress shirts and blue and white checkered bandanas tied around their heads.

"Come on man my feet is killing me," said a short kid with an emerging moustache. The tattoo of a plumed serpent twined its way up his forearm.

"Shut up Chico," a cop with two stripes on his sleeve said.

"That's not my name. You busted me enough to know that."

The guard took the papers from the cop. "Back again so soon Herrera?"

The cop said, "They missed the accommodations here. I caught them hanging around the corner of the building."

Herrera was the only one who spoke. "Yeah, we missed Sloppy Joe day."

The black guard scowled. "You and your buddies take a seat and try not to piss me off."

Herrera turned his head and looked at me slumped down in my chair. "Who's the punk?" he asked.

"What's it to you," the guard answered.

"He's in my chair."

"Find another."

"What you in for homeboy?"

"He's a real hard case that's all you gotta know, Herrera. Now go find a seat before I make you stand in a corner all night."

"Him a hard case? Don't make me laugh. He looks like a puta."

"He's hardcase enough to get himself busted by the Highway Patrol with a shotgun in his bag."

Herrera gave me a thumbs-up and took a chair at the other end of the room. He nodded and his friends joined him. The white guard stepped out of his office. He had an empty bag of Doritos in his hand. He licked his fingers, dipped them into the bag, and sucked them clean. He crumpled up the bag and threw it at my head.

"You, yeah I'm talking to you. Have you decided to give us your name and address?"

"No Sir."

"Don't give me that Sir shit."

"Come on tell us," the black guard said. "You owe me. I did you favor. Chico, over there, thinks you're a real gangster instead of just another pansy-ass white boy running away from Mommy and Daddy."

I stood up and hurled my plastic chair across the room. Two-seconds later I was face down on the asbestos floor.

The black counselor had his knee in my back and my arms pulled up in a hammerlock. "Calm down, calm down. You'll hurt yourself if you keep struggling."

"Christ! What'd I do to set him off?" the other guard said.

I felt the bite of handcuffs back on my wrists.

"Beats me."

As the black guard escorted me out of the holding room, I heard Herrera say, "Crazy man, he's loco. But means more Sloppy Joes for us tomorrow."

The black guard stopped in front of a thick metal door that had Observation stenciled on the wall above it. He removed the cuffs and then pulled back a bolt. "Strip down to your shorts and get inside."

I spent two nights in isolation with the lights on. I had a private cell and room service. With the exception of the suicide watcher peeking in every hour through a small window I was left to myself. On the morning of my third day the door opened and a thin counselor who looked barely older than me said, "Times up. Some boys checked out unannounced last night. We got three vacant cots."

I stuck out my hands to be cuffed.

"Cool it, you think this is Alcatraz?" He looked over his shoulder at a black kid with orange hair and freckles. "Juice, take him down to the supply room then over to Assessment."

I followed the kid to the same room where I had thrown the chair. He disappeared into the office and returned with a stack of neatly folded clothes consisting of two white T-shirts with LA Juvenile Hall printed on the back, two pairs of white cotton slacks, two pairs of underwear, two pairs of socks and a pair of blue canvas deck shoes.

"Heard about the shit-fit you threw, man," he said and handed me a form to sign saying that I had received my wardrobe. "You must be in some serious shit to go crazy like that."

"I got tired of being asked the same stupid question."

"That's it? That's what made you pop a cork?"

"That's it."

"You in for a short or long ride, Chairman?"

"Chair what?"

"Word got around about you busting that chair to pieces. So how long you intend to stay?"

"I don't know."

"Me, I'm inside for nine months for boosting a car. It's my third go around." His chest swelled up as he smiled. "Next time I'll do real time if I'm caught. But I ain't gonna get caught."

Juice took me down the hall. We passed through double gates into another corridor. Along both walls were closed doors. He walked me to the only open office in the wing and knocked on the door jam. A head of silver hair rose from a stack of papers spread out on a steel desk. A prematurely greying woman in her late twenties or early thirties crooked her finger at me. She tucked a pencil in the bun behind her head.

"Miss Reitz, I brought the boy from Observation for his assessment," Juice said.

"Thank you. Go back to your wing. I'll call you when I need you."

The Social Worker stared at me a minute then looked at the papers on her desk. "It says here you refuse to give us any information on yourself. You also caused quite a commotion on your arrival." She glanced up from the desk. "Why are standing?"

"I'm waiting to be asked to sit."

"Hmm, interesting." She removed the pencil from her bun. Flipping open a steno pad, she wrote something in it. "Do you want to sit?"

"Yes Mam."

"Yes Mam? Hmmm, interesting." She scratched something in her pad. "You know, we can't help you if you don't tell us who you are."

"I don't need help."

"If I released you today where would you go?"

"San Francisco."

"Do you have family there?" I didn't answer.

"Why don't you tell me where you're from?"

"Maybe I like it here."

"That's a possibility. Based on how frequently they return I think a lot of our young guests like it here." She shuffled through the papers again. "Can you at least tell me how old you are?"

"Seventeen."

"Good thing you look closer to fifteen than eighteen or you might have ended up in LA County jail. Anyway, I don't have the time to play games. You are here until we find out who you are. You'll be assigned to a work group and will be expected to attend school two hours each afternoon. Do you have anything to say?"

"No Mam."

"No Mam, huh?" She took a cigarette out of a pack on her desk and lit up. As she exhaled her words mingled with the smoke. "Things must be pretty tough for you to prefer staying here to going home. Don't answer. It's not a question, just an assessment."

Juice escorted me to my dorm. A couple of guys passing by greeted me with, "How's it going Chairman? Don't go blowing no one away on your first day."

The 22/20 Remington I'd been busted with morphed into a pump action 12-gauge riot gun in the minds of the residents. This gave me a measure of status in the dormitory. The first time I entered the room Herrera sat at a table playing a game of bottle cap checkers with another Spanish kid. He waved at me, then double jumped his opponent's blue bottle cap with a red one.

I made it through the night without getting the shit kicked out of me or becoming the end piece in a daisy chain. My sector was a short-term detention area for boys on their way to a county ranch to get rehabilitated in the fresh air. The hard cases, real gang-bangers, and serious bad guys were assigned to another wing. I spent my days staring through the thickly screened windows or watching others play cards or dominoes. After lunch I attended remedial education classes in the cafeteria.

A young man sporting a surfer tan and sun-bleached hair that fell across one eye was the instructor. He covered math on Mondays rarely getting past 8x8 in the multiplication tables. On Wednesdays he concentrated on history and how your government works for you. Reading and Writing was on Fridays. My second Friday in his class he read the short story, "The Monkey's Paw" aloud. He asked us to write an essay on the danger of wishing for something without considering the consequences. He passed out four sheets of notebook paper and pencils that were too stubby to be used as weapons to each student. I went to work filling my papers to the last blue line without lifting my head to look at the other reform school scholars chew on their erasers or draw representations of male and female anatomy.

The following Monday the surfer teacher broke off his multiplication table drill and held up four sheets of notebook paper written from top to bottom on both sides. "Class, I know reading and writing day isn't until Friday but I want to tell you about one of your friends who really seems to have developed an understanding of the danger of not making the right choice."

He began to read my essay in a sincere voice, pausing for dramatic effect.

The Monkey's Paw is not about consequences but about choices. It has occurred to me that the choices one makes on the journey through life are not choices but predetermined destinations. Up until recently I have been very good at following directions, rules, walking straight lines all the time deluding myself into thinking I did so by choice. But this is a lie. I did so out of fear, fear of what would happen if I ever did make a real choice and open the door to see what was on the other side ...

He finished reading and put the essay on my desktop. "You got an A. It's a standup A. You would have gotten the same mark in any class on the outside."

It is not a good thing to be singled out for praise in a place where a debate on the literary merits of The Incredible Hulk versus Spiderman can result in a trip to intensive care. I felt my ass pucker. Maybe I was scheduled to experience a daisy chain after all.

The surfer teacher droned on and on about how my writing and my having an understanding of the multiplication tables and knowing that George Washington was the father of the country would provide me with an exit out of a life of crime before it was too late. I avoided looking at him as I took the paper. Folded into four parts it ended up in the trashcan on my way back to the day room. I parked myself at a window and watched the cars speed by beyond the eight-foot-high chain link fence. My reverie was interrupted by the thick Hispanic accent of someone saying, "Hey Chairman, you write real good."

I looked behind me and saw Herrera and a tall Latino with a bandana tied around his forehead walking toward me. The tall one was one of the more senior residents, so senior that his five o'clock shadow was darker than a full day's growth on a lot of grown men.

"Thanks." I stuck out my hand. The tall one shook it and then banged his clenched fist against my knuckles.

"Sheesus man, you got something good. Me too I got talent."

"It's true, Rico's a painter," Herrera said.

"That's how I ended up here. I painted a mural on the side of a wall next to a church and got busted."

"Of what?" I asked and glanced around the room to see if there were any counselors lurking about when he handed me a cigarette.

"Bitches, big boob bitches wearing nuthin but smiles, man. It was stupid to do it near the church where my mother goes."

I took a deep drag off my smoke.

He didn't speak for several seconds. He fixed his gaze on the fence that cut the detention center off from the outside world. "I gotta get out of here," Rico said.

"You're not the only one," Herrera said. "It's not hard to blow this pop stand. I do it once a month. Go over by the trees where the hill slopes down to a ravine and hop the fence. I come back after a few hours on the street."

"You escape on a regular basis and come back?" I asked.

"Sure. Why not? The guards are okay for guards. Besides it's a lot safer here than it is in my barrio, safer than it is in my apartment. The food's not bad. The place is clean and mostly people leave you alone."

"So you're cool with this scene?" I said, trying to sound street smart.

Rico sighed, "Next year I got to straighten up my act or I'll do real time in the joint."

"It's not such a bad place here when you get used to it," Herrera said.

Chapter 42

It had been a few weeks since I had caved into Eliot's plea. I was staring up from my cot at brown splotches on the ceiling tiles when the guard who had first led me into the unit came to fetch me.

"You know, you're a real genius," he said. "Next time you want to keep incognito don't write your fucking name, address and phone number in your books.

You would have been out of here sooner, but it took some persuading your old man to spring for the return airfare. The thing that clicked with him was when the director told him how the taxpayers of California were paying to take care of his problem son. If I was you, I'd keep my head down when I get home."

*

Once inside the jet, police officers took off my cuffs. A girl dressed like a gypsy was also escorted handcuffed into the cabin and seated next to me. The girl's name was Chloe. Her granny had scraped together enough cash to rescue her from the Children of God cult that had persuaded her to run away with them.

"Travel all that way and I get busted stealing ground beef in a supermarket in Hollywood. Do you believe it?"

I would have accepted any story she told without question, just so long as she left her hand on my knee. We talked non-stop from LA to Dallas, getting charmingly tipsy on free daiquiris swerved by the flight attendant to keep us under control.

About two hours into the flight Chloe grew morose, pensive. When the Captain announced our descent to the Dallas airport, Chloe kissed me with a passion reserved for love affairs that begin and end in sinking lifeboats.

"Give me your address and I'll call you," I said.

She scribbled something on a napkin, folded it in half and tucked it into my jeans pocket.

The plane taxied to a stop. A gangway rolled up to the exit. As the door opened, fresh air filled the interior of the plane. Descending the stairs to the tarmac I saw my father leaning against a wall behind a waist high fence. Next to Dad stood a black woman. Chloe waved at her. The woman looked hardly old enough to be the girl's mother much less her grandmother. I walked so close to Chloe that we could have been holding hands. As the fence grew nearer Chloe widened the distance between us. She rushed over to the woman. I pulled the napkin out of my pocket. "Bye-bye" was all it said. Although I thought she looked back at me I could not be sure. Dad dug his fingers into my upper arm and jerked me to the parking lot. When we reached the car his fist nailed me in my lower back. He flung open the passenger door and pushed me inside.

"You had your mother near out of her mind." He punched me again, this time below my ear.

"At least you didn't go calling me for help when you got in trouble. I guess that counts for something." He rubbed his knuckles on top of my head playfully. "Hungry?" he asked. "I once ran away to New Orleans when I was about your age, actually I was a year younger."

"What happened?"

"Before or after I came home?"

"Both."

"I got rolled in the Quarter and had to hitchhike most of the way to Birmingham. I called the Chief from Mississippi to ask for help. Your Grandfather said, 'Ernie if you're man enough to go to Mardi Gras then you're man enough to find your own way home.' Eventually he sprung for a bus ticket. When I got back the Chief put me to cleaning the squad cars to pay him back. Could have been worse. He once cracked my rib for calling policemen cops."

"What do you have in store for me?"

"Nothing. You did your time like a man and didn't call me begging and crying to bring you home. You do owe me for the air fare."

"I have money in the bank."

"Okay, then were even. But I warn you about one thing," he said as he pulled into the driveway. My mother, brothers, Janet, and Fred were in the yard. Mom walked up to the car just as Dad backhanded me across the mouth, splitting my lip. "If I ever find out you are associating with low life hippies and commies again, I'll make you wish they gave you the gas chamber in California. Now get the hell out of the car and smile. Your Mom has fixed something special for your birthday."

I had forgotten that it was my birthday. Turning eighteen was my ticket out of the Colonel's stockade.

"Monday you register for the draft," Dad said.

(1969-1972)

"A revolution always seems hopeless and impossible the day before it breaks out and indeed never does break out until it seems hopeless and impossible."

George Bernard Shaw

"I can deal with the dope smoking, the screwing around, but I will never tolerate having a traitor as a son who not only spits on my flag but induces others to do the same and in the name of what, change, revolution? When the fuck has change or revolution accomplished anything?"

Lt. Colonel E.H. Brown (U.S.A.F. Retired) 1925-1997

Chapter 43

At the start of my last year at MacArthur, Eugene Lesman occupied the entrance of the school with his apprentice stooge, Trevor Graves. Graves was campaigning actively on this first day of the new semester to become the President of the Student Council. He was one of the few people I have met in my life who could suck and blow at the same time. On a couple of occasions, he'd ventured across the street to the Gazebo to score weed and concurrently take notes for Lesman on who frequented the plaza in contravention of the city ordinance.

Trevor checked off names for Lesman from a list of individuals singled out for a "talking to" while Lesman culled students from the herd based on the length of their hair, style of dress, and perceived political affiliation. To hide from the vice-principal I lowered my head, held my books up to my face and inserted myself in the middle of a group of cowboy hat wearing shit-kickers. In my brushed denim slacks and long sleeve dress shirt I stood out like a red tie on a yellow shirt.

"You there you, you there, stop!" Lesman shouted. "Get over here."

The cowboy hats clung to the walls leaving me completely exposed.

"When I say get, I mean get!"

"What do you want, Mr. Lesman?"

"Don't go getting huffy with me." Lesman pulled his jacket open and revealed a paddle hanging from a homemade leather holster.

"Generally I make it a rule not to use the great equalizer on anyone during the first week of school. I like to give students a chance to make amends. But some people are beyond redemption, second chances are useless."

Exhausted from listening to hours of my father's lectures since I returned from LA, and Mom's operatic wailing about the mess her children were making of her life, I walked past Lesman. He reached out to pull me back. I knocked his hand off my arm. My nostrils flared and my voice dropped so low, he could not hear me say, "Don't push it."

The blood rushed to fill the hollows of Lesman's acne-pitted cheeks. "What did you say, boy? You best be ready to start the new school year with a new attitude. From what I hear you had a real interesting summer. From what I hear you almost made the big time. Too bad those limp wrists in California let you off so easy. If you got picked up in Texas we sure as heck would have known what to do with you. You know what would have happened?"

"Nothing would have happened," I said. "It's not against the law to hitchhike or carry a broken-down shotgun in this state."

"You getting smart with me?"

"All I want is to make it through the school year without getting in your way or getting in trouble."

"Good, seems you learned a thing since last year. Keep your nose clean and you might make it through the next nine months. But you go smarting off or causing disturbances I'll lay the board on you until you wise up. This is your warning. This is your second chance."

I shrugged and walked away. I didn't get far. Mr. Berk's massive body blocked the hallway. He held up a hand like a traffic cop. "Brown, I didn't hear you thank Mr. Lesman."

Berk stretched out a thick finger and tapped my right ear then my left. "What Mr. Lesman told you went in one side and out the other side of your bonehead. You march over to Mr. Lesman, apologize, and thank him for giving you a second chance. There are new rules at MacArthur and at the top of the list is showing respect to your betters."

It would have been easy to simply tuck my prick between my bum cheeks and slink over to Lesman and do as I was instructed. But Berk's pretense that Lesman was my better lit my fuse.

I said, "I don't think so."

I was halfway down the hall before Berk shouted, "Things have changed around here."

My first course of the day was Latin with Miss Percy. She hobbled around the class on two canes and was so old that she probably had a front row seat when Julius Caesar crossed the Rubicon. I liked her. She was notorious for her absent-mindedness, bordering on dementia. A rumor circulated that one semester Miss Percy gave the same test six times without realizing it. At semester's end every student received an A without ever getting past the conjugation for amor or getting straight whether Caesar veni, vidi, vicied or vicied, vini, vidied.

In my opinion, she faked her bouts of forgetfulness. Her senility allowed her to get away with things that any other teacher would have been pilloried for. She insulted Nixon, Kissinger, and every Texas politician she could remember, as "lean and hungry men" not fit to clean a cuspidor much less run a government.

Her favorite book was The Satyricon which she read aloud in Latin and translated as she went along. She braced herself against the blackboard and told us that she acted as Irving Texas' arbiter elegantiae and declared the first Tuesday of each month to be Toga Day and if the school didn't like it, they could choke on a feather.

She started by saying that she was obliged to read us a new set of rules of deportment and conduct given to her by the par nobile fratrum, Mr. Berk and Eugene Lesman. She read six memorable regulations aloud in a nasal imitation of a British school matron.

A. **No PDA (Public Displays of Affection) on or within 1/4 of a mile of the school property.**

B. **Strict adherence to dress code (No tie-dyed shirts, collarless shirts with embroidery, gypsy garments, or fringed clothing. Girls' dresses and skirts must neither rise more than one inch above their knees while kneeling nor go below their ankles while standing.)**

C. **It is forbidden to engage in politicking or support in an overt manner any organizations and causes not sanctioned by the school.**

D. **The wearing of badges, ribbons, insignias, or other items of clothing (e.g. letter jackets from schools other than MacArthur) that have been deemed by the administration as expressing a social or**

political message against community standards is prohibited.

E. **If by mouth, written word, or deed, an individual expresses a view or idea which is contrary to the mores, standards of decency, and goodwill of the community, that person will be held accountable for inciting violence should any incident occur.**

F. **Should a student no longer reside at home with his legal guardian(s) he will no longer be allowed to attend MacArthur Senior High School.**

Miss Percy finished with, "Sic semper tyrannis," and crumpled the sheet of regulations.

"Seems like the Bill of Rights is a subversive document in Heil Hitler High," Dan said. "What are we going to do about it?"

I gave a blunt answer. "Nothing, this is my last year. I don't need any more trouble."

"That's cool by me," Johnny said. "But do you really think that Lesman and Berk will ease up on you?"

"They have no choice. If I don't give them anything to squawk about, they have to leave me alone."

"I wouldn't lay odds on that," Johnny said.

Nina and I agreed that we would fly below the radar. We got the word that we had made the administration's list of undesirables along with Dan, Johnny, Floe, Hugh, and Muffy. There was a second roster that included my brother, Vince Crane, and Albert but because they were deemed potheads instead of radicals, they received less heat.

317

Things had gotten considerably more complicated since the end of the last school year. Vernon and a few other shit-kickers decided to do their duty. They enlisted in the Marines after a recruiter spoke at a pep rally dressed in an organ grinder's monkey suit. Others would join them as the year progressed. A few students returned in body bags and had their names engraved on a brass plate that read "In Honor of Those Who Served." The plate hung inside MacArthur's trophy case.

Hugh Swift was suspended the first week of school for reading an underground paper. The paper's headline was a quote from the late Malcolm X "The Chickens Have Come Home to Roost". It was an article written by a guy on the lam from the Feds, a Weatherman. The crux of the article was that JFK was a reptile. The piece claimed the dead prez jumped on the communist bashing bandwagon even before Tricky Dick. Kennedy then moved on to plant nukes around the world and as a final act sent in military advisors to prop up a puppet prick in Vietnam after arranging to have the former president snuffed. The bit ended with the assertion that if JFK had taken a bullet in 1961, Americans would not be dying and killing civilians in Asian rice paddies eight years later.

Hugh, actually a fan of JFK, was reading the article in order to write a rebuttal. Lesman warned that if he didn't get a haircut and start toeing the line he was going to be expelled for good. For added emphasis, Lesman beat him so hard with the paddle that Hugh's screams could be heard outside the school. When Eugene was finished, Hugh needed assistance to limp out of the building.

After school, I reluctantly went with the flower power brigade, Floe, Muffy, and two bead-wearing twins, Travis and Deacon, to comfort Hugh. I was worried that if I were spotted with them, my hassle-free stint at MacArthur would be jeopardized. Hugh's mother answered the door. A San Francisco transplant she taught piano at home while her husband thought of ways to make transistors and computer chips smaller at Texas Instruments. She held out a piece of paper and asked us if we would sign a petition demanding the abolishment of corporal punishment at MacArthur High School.

"My husband is adamant that it is time for the Bill of Rights to come to Texas. He's going to send a letter to our congressman and state representative. Bury the editorial pages from Dallas to Boston. Work to dismiss abusive school officials and bring class action suits against boards of education that condone beatings."

Mrs. Swift waited patiently for us to sign. I retreated into a corner, hoping she wouldn't notice my failure to put down my name.

"Of course," she said, "Hubert Senior and I realize that making an issue out of paddling will not endear us to our neighbors. Mr. Swift may even lose his job, but we've had enough of the daily bullying and intimidation our son faces with the sanction of the school administration."

Hugh's reedy voice sang out from the back of the house, "Come on, Mom, they came to see me not join the revolution."

Hugh lay on his stomach on a couch in the den. A beach towel covered his pantless lower body.

"I'd get up, but I don't want to embarrass you."

"Does it hurt," Muffy asked.

"Don't be an airhead. Of course, it hurts," Floe said.

"Not as bad as you'd think. Sure, it stung but that wasn't the part that got to me. Having to reach down and hold my ankles while he hit me was the worst part. Lesman told me that I was lucky to be getting off so easy." Hugh smiled. "He thinks this will stop me from speaking out. He's wrong. Come October 15th Mr. Lesman and Mr. Berk are in for a real surprise. I am going to organize students to support the national moratorium against the war."

"That's not such a great idea," I said.

"It's only part of my idea. I think we should run candidates in the student council elections, including for school president."

Floe bounced across the room and hugged Hugh. "I'll support you for president, and I'll run as vice-president. It will be cool. We can make posters, and have teach-ins at the park, and..."

Hugh shook his head. "No one will take a bunch of peace-loving hippies seriously. David, do you see where this is leading? Do you see a place for yourself in this?"

"No."

"You're a jock, an honor student, and someone who doesn't take shit or back down. You can run," Hugh said.

"Nobody will ever mistake David for a pacifist," Travis piped up.

"Forget it," I said. "Take it easy and I'll see you in school."

Floe said, "Why bother? The only thing he knows how to do is fight and cause trouble. He doesn't give a damn about anything."

She was right. The prospect of drawing fire for a cause, even one I marginally supported, was not in the cards. If I could walk the line until June, then it was possible to get an out of state scholarship and leave Irving in the rear-view mirror. It wasn't much of a plan, but it was the only one I had.

*

I was called to the office almost daily to defend myself against some infraction Lesman concocted. My mother unwittingly supported him in his interrogations. She had embarked on a letter writing campaign to public officials, newspapers and senators. She flitted from cause-to-cause, obsession-to-obsession.

One week she condemned the hypocrisy of organized religion as exemplified by everyone from Oral Roberts to the Pope. The next week she called for a dialogue between theologians and scientists to find a mutually acceptable way of merging creationism with Darwin. Her favorite rants by far concerned the supposed threat to morality posed by rock music, The Catcher in the Rye, and movies.

Mr. Lesman once waved a sheaf of letters my mother had sent him at me. "Your Mama is worried, crazy worried about you. I have met her. She is a good woman. She's worried, as she has every right to be, about the people with whom you have been associating. She's right to think that they are unwholesome and hold dangerous and perverse views."

My silent response infuriated Lesman. "One day you'll cross the line and I'll bend you over and give you something your daddy should have given you a long time ago."

I came close to cracking his fuzzy skull like a walnut.

My intention to stay out of the fray ended the third week of school. On Monday a logjam of people had formed outside the entrance of MacArthur. As they entered the doors, students were segregated by gender. Boys were hurried into class. The girls were ordered to wait their turn to have their hemlines measured. On one side of the corridor girls in short skirts knelt on the tile floor. Another group of girls stood on the other side with their backs to the wall. Two male teachers supervised the measuring done by the office secretary and the school nurse. The girls failing to meet the standard that had been delivered on the first day of class were directed to proceed to the vice-principal's office. Most of the girls were given a warning and told to go home and change. The ones who got reprieves were cheerleaders and pom-pom girls.

"You, get moving!" Coach Worell barked when I paused on seeing Muffy standing outside Lesman's office. She was dressed in a yellow granny dress decorated in peace symbols and flowers. Her hemline dropped below her ankles.

About forty minutes later the sound of an ambulance's screams shattered the monotony of our morning lectures. Several of us rushed to the window. After a few minutes the paramedics rolled Muffy out on a gurney.

At lunchtime I found a corner in the cafeteria away from Floe and the other flower children. Their heated discussion overflowed into other areas of the lunchroom. I sloughed it off and ate my sandwich. Tory and a couple of his buddies stopped to argue with Floe and her group.

I looked up when Floe cried out, "Deserved it! Lesman beat her so badly he burst the blood vessels on the back of her legs and then he kicked her out of school for a week. Who deserves that?"

"Your dyke hippie bitch does." Tory smiled.

Floe slapped him fast and hard. Tory tripped on a chair while dodging the next slap and spilled his strawberry milkshake on his black, pearl-buttoned shirt.

It was bad move on Floe's part, considering her clique was composed of non-violent yogurt eaters and tree huggers. Her friends dispersed leaving her to face Tory alone. He kicked the chair out of his way. He and his buddies closed in on her. My head turned toward the entrance of the lunchroom. Monkey Man Sims and Mr. Lesman stood framed inside the open double doors. They did not budge an inch until Dan and Johnny raced over and stood between Floe and Tory. The Monkey Man blew his whistle. The rednecks backed away when Lesman trotted over.

He glanced over his shoulder at Monkey Man. Sims carried over a paddle. "You hippies just won't learn," Lesman said in a mealy voice. "It's your choice, either take your licks or you're out for the year."

"What about him?" Floe pointed at Tory.

"The way I see it, girly, you started it then called your friends to come and gang up on him. Now bend over and grab hold of your ankles."

Floe complied. The vice-principal laid on six strokes of the board but she did not whimper. When he was done Floe straightened up.

"Now what do you say for my taking the time to set you on the right path, girl?"

Floe's face was twisted in an expression of defiance. "Thank you Mr. Lesman."

Johnny bent over without being asked and shoved his ass out and up in an exaggerated stance. Lesman hit him eight times.

"Now what do say for my taking the time to set you on the right path, boy?"

"Is that the best you got?"

"I'll show you what I got!" Lesman laid the board on full force and would have continued to beat Johnny if Monkey Man had not held his arm.

Lesman sucked air. "Your turn."

Dan crossed his arms over his chest. "Get real."

"Are you disobeying me?"

"Yeah, I am."

"I'll have you kicked out of MacArthur for good. I will see to it you can't attend high school in this county or in any other in Texas."

Dan filled the space that separated him from Lesman in two steps. "You flat faced pervert, do you think I give a shit if I graduate from your or any other Texas High School? I'll pass the GED and take my chances."

Dan pushed Monkey Man out of his way. He strolled out of the cafeteria, winked at some people and flipped the bird to others. He stopped at my table. "Are you ever going to take a stand?"

"My legs are asleep."

"That's not the only thing that's asleep. If you ever decide to wake up give me a shout."

A quiet mutiny of the student body was taking place and I was trying to ignore it.

Nina and I went over to her house after school. Her parents were out of town. We used their bed. She quizzed me on what had happened.

My admission that I had not acted put a damper on our foreplay. I recounted my discussion with Hugh the day before and we went from talk to full tilt sex. I rested my sweaty cheek on her naked breasts and said, "I'll run for president if you want me to."

She kissed me. "I'd like that. Have you spoken to Muffy?"

"Muffy's parents called Hugh's parents. They were going to join them in a lawsuit against the school board.

"That's great."

"Not really. The school commissioner called her parents and told them that if they didn't back off, the board would include Muffy in an investigation on drugs and sex in the school. They would make her name public and how would that look to her father's parishioners?"

I had known Muffy for half a year and knew nothing about her. She was like a bit player in a B-grade Hollywood psychedelic movie. She was the eye candy in the background shots, flipping her blonde hair from side to side and saying inane hippie clichés while her best friend shared tongue with Jack Nicholson or Bruce Dern.

On Monday I ran into Floe and Johnny at the 7-11 where a lot of kids congregated since the order banning assemblies at the Gazebo.

Floe said, "I begged my parents to let me quit school. Theytold me I'd be throwing away my future. They told me to stick it out and later I could work to change the system from within."

Johnny asked, "Why the heck would you come back here to change something from within once you've found a way out?"

"Big John must want to kill Lesman," I said.

"That's why I didn't tell him."

Nina drove into the parking lot. She went into the convenience store and came out sipping a cherry Slurpy. "Hi guys, are you going to help David run for student council president?"

Floe had never warmed to Nina. "That's not funny."

"It's true," I said.

"Trevor Graves has already started hanging posters," Nina said. "He's pushing for more vending machines. He's a worm but he's popular. Trish Steuben, Miss pom-pom squad leader, also signed up to run."

"To win, you got to pick a cause the other candidates are afraid to touch," Johnny said.

"Like abolishing corporal punishment, and protesting the war," Floe said.

Nina shook her head. "The first part's okay. Most kids are against paddling, but I don't think they'd buy into the war thing. This is Texas after all."

"Then what do you suggest, a movement against clashing colors?"

"Nina is right," Johnny said. "How about eliminating paddling, freedom of assembly and free speech as issues?

There are other kids besides the freaks and radicals who object to being banned from the Gazebo."

At lunch, Floe, Johnny and Nina went with me to the school office. The secretary did not glance up from her copy of Readers Digest until I cleared my throat. She flipped the magazine face down.

"What do you want?"

"I want to add my name to the list of students running for the student council."

"Really? For what position, class representative, school beautification officer, officer of school spirit?"

"Student Council President."

"You need a C+ average and three nominating signatures for that."

"I got it and brought them."

My backers signed their nominations as the secretary looked through a filing cabinet at the back of the office. She pulled my record and pursed her lips. "You got the marks, but you haven't been here long to know what the school needs."

"Long enough to know things need to change," I said.

She handed me a list containing the signatures of the candidates and their group or party affiliation. Next to Trevor Graves's name was written Reach For Excellence. Trish's party was called MacArthur Forever.

I signed my name then printed, PAS and in brackets next to it wrote, Progressive Association of Students.

In the evening Dad was in an especially jocular mood.

"So what did you do today?"

I knew Dad was talking to me because Jeff was at school allegedly trying out for the football team. In truth, he was over at Vince's testing a new hash pipe.

"I signed up to run for student council president."

"That'll look great on your college applications. I got some good news myself. I'm in line for promotion. You know what that means?"

My Mother's voice drifted across the kitchen. "It better not mean we're moving again."

"Norma, we're staying put. What it means is that with the extra pay we'll be able to start looking at developing that land we bought in Colorado."

'Nope, that's not what it mean' I thought as I told Dad how great his news was. If the back draft of my run for presidency torched my father's career it meant that I was living on borrowed time.

Chapter 44

The school and the surrounding neighborhood were papered with posters urging people to support me for president. Floe and Hugh had enlisted several of their artsy friends to come up with posters and slogans such as "Beat the clock not the students" and "Support PAS not the Past."

More radical messages were stapled to light and telephone poles off school property. At the most benign level they advocated freedom of speech and freedom of assembly. Others were so militant that I cringed when I saw them. The most radical ones called for direct action. "Break the tyranny, break rednecks; vote for PAS." I sought out Floe and Hugh when I ran across, "You got to burn it down before you can build it up" nailed on a tree near the fire station.

"Ask your crazy radical friends. We had nothing to do with that. We're pacifists," Floe said.

Hugh said, "We've spread the word that there's going to be a meeting for people who want to play a role in PAS at the Gazebo tomorrow after school."

"Don't you think that's taking a chance?"

"It's okay," Floe said. "I got clearance from the mall owner. He's sick of Texas. Before going back East he's going to thumb his nose at the city ordinance and let the kids have one more fling."

"You know David, it will be a good opportunity to practice the speech you have to give next week at the assembly."

That evening while I prepared my speech, the telephone rang. With the assembly on Monday, September 30th and the election on Wednesday I was pressed for time. My Mom yelled for me to pick up the receiver in the den.

"Hey, how's the election going?" Dan asked. "I heard you woke up so I thought I'd give you a shout before you gave me one. Farron told me to tell you hello."

"So you're hanging around that asshole again?"

"Yeah, we've taken an active interest in your campaign."

"Tell Farron to screw off and stop putting up those crappy posters."

"You tell him. Farron and I are going to the rally at the Gazebo. Pretty gutsy to hold it there. Oh, by the way, if you need help writing your speech you can count on me and my friends."

"I'll write my own speech."

"Have it your way, man. See you later."

*

Nina and I walked over to the plaza. A girl who resembled Twiggy ran past us carrying a large gym bag. I was surprised to see how many young people had shown up at the Gazebo. A cross section of freaks, cowboys, moderate closet dope smokers, and regular students mingled. Trish Steuben and Trevor Graves were at the plaza. They worked the crowd like experienced politicians doing everything but listening when they asked someone for their opinion and their vote. On the fringes of the gathering were the shitkickers and the serious leftists. Since neither group had enough supporters to present a threat, they refrained from goading each other.

Floe strummed her guitar while she stood on one of the semi-circular benches inside the Gazebo. Hugh stood next to her. He had a wire contraption around his neck that supported a harmonica. They launched into "The times they are a changing."

When the music stopped, Trevor and Trish led the applause. "I love the New Christy Minstrels," Trevor said. He jumped on a bench in front of the Gazebo, extended his hand to Trish and helped her up. Trevor flashed his perfect teeth at the girls while Trish thrust her best feature, her tits, at the guys in the crowd.

"That song was really cool, really out of sight Sue," Trish said.

"My name's Floe."

"What counts is that we're friends. When you go to MacArthur you can count on all of us being friends. I mean that."

I half expected Trish to jump into the air and do a split while waving red and white pom-poms at the crowd.

"Trish, you have the locker above mine and you still have no idea who I am," Floe said.

"That's not important. That's not what we are here for," Trevor said.

I walked up to Trevor's bench and hopped onto it. "What are you here for, Graves? I don't recall inviting Ken and Barbie."

"That comment is exactly why we're here, because of your penchant for starting trouble."

"Penchant? Christ, Trevor when did you buy a thesaurus?"

Trevor sighed. "I got wind of your rally and thought I should come over to tell your friends that if they are against corporal punishment and want more of a voice all they have to do is write to the school paper."

"Is that the same rag that ran an article called Vietnam the New Crusade?" Johnny yelled out.

Floe plucked her guitar. "How about the article, Sacred Love Versus Lust?"

"Fucking commie bitch," a voice in the gathering shouted.

"I see you brought the debating club with you," Floe said.

"I've talked to Mr. Lesman and he's willing to listen to us," Trevor said. "He's aware that outside agitators are responsible for the incidents at school and is willing to forgive and forget."

"Provided," Trish said, sticking her boobs out so far that they looked like freeway warning cones. "Provided that we vote with our minds," she raised her finger to her temple, "and not our hearts." Her hand moved down to her left breast.

Nina said, "What the hell is that supposed to mean?"

Without losing a step Trish threw her arms out in front of her in a loop and pulled them back as if harvesting an enormous bouquet of flowers. "I'll run because I promised my Pom-Pom squad I would but I'm throwing my weight behind Trevor. He knows what it means to compromise."

"Kissing ass isn't the same thing as compromising, Sweet Cheeks," Jeff shouted. He galloped across the plaza and did a running broad jump landing next to me. "Heard about the rally and came to support you." The musky aroma of hash clung to Jeff. When I told him about my plan to run for school president he'd smirked and said, "Big Brother I'm with you, provided PAS agrees to place free condoms in fishbowls throughout the school."

I looked over the heads of the crowd and saw Vince Crane waving. "Right on, go for it," he shouted.

"Jeff, you don't know what you're doing," Trevor said.

"Neither does David so that makes us even."

"You have to work within the system to change it," Trevor said.

"Graves, I don't want to change the system. I want to bury it. I don't want to mourn it. I want to burn it."

"That's just great, Dave," Trevor said. "You're willing to put us all in trouble to promote your leftist nonsense."

"Let me get something straight. I'm not a raving commie. I'm just fed up with dick heads like Lesman abusing us and getting away with it."

"Maybe the people he disciplines have it coming."

"Lesman beat Muffy so badly that she couldn't walk. And for what, because her skirt was too long and had peace signs on it?"

"You can't say she wasn't warned," Trish said.

"Keep out of this," Floe growled. "Your dress doesn't reach your knees and you got more cleavage showing than the Royal Gorge. There are two standards in Lesman's cow palace. You get away dressing like a Lone Star slut and those hicks out there-" Floe pointed at the cowboy hats in the crowd, "get away dressing like midnight cowboys. Meanwhile we get beat and kicked out of school because our views offend the administration."

"Dave we can talk about what's bothering us with Mr. Lesman and Mr. Berk," Trevor said. "If we put our points across in a logical non-threatening manner they will listen and may even relax some of the rules."

"Graves, I'm not interested in having a debate with you, them, or anyone else in this shitkicker school. Come next week the students will decide if they want a candy ass bootlicker running the student council or a person who will lay it on the line."

"If we win you lose and if you win we all lose," Trevor said. "Things will get even tougher for us." He stepped off the bench and walked away from the plaza followed by Trish and their friends.

"Graves, what do you gargle with to get the taste of Lesman's ass out of your mouth," I shouted.

"Far-out," the girl with the large gym bag sang out. She unzipped it and dragged out a dummy dressed in a white shirt, pin striped tie and grey suit. It had a stuffed pillowcase for a head. Around its neck was a cardboard sign with the words U-gene Lesman.

Jeff shinnied up a pole and suspended the dummy from a beam. The effigy of Lesman slowly twisted in a circle. Stillness fell around the Gazebo.

"Far-out," the girl repeated. Jeff swung from the beam like a trapeze artist and dismounted landing next to her. She pulled him to her, gave him a kiss then ran away.

"Who was that?" I asked.

"I have no idea, but I'm going home and make an army of dummies," Jeff said.

Chapter 45

On the morning of the student council election assembly, Lesman, Berk and four policemen stood at the curb side before school began. When students approached the entrance, Lesman either pointed them out to the cops or shook his head. When I walked by with Nina, he told me to stop. One of the cops looked me up and down then wrote something in his notepad.

"Move along to the auditorium," Berk said.

"Bet you got a whizzer of a speech prepared," Lesman added.

And I did. I'd spent the weekend writing, revising and practicing my speech with Jeff until he said, "Lay off, I'll vote for you twice if you shut up."

*

The auditorium was MacArthur High School's show place, ultra-modern and outfitted with the most advanced audiovisual projection and sound equipment. I sat with the other candidates on the stage. The school's mascot, a bright red cardinal, was projected on a screen behind us. Mr. Berk walked out from the right wing of the stage and stood behind the podium.

"Quiet down," he ordered even though no one had made a sound. "We are here this morning to learn about the various people who want to represent you, the student body. Each person up here will give a speech telling you why they think they are best qualified to serve your interests."

He rapped on the microphone again and looked up at Lesman when he entered the auditorium with the cops. They stood at the back of the room preventing anyone from making a break for the doors.

"Rowdiness and cat calls are not permitted. Hold your applause until your favorite has completed his or her speech. One other thing, I know that the vote was to have been on Wednesday but because of a scheduling conflict the ballot casting will be done today during the three lunch periods. By day's end we'll announce the results."

A collective grumble rose from the auditorium. Someone yelled, "Fix!"

"That'll do. Anyone making a scene will have to answer to those officers back there." Berk read a name, "Sammy Marsh," off a list. "You all know him as the leading scorer on the basketball team, and captain of the cross country and baseball teams. Sammy is running as vice-president of the school improvement committee."

Sammy loped over to the podium. His friends on the basketball team, occupying the front row of seats, cheered him. "Thank you, Mr. Berk, thank you, school friends. I say friends because we are all friends at MacArthur even if we don't know each other's names." The essence of his fifteen-minute speech could be distilled into one line:

–In this great school in a great country we should be grateful and strive for greatness so vote for me.

Mr. Berk clapped. "I know some of you are only here for a good time, but this school election is a serious lesson in how government works. Everybody knows our first speaker from the numerous heart and spirit events she has organized to support our sports teams."

Trish's tinkling laughter filled the auditorium like wind chimes. Once behind the podium she immediately launched her speech. "My fellow boy and girl students. Although I would really love to be student council president there is something even more I want to be. I want to be a proud American. Some of the people around here think they know better about what is going on in our school and nation than our leaders. Well, they're wrong. I place my faith in people like Mr. Berk and Mr. Lesman. They are like our fathers. We may not always agree with our daddies but at the end of the day we have to admit they are mostly right. I am not going to ask you to vote for me. Actually, I would rather you vote for almost anyone up here if it means keeping out a person who mocks our school, our country, and God. But if you do vote for me, I won't let you down. Go cardinals!"

Five more people came to the podium to stump for such positions as head of school spirit, civic pride leader, secretary/treasurer of the student council. Trevor Graves woke me with his silky baritone voice.

"It's easy, so easy, to say what is wrong with the world. It's more difficult to see what's right." Trevor turned sideways and leveled a finger at me. "Some people assume by shouting and causing trouble that they will change the establishment to conform to their idealistic visions of what the world ought to be. All I have to say to these infant socialists and anarchists is that I like my world the way it is. I enjoy the freedoms that other countries' students would beg to taste. If I am elected student council president, I will work to bring more soda and snack vending machines into school. The money raised from these machines will be spent to improve our school events and dances like the Valentine dance, Sadie Hawkins day, and Halloween Party. Do what you know is right. Vote for me."

Mr. Berk glanced up at the clock hanging above the entrance doors then looked at me and then down at his wristwatch. "We're running late so you won't have time to make your speech. I'll go up to the podium and tell them your name and what office you are running for."

"That's not fair but it is typical," I said.

"Okay, I don't want it coming out later that I denied you the right to speak. How much time will you need?"

"Not much." Before Berk could stop me, I stood behind the podium. It was comfortable to face an auditorium full of people. I spread out a sheet of blank paper and pretended to be reading from it. "My fellow classmates I'm running for student council president. I haven't been here long..." I paused and swept the auditorium with my eyes. "But I've been here long enough to say what is on my mind without reading from a prepared speech." I crumpled up the paper and tossed it into the audience.

Unhooking the microphone from the gooseneck I stepped from behind the rostrum. "I've heard a lot about how we're here practicing democracy in action. I have been told how this school is training us to be responsible voters and knowledgeable citizens who respect what this school and this nation stands for. I got news for you. MacArthur's version of what it takes to be a good, knowledgeable citizen obviously doesn't have room for such concepts as freedom of speech, freedom of assembly, freedom of press. God

340

forbid we exercise the subversive principles that our founders saw fit to include in a little document called the Constitution. Heck no, that would go against what Mr. Lesman and Mr. Berk see as contributing to being good students, good Americans. It sickens me to look out over you, the student body, and realize what a joke this election and this school is."

Mr. Lesman pounded a path down the center aisle. Mr. Berk tried to take the mike from me. I wasn't done. My tongue was on fire. "We are allegedly here to be prepared to be intelligent, discerning citizens. Nonsense! We are here to be cast into a quagmire of unthinking obedience where the only right we have, is to say, Yes Sir, to whatever bs they choose to feed us. All I've got to say is, No Sir! No Sir! I will not buy your lies. No Sir! I refuse to allow you to beat us. No Sir! I will not accept your attempt to silence us and restrict our freedoms. No Sir!"

I had not set out to be a radical or more accurately a shit disturber but just happened to be caught up in the convergence of all the elements that constitute a cultural and historical tsunami. My rebellion was not aimed at Lesman it was locked on home. The face of my father was etched in my mind as I shouted, "No Sir!" one more time. Perspiring I ended with, "Vote for me or vote for them."

Hopping off the stage before Lesman or Berk could grab me, I strolled up the aisle past the cops, one of whom opened the door for me. "Good speech, kid," he said. "But I wager it's gonna be your last one."

As I pushed the doors open, I heard a commotion behind me and turned to see people standing on their seats whistling, stamping their feet, and applauding. Mr. Lesman and Berk were shouting for the students to sit down and shut up. A small band of radical PAS supporters rushed the stage screaming "No Sir!" They unfurled a banner, which repeated the slogan I'd seen by the fire station, "You got to burn it down before you can build it up."

Outside the auditorium, effigies of Berk and Lesman dangled from the railing above the lobby. All morning, students greeted me as I walked down the hall. Even some hard-core shitkickers and Bible thumpers told me they agreed with my speech. Insults and threats were also delivered, though generally not to my face.

On my locker someone had scrawled, "Yankee Commie bastard go home." On the blackboard in my Latin class a message in red chalk warned, "All you pinko PAS faggots and lesbos better watch your backs! We know how to deal with your kind in Texas."

Despite my theatrics, Berk and Lesman didn't call me into the office for inciting a fracas in the assembly. They were busy overseeing the election. When I approached the table to vote Lesman almost fell out of his chair reaching for my wrist. He snatched the ballot out of my hand and tore it up and threw the pieces in my face. Some kids standing behind me gave him a prolonged raspberry.

Berk who always maintained a safe distance from overt conflict said, "Gene, go get us a cool drink."

"I ain't going anywhere until I'm satisfied this election is going the right way."

The skin around Mr. Berk's eyes grew taut. His nostrils flared. "We need a cool drink, Eugene. Go for it."

Mr. Lesman stamped off. Berk picked up a ballot and swiped a space with a pencil. He held it up so I could see a √ next to my name. "Satisfied?" He folded the ballot in half and pushed it through the slot of a sealed cardboard box.

After lunch my brother, Vince and Albert located me in the courtyard of the school. Vince had come up with the idea of conducting an exit poll. They asked almost every student leaving the cafeteria which candidate they had voted for.

"It's unreal, man," Vince said. "From my survey I'm convinced that the impossible has happened. You've won."

I wanted to win. I'd convinced myself that PAS could force through some real changes.

Berk's voice came over the intercom as I started for my class. "Attention, attention MacArthur students. The votes have been tallied. Sammy Marsh is your new student council president."

Exclamations of disbelief and outrage echoed down the corridors of MacArthur.

"You're most likely wondering how Sammy was chosen as president when he wasn't even running for the position," Berk's voice crackled through loudspeakers. "It became clear that the votes cast for the people running for president indicated that no one would have a substantial majority so the administration awarded the position to Sammy who clearly had the most votes of any person running for any of the student council posts."

Many students who had sat on the fence sought me out to tell me that Berk and Lesman screwed me over. A few went so far as to ask to join the Progressive Association of

Students. By the end of the day PAS had become more than just a cute acronym, it was a real movement. Floe and Johnny worked the sidewalk beyond the school grounds encouraging kids to show their disapproval by refusing to support school events. By week's end posters appeared in the hallways urging students to boycott pep rallies, bake sales, and all sports activities. Lesman spent a couple of hours each day tearing down the offending posters. By Friday the police patrolled the halls to make sure no anarchist with a handmade sign and a roll of masking tape would undermine the foundations of God-fearing America.

Chapter 46

Hugh Swift discovered a way to push the administration over the edge. On the Monday after the election, he returned from his suspension and circulated a petition. He asked students to sign their names in a show of solidarity for the national moratorium against the war in Vietnam scheduled to take place on October 15th. Over two million people across the country would demonstrate their opposition to the war by wearing black arm bands, holding candlelight processions, and giving speeches on college campuses, in church basements, parks and shopping malls throughout the nation. My brother and Vince were among the first to sign.

"You do know that what you signed was a petition against the war?" I said.

"Bummer," Jeff said. "I thought it was a list of people who wanted to go to a party at SMU."

As I walked home from school a car whizzed past, then reversed at breakneck speed. The window on the passenger side rolled down and a half full beer can rocketed out and struck me above the left corner of my eye. I recognized Ham's voice.

"You owe me a Lone Star the next time I see you, Brown."

Blood poured down the side of my face. I was too angry to go home. Despite my aversion to firearms, my Dad's arsenal was too tempting to chance it.

When I knocked on Nina's door she cried out and pulled me into the bathroom where she administered first aid and tried to calm me down. It took a while.

Her efforts led us to a cabana by the pool in her backyard. We made love until the sound of a car pulling into the driveway sent us scrambling for our clothing. I managed to clear the fence before her father called out from the front yard, "Is anybody home?"

I arrived home after dark. Supper was on the table. My mother and Tommy were eating. Mom was sheltered behind one of my textbooks. The book, standing on its spine, hid her face.

"Where's Jeff?" I asked.

"Out of town. He'll be back tomorrow evening." With each threat of a new transfer Mom's voice had grown flatter. It conveyed as much passion as a telephone time check.

"Jeff's out of town?"

"I thought you were asking about your father. Your brother hasn't come home yet." She closed the book and stared at me a few seconds.

"Your eye."

The beer can left a half moon gash at the corner of my eye. "It's nothing."

"Better put a bandage on it just in case."

I finished eating and headed for the garage. Just as I entered, Jeff raised the garage door so violently it skipped off its tracks. He went straight to the workbench and started rooting through a box of tools. He hefted a heavy rock chisel in his palm, closed his fingers around it and threw a straight arm punch at a piece of plywood that leaned against the wall. "Shit!" He dropped the chisel and stared at his bloody knuckles.

"What's going on?" I asked.

Above the workbench a ball pen hammer caught his attention. He took it down leaving its black outline traced on the pegboard. A galvanized trashcan sat on top of the bench.

Jeff swung the hammer and punched a hole in it. Jeff wheeled around. His face twitched and the muscles on his neck stood out. He stared at me as if trying to determine if I was the enemy. He stretched out his fingertips and touched the scab forming on my cut. "Where did you get that?"

"Some cracker nailed me with a Lone Star."

"Count yourself lucky. Vince is in emergency. I went with Mrs. Crane to the hospital to see him. After school Vince stayed to watch me at football practice. Coach Worell ordered Vince off the field. Lesman was sitting on the sidelines with Tory, Roddy and some other guys. When Vince left, they also left. He got as far as the 7-11 when a car slows down and starts dogging him. Tory was at the wheel and Roddy sat on the passenger side. Two other guys were in the back seat. Roddy yelled, 'Faggot, you make me sick.' Vince flipped Roddy the finger." Jeff cracked a smile. "You know what a wise ass Vince is. He shouted, 'That's rich coming from a guy whose idea of fun is sneaking up behind a good-looking goat. But hell, if it was good enough for your mama why should you break the mold?' Vince didn't have a chance."

347

Roddy had fought golden gloves for a couple of years and had racked up a string of victories.

"He beat Vince until he couldn't lift his arms to block the punches. When he fell to the ground and curled up in a ball the other two guys jumped out and helped Roddy put their boots to him. Tory stayed inside the car."

"The tools, you planning to use them for offense or defence?"

"Neither, I'm blowing off steam to keep from hurting somebody real bad."

"Cool. I'll leave you alone then."

As I walked back into the kitchen the telephone rang.

"I guess you know about Vince." I recognized Jardin's voice.

"My brother told me."

"I was at the Dairy Queen with Dan when Tory and his nitwit friends came in. They were bragging about the ass whupping they gave Vince. The DQ's owner is a friend of Lesman. He egged them on to tell him how they trashed Vince. The son-of-a-bitch said, 'that ought to teach him and his kind. I'll give every boy here a free milkshake for every hippie faggot they stomp'."

I returned to the garage and picked up a can of paint thinner. "Jeff, if you really want to get even with these shit kickers then you got to make them more scared of what you might do than what you will do."

The next morning, I waited for Roddy to leave his house. I hollered, "Hey, you redneck mother fucker," and held up the paper bag.

A smile crept across Roddy's face. "You better not be talking to me." The smile disappeared when he saw Dan and a couple of other guys leaning against a stop sign on the corner.

"You're real brave when it's three against one," I said and removed the paint thinner from the paper bag and doused him with it until he reeked. "Next time I'll bring a match."

Screaming, "I'll call the police," Roddy backed away from me.

"Go ahead. You know what my friends in the movement taught me? They taught me how to run a copper wire from a car battery to the gas tank. Technically it's not a bomb when it blows but who cares what it's called."

I had no idea what I was talking about. I had never seen, much less made a bomb. Roddy did not go to school that day or the next day or the day after that. He moved to Tulsa to live with his grandmother.

When word got around about what I'd done to Roddy Jeff said, "You're fucking nuts! Don't you think that was a little extreme?"

"You wanted to drive a chisel through his gut."

"Yeah but he would've got over that. What you did wasn't normal."

*

As the October 15th moratorium grew nearer, Lesman's vigilantes increased their attacks on people they were sure would not fight back. At some point renegade factions of the student left decided enough was enough. Lesman's goons now found slips of paper with their telephone number, home address, and the names of their family members and girlfriends taped to their lockers. Singled out for special treatments were Tory and Ham. Their car door mirrors were ripped off, taillights kicked in, and on their hoods, someone scratched what was now the official slogan of MacArthur's secret underground, "NO SIR". Cans of paint thinner were left on the roof of their cars. The same message appeared on the blank walls and garage doors of their residences and on those of the most conservative school board officials.

An orgy of graffiti and a proliferation of Lesman and Berk effigies dangled from tree limbs, light posts, and jungle gyms throughout Irving. For added emphasis someone had painted "You got to burn it down before you can build it up" on the sidewalk in front of the school.

A few days before the moratorium against the war Hugh and Floe cornered me as I walked down the hall with Nina and Johnny. Floe accused me of orchestrating the campaign against the other side.

"Come on, David, the word's out on how you scared Roddy so badly he left town," Floe said.

"Ask Nina, we've been together almost every day. She'll tell you that I haven't had the time to do anything."

"We've been writing applications for universities. Tulane, the University of Chicago, Stanford, anywhere out of state," Nina said.

The idea of escaping Texas channeled the conversation in a more amicable direction. As we discussed the merits of one university over another Sammy Marsh and Trevor Graves appeared. Sammy unrolled a poster, smoothed it flat with his hand and taped it to the wall. Stand Up for America Rally October 15th 2:00 to 3:00 was printed over the picture of a smiling, short haired male in an ROTC uniform and a girl in a red, white and blue cheer leader's outfit.

The poster went on to say how the true youth of America must declare their support for our boys in Vietnam and their love for America the Beautiful. It ended with the promise of hot dogs, chips, drinks and door prizes.

Hugh said, "Perfect, while we hold a teach-in and wear black armbands to protest the war you guys will eat slaughterhouse scraps and chug Dr. Peppers to support it."

Trevor moved the stack from under his armpit and peeled off four sheets of cream-colored paper. "I don't think you'll be doing much of anything." He handed us a mimeographed bulletin bearing the school letterhead.

To All MacArthur Students:

It has come to my attention that on Tuesday, October 15th certain elements in school plan to wear black armbands and participate in a rally against the war in Vietnam. Although political dissent is a necessary part of a democratic society, the public good and its sensibilities must take precedence. Therefore, students wearing symbols that clearly define their anti-war, anti-America feelings will be suspended from school. This should not come as a surprise to you as the following rules were stated at the start of the school year:

A. The wearing of badges, ribbons, insignias, or other items of clothing that have been deemed by the administration as expressing a social or political

message against the community standards is prohibited.

B. If by action, word, or deed an individual expresses a view or idea, which is contrary to the mores, standards of decency, and goodwill of the community that person will be held accountable for inciting violence, should an incident occur.

See you at the Stand Up for America Rally October 15th 12:00 to 3:00.

Mr. Berk

Mr. Berk, Senior Principal

"You guys just don't know who's on top," Trevor said.

Sammy's shoulders slumped. "Be quiet, I think if y'all want to meet and wear black armbands then that's your business. As long as no one gets hurt, who cares?" I could see why people liked Sammy. After the election he'd gone out of his way to find me and shake hands. "I think you got a raw deal," he said, "but what the heck, we can work together on things we both believe in."

"So what do we do?" Floe asked. "I can't afford to get suspended. It will kill any chance I have of getting a scholarship."

"We can hold the rally before school at the park," Johnny suggested.

"The rally isn't important. It's the arm band that counts," Hugh said.

"Okay, we'll wear them off MacArthur property," Floe said.

Hugh looked grim. "What will that prove?"

"It will prove they've won," Nina said. "I'm going to wear an armband to school."

"Even your boyfriend isn't that much of an idiot," Floe said.

"What David does is David's business. I have to do what I feel is right." Nina took my hand.

That weekend I mulled over what I should do. It was certain that if Floe didn't wear an armband at school others would follow her example. It was also clear that Nina, having stated her intention, would follow through on it and that Hugh would too. Johnny would decide at the last minute. He was against the war but the whole incense-and-cinnamon mentality of the flower children put him off.

Jeff said, "Lie low, stay clear and walk down the hall with blinders. As for me, I got an in with Berk. He feels sorry for me 'cause he thinks you're a bad influence. That's a trip. I smoked dope and was banging nubies before you found out they existed. But to him you're public enemy number one. He thinks you're part of a conspiracy to import all sorts of subversive ideas from Nebraska."

"What a load of crap."

"Crap or not he believes it. Twice a week he calls me into the office to pick my brains, feels me out about where you're going, who you're seeing, even what you're reading."

"So what do you tell him?"

"Nowhere, nobody, nothing," Jeff said. "Anyway it's not important what I tell him. What is important is what he tells me. He tells me that he won't tolerate your blatant insubordination anymore and that if necessary, he'll see to it that you're not only expelled but that you end up in jail."

Monday morning three squad cars were parked in front of MacArthur. One kid had a peace symbol stitched to his sleeve. He was ordered to take off his jacket. A cop flicked open a pocketknife, cut the patch away then handed the denim jacket back to the student. Policemen with bolt cutters accompanied Lesman down the corridor. They snipped the locks off lockers and swept the contents onto the floor in their search for drugs, weapons, and incendiary literature.

Girls were ordered to remove big loop earrings, wipe off makeup and lipstick and go home and change into appropriate skirts and blouses. Boys got the same treatment with the added thrill of being frisked. Four times during the day Lesman pointed me out to his cop and I had my face pressed against cold wall tiles. I counted myself lucky. Travis and Deacon were hauled off in cuffs after a zealot cop discovered a baggie with less than a thimble of marijuana in their locker. When Mr. Berk's voice came over the PA system it was clear that this was a dress rehearsal for what was to come.

"This is your senior principal reminding you that Wednesday is the Stand up for America Rally. This activity will take place during normal school hours. It is mandatory that all students attend. All other activities in the school are forbidden. The display of armbands, buttons, or slogans not sanctioned by the administration will result in immediate disciplinary action. Policemen will be stationed throughout the school for the next week to ensure disturbances do not take place."

On October 15th across America students and citizens wore black armbands, listened to music in the parks, and marched down city streets chanting anti-war slogans. In Irving Texas a fleet of patrol cars lined the curb along MacArthur High School.

Cops roamed the halls slamming known liberal miscreants and flower children into walls, conducting body searches and confiscating armbands and peace symbols even if they were hidden in school bags.

Floe and a few other students skipped classes to attend a last-minute gathering at the Unitarian Church. I had not seen Nina but heard that Berk sent her home for wearing an armband and a colored glass peace symbol around her neck. I remained armband free and dressed in clothes that even Pat Boone would have considered conservative.

At noon Berk's voice blared through the loudspeakers instructing all students to proceed to the athletic field house. At about the same time a low chorus of voices could be heard from outside the building. Several people who had attended the healing and peace gathering at the Unitarian Church congregated across the street singing "Blowing in the Wind". A couple of cops were dispatched but they returned in a few minutes looking dejected. The minister, a veteran of civil right's marches, had shown the cops a parade permit.

Jeff intercepted me on my way to the field house. We talked a little about Dad and how pissed off he must have been by the national moratorium and the politicians who lent their support.

"Tonight would be a good night to keep busy and stay out of the Colonel's way," Jeff said.

When Jeff and I headed for the brick courtyard of the school we saw the backs of three guys standing in a semicircle. Ham turned.

Hugh Swift was on his knees. His shirt was torn. His bloody knees poked through his jeans. Tied around one bicep was a black armband. Tory stood beside a new recruit to the goon squad. Tory snatched the piece of ribbon off Hugh's arm. Hugh stuck his hand into his pocket and pulled out another armband and fumbled to tie it on.

"I thought you'd have learned last time." Ham plucked the ribbon from Hugh's fingers.

"Either you take that thing off on your own or we'll beat you till you can't walk," Tory said.

Jeff grabbed the ribbon out of Ham's hand. "Knock it off."

I helped Hugh to his feet. The stubborn little hippie slipped a curled up black ribbon into my fist. "Peaceful resistance, David. If we do as they do, what have we proven?"

"Get out of here, Hugh." I pushed him into the middle of the courtyard.

"You're interfering," Tory said. "Mr. Lesman made us hall monitors."

"Lesman gave you the right to stomp on some kid who couldn't fight back even if he wanted to?"

"He asked for it. Those damn ribbons are an insult to our boys dying in Vietnam."

356

"Fuck you," Jeff shouted. Tory's eyes moved from me to my brother. Jeff had taken a ribbon and tied it around his upper arm. I followed suit.

"There are three of us," Ham said nervously.

"So what?" Jeff replied.

"We'll report you."

My response was swift. I nailed Tory in the throat and kicked him in his balls. I circled behind him when he was on all fours struggling to breathe, drove my knee into his back and put a chokehold on him. Jeff picked up a loose patio brick and slammed it into Ham's gut and started pounding him on the back with his fists. The new recruit hid behind a potted plant while his friends were being beaten. He begged us to stop.

"Stick around and you're next," I said.

Jeff and I took turns kicking Tory and Ham. I leaned over Tory and spit in his face. "Maybe you'll get it through your thick head that I'm not a pacifist."

Jeff went on to the rally. Tory and Ham did not. Floe told me that the Unitarian minister drove them home when he saw them stumbling out of the school. He mistook them for kids protesting the war. He told her that they looked like someone had worked them over with a metal bar.

I blew off the rally. Lesman caught me on my way to my locker. He was wandering the halls looking for skippers. He grabbed my arm and tried to drag me down to his office. I shook him loose. He ran after me panting and screeching, "You come back here! I said come back here. I'm gonna whup you till that smirk falls off your face."

357

"You raise a hand to me and they'll be scraping you off the walls for months to come."

"That does it. You're expelled."

Chapter 47

The doorbell tolled like a death knell the evening of October 15th. My father hated being interrupted at dinner. It didn't take Edgar Casey to predict my future when Lesman and three school board members stood on the doorstep. A guy with a crew cut and a white shirt, black suit and black tie stood behind Lesman's group. He handed Dad a business card that identified him as an FBI agent.

About twenty minutes passed while Dad listened to what Lesman and the others had to say.

When I entered the living room, Lesman and his committee were squeezed primly together on the sofa. Sitting in the armchair was the FBI agent with an open notebook in his lap.

"Go ahead, tell my son what you told me," Dad ordered Lesman.

The vice-principal's voice cracked. "Your boy is a bad influence."

"I didn't ask you about his moral character, I asked you to repeat what you told me."

"Yes Sir," slipped out of Lesman's mouth. "Your son is thought to be responsible for organizing a student movement at MacArthur. This movement is anti-war and anti-American in thinking. In the speech he gave while running for student council president your son accused us of dropping people into a mud hole and telling them what to think and said that we didn't believe in the constitution."

"That so, David? Is that what you said?"

"No Sir. I said into a quagmire of unthinking obedience, where the only right we have is to say Yes Sir to whatever crap they feed us."

Dad pressed his lips together and smiled briefly. "Not too shabby, has a lot of punch to it."

The FBI agent coughed. "Colonel Brown, I have reason to suspect that your son has become an unwitting dupe of the left wing fringe. The bureau believes that the speech he gave was written for him."

"With all due respect, my son is quite capable of writing a cliché laden diatribe. It doesn't take a genius, only someone who knows the difference between a verb and a noun."

"Let's assume he did write the speech," the agent said. "Then that means your son supports a movement which flies in the face of everything the uniform you wear stands for."

"Did you say you were against the war or America?"

"I said I was against corporal punishment."

"Are you against the war?"

I did not respond.

"One more time, are you against the war?"

"I guess I am."

"Why?"

I scanned the room and stopped at Lesman. "Because if that idiot is for it then it has to be wrong."

"You heard him," Dad said. "Now please go."

After the room cleared my father pivoted on his heel and slugged me in the stomach. He left me curled in a ball on the carpet and went back to his meal. The rest of the evening he did not say a single word.

In the morning I awoke when I was lifted out of bed and flung across the room. My father threw the clothes I had worn the day before at me.

"Get dressed, you're coming downtown."

I knew better than to inquire why and pulled on my clothes and dashed to the car ahead of him. We rode to his office in the federal building without speaking. He pulled into the underground parking garage.

"Get out."

I waited by the elevator for him. Instead of pushing the button for his floor he pressed the one below it. The elevator opened up into the main lobby. Along both sides of the corridor were recruitment posters for each branch of the armed forces hanging next to their respective office doors. Dad walked up to the Marine recruiting station and rapped on the door. A burly Sergeant Major decked out in his dress uniform saluted when he stepped into the hall.

"Good morning, Colonel Brown. This must be your son." He stuck out his hand, but I did not take it. "Your father told me that you want to see how the corps can do right by you and you can do right by the corps."

"I don't know what you're talking about."

The lifer looked confused. "Your father called last night to tell me you were coming in to enlist."

"If he told you that, he's lying. I got no intention of fighting for you, for my country, or my father."

The Marine's ears turned red. His chest puffed up. He placed his hands on his hips and bellowed, "You are not man enough to be a Marine!"

"If by man enough you mean I'm not someone who can be taught to jump like a dumb beast when you bark out an order then you're right. I'm not man enough to be a Marine."

I walked off leaving my father spewing out apologies to the recruiter who kept yelling how it was kids like me who were ruining this goddamn country.

Before my father returned home that evening the scene at the federal building had replayed in my mind so many times that whatever he planned for me would seem anticlimactic. Mom and Tommy had gone out for dinner. Jeff urged me to take off until things cooled down.

"Dad might be a God in the world of toy soldiers but he's not my commander and chief," I said. "He stepped over the line by taking me down to the recruiting station to pawn me off like a slave. Back in Omaha I told Dad I'd sign up and got my face punched in for it. Now he can go to hell."

"It's your funeral," Jeff said and headed for the back door when a car pulled into the driveway.

Dad slammed the front door behind him and marched straight to the back of the house. A minute later he yelled, "Get your queer ass in my office! Don't make me ask you twice."

My stomach was in knots. With my mother and brothers out of the house there was no one to restrain him. When I opened the door of his study my father was sitting behind his oak desk, still dressed in his uniform with his arms flat on the glass that protected the wood. Beside one elbow was his hat, the silver lightning bolts visible on its shiny black brim. In his hand he clutched a Colt Woodsman semi-automatic 22 target pistol.

The pistol's full clip was in an ashtray. He raised the gun, leveled it at my face and squeezed off a dry shot. The click of the pistol sent a convulsion through my body.

"Relax you're not worth a bullet. Not that I didn't think about it. But then I would have to explain it to your mother, and it would make life hell for your brothers. I'm sure I'd get off when the court saw what a favor I did by taking one more faggot coward off the streets. Pretty sure, but not totally sure."

Dad sprang across the desk with the pistol in his hand. "That man you insulted is not only my friend, he is a decorated war hero!"

I keeled over when he sideswiped my ear with the grip of the 22 then clubbed me on the side of my neck with its barrel.

"I can deal with the dope smoking, the screwing around, but I will never tolerate having a traitor as a son who not only spits on my flag but induces others to do the same and in the name of what? Change? Revolution? When the fuck has change or revolution accomplished anything? You got until the morning to decide how you are going to apologize to the Sergeant. You got until the morning to decide to enlist in the military. I don't give a flying fuck what branch you pick but you better pick one or I'm going to do my country a favor, jail or no jail." He pushed me to the floor on his way out of the room.

Dad locked the door from the outside, a practice he started when he discovered that Jeff and I were sneaking into his study and raiding the supply of olives and cocktail peanuts stashed in his closet. I peeked out the window when I heard his car start. He burned rubber backing out of the driveway and sped down the street.

I tried the doorknob. It was locked but posed no real problem. In the desk drawer was a screwdriver with multiple interchangeable bits. The flat head was thin enough to force between the jam, perfect for popping the hinges. Once in the hallway I ran to my room and stuffed whatever clothing and toiletries I could find in the same green duffel bag I had taken to California. I left the shotgun on Dad's desk.

One side of my face was swollen and numb. On the other side my ear was sticky from fluid and blood. I swore that this would be the last time I ever let Dad strike me. Screw "honor your father".

I slithered out of the patio door and hopped the backyard fence. I lit off without looking back, running faster than I had ever run.

Chapter 48

North Texas is not the arctic, but it does get chilly in late autumn. I caught a few moments of sleep on a park slide hidden behind a set of monkey bars. I awoke to the wailing of a fire engine and wandered the streets, pondering what I should do.

With no place else to go I went to where I heard Eliot now lived. Cheryl ditched Eliot after two nights in Los Angeles. She and Cotton caught a bus to Tucson and joined a Christian fundamentalist commune. Eliot returned to Texas and managed to find a bed to share with a waitress who was older and less hospitable than Cheryl.

Visibly agitated by my 4 A.M. visit, Eliot reheated the remains of the previous night's coffee. I gave him a summary of the events of the last few weeks and said I needed a place to crash while I got my act together.

The woman clumped out of the bedroom smoking a cigarette. She wore a short terry-cloth robe that barely covered her potbelly. "Bubba, that's your problem," she said. "Don't want or need your kind of trouble round here. You're welcome to catch a few winks on the sofa and have breakfast but you best be gone when I get home from work."

"But darlin'—"

"But darlin' nothing. Either he's gone or you're both gone. End of story."

"Marcy isn't a bad sort once you get to know her."

"That's okay. I'll figure something out." I lathered a slice of toast with Cheese Whiz.

*

Without realizing it I headed toward the school. Using my duffel bag as a pillow I lay down on a bench under the Gazebo. The morning dew immediately soaked through my clothes.

The smell of sandalwood and marijuana roused me from my sleep. Johnny Jardin knelt in front of my bench. Nina stood beside him. "We've been looking all over for you," he said.

A strong breeze sent a shiver through me. Nina removed her jacket and draped it over my back. She took my hands and rubbed them between her palms. "Jeff called me last night to see if you were at my house."

"Did he tell you what happened?"

Nina gasped when I turned the opposite side of my face toward her. My ear was crusted with blood. My cheekbone and neck were tattooed with bruises.

Johnny gritted his teeth. "Your old man did that?"

"Good guess."

"Your father called after your brother did," Nina said. "He told my dad that you're a drug addict and a communist sympathizer and that he should send me away unless he wants to end up supporting a bastard child."

"Big John says that if you need a place to crash, you can stay with us until you're on your feet," Johnny said.

*

With their front yard of knee-high grass and towering sunflowers interspersed with twisted metal sculptures, the Jardin's specialized in antagonizing the staid denizens of Irving. As a further affront, Big John strung the banner of the International Workers' Party above his garage door on May Day and held a barbecue for union organizers from the various Dallas locals.

When Johnny brought me through the front door his father charged across the cluttered living room like a water buffalo. He stopped short of running me over. "So we meet again, Vladimir." He frowned. "Boy, the jackboots really did a job on you."

"His old man did that," Johnny said.

"Excuse me for saying so, kid, your father, the General, is a coward."

I wanted to tell him he was wrong. "I'm okay, Sir."

"Do you see me walking on water in here, are sparks coming out of my ass? Don't call me Sir. Call me Big John or Mr. Jardin if you feel like you gotta tickle my balls."

Big John threw his big arms around our necks and walked Johnny and me into the kitchen. Seated at one end of a butcher-block table a boy played a single note at a time on a wooden recorder. He peeked over the rim of his John Lennon sunglasses and flashed the peace sign with both hands. A woman standing at the stove lifted the lid of a simmering pot. Her thin body was covered in a light blue painter's smock. She flipped the silver ponytail that trailed down her back over her front shoulder, turned toward me and smiled.

Big John plopped down on a cane chair. He brought his hands together in a loud clap. "This here is David, he'll be staying with us a while."

The woman wiped her palms on her smock and held out her hand with her fingertips pointing toward me. "I'm Eunice."

"I'm glad to meet you, Mrs. Jardin."

"Bernier, Eunice Bernier," she corrected. "Johnny will explain it to you."

That evening we ate sourdough bread made by the recorder player and barley soup out of heavy clay bowls. For dessert Eunice served stirred yogurt with strawberry and rhubarb preserves.

I stayed with the Garners for three weeks. They were the antithesis of everything I had been inculcated by prime-time television to believe constituted the average American happy family. Eunice had lived with Big John common-law for thirty years, bearing him three children, one of whom was working with the Peace Corps. She was a graduate of a northern liberal arts college. All the left causes were the right causes in her world. As a young woman she wrote letters to Truman and Eisenhower, pleading that the Rosenbergs be spared the chair. She marched for the integration of white only beaches on the Chicago lakefront and condemned American involvement in Southeast Asia long before anyone knew where Laos and Cambodia were. She met Big John when he came to her campus to speak about unionizing the automobile parts factories near Detroit.

One night, Big John asked, "So David, what ya intend to do with your life?"

"I guess go to university and study journalism or law."

A sour look came over him. "In the meantime though you gotta make an honest living. I need somebody to help me organize some of the larger construction sites. To get ahead you have to have a high school diploma or the equivalent. Don't worry about it I'll put you in with a group that's taking the GED from the local brotherhood."

I aced the test and received my GED, making up for the year I lost when I was put back in grade four. Big John held a mini-graduation ceremony for me. He invited Nina along with some guys from the union hall. He served cheese and Joey's bread. We washed it down with his home-brewed beer. Eunice and Joey performed a recorder and zither duet of bluegrass and folk music. Eunice's voice rose in a striking rendition of Woody Guthrie's ode to migrant workers "Pastures of Plenty". Big John rolled in a wheelbarrow overflowing cans of soda and more bottles of brew on ice.

The party atmosphere turned somber when one of Big John's union buddies, a short black guy with a shaved head, said, "It's all well and good to try to sign up the sites John, but it don't mean spit if the only ones biting is the brothers and the Mexicans. Those that join will be blackballed from construction work and those that don't will still be making three bucks an hour less than white boys doing the same damn work."

"What would happen if all the Blacks and Mexicans walked off the sites at the same time?" John asked.

"They'd hire more."

"And if those fellows walked too?"

"What's your point John?"

"If you don't have the Blacks and Mexicans to haul dirt and tote bricks and beams, the sites will have to shut down."

"Hell John–" a lanky white guy in a baseball cap held up his right hand. The tips of his index and middle finger were missing. "This is Texas not Detroit."

Big John snorted and launched into a speech about how he'd gone toe-to-toe with motor city goons and scabs in the forties and fifties.

"Shit John, the boys down here don't hire goons. They thump you themselves or put a slug between your eyes. You got no friends in Big D or Cowtown 'specially since your national came out against the war. Even I got a hard time standing by you. I'm a loyal union man but I'm also a loyal American."

"You can be both, Russell," Big John said.

"Don't see how."

Russell finished his beer, tipped his baseball cap to Eunice and left the house.

On Monday Big John packed Johnny and me into the back of his station wagon. His office, a twenty-four-foot trailer, sat on cinder blocks in a vacant lot.

The inside of the trailer was gutted. A few folding chairs and tables stacked with literature were lined up along the walls. At the rear of the tin house, where the bedroom used to be, were two steel desks. A fat man at the smaller of the heavy desks sweated bullets as he pecked at an Olivetti typewriter circa 1940. Big John sat behind the bigger desk in a leather chair. In several places the chair had been repaired with duct tape.

Harold pushed himself out of the chair. He plodded over to the literature tables and deposited a bundle of pamphlets in two "Union of Bricklayers and Allied Craftworkers" bags.

"Let's hit the bricks rookies," he said and shoved the bags in our arms. About forty minutes later Harold dropped us off across the street from a high-rise construction site.

"Make sure that when you boys pass out literature you keep outside the site. If you put one foot inside, you're liable to get busted for trespassing or worse. I'll pick you up at three."

Most of the workers ignored us when we tried to hand them literature or took it then tossed it on the ground. By 1 o'clock we were discouraged and bored.

"Let's go on site and talk with the workers one-on- one," I suggested.

Johnny shook his head. "Not a good idea, man. It would be seen by the courts as a provocation for some foreman and his crew to take you apart."

Johnny hoped that there would be more action than this when he went to DC in November. Over a half million anti-war activists were going to descend on the capitol. He talked about sit-ins at the justice department and how a peace chain of people linked by their arms would encircle the Pentagon. The event sounded like a massive demonstration of Thoreau's passive civil disobedience in action.

"I'll go with you," I said.

Johnny brightened up. "I thought I'd be on my own. Everyone else I've spoken to is more concerned with making it through senior year."

*

I kept tabs on the home front through Jeff. We met at Lee Park, the hippie hangout in Dallas, or at the Nature Trails. According to Jeff, Dad raged that my resistance to taking discipline like a man was an indicator of my deviant leanings. He should have clued in earlier. Even my sports preferences were, when you came down to it, questionable pastimes.

My father knew where I was but chose to let me wallow in my life of filth and depravity. For this I owe him a measure of gratitude. While I stayed with the Jardins no one raised a hand to me. I was spared hearing the Colonel calling me names or insulting my mother and siblings. I could see myself plotting a course happily through life without him. Maybe I'd pick up a trade and continue to work as a union organizer until I earned enough money to go to college. That was the plan.

Three days before Johnny and I were to leave for Washington a violent knock shook the house. I was seated at the kitchen table with Johnny going over the list of possible places to stay in DC. Eunice dropped the pottery bowl she was casting.

"Who the hell do you think are, General Patton?" Big John's voice boomed when he flung open the door.

"I'm Colonel Brown and I'm here to pick up my son. Now get him out here, now!"

The sound of my father's voice felt like a blow to the gut. My throat constricted.

"You wait here. I'll go see if he wants to see you, Ernie."

"Mr. Jardin, my friends call me Ernie, my subordinates call me Colonel Brown."

I entered the foyer and stood next to Big John. The colonel lunged at me but Mr. Jardin stepped between us.

"Your Grandfather died last night. The funeral is in two days. Get your things."

Stunned by the abruptness of his announcement I asked, "How? Granddad Agerton was in perfect health."

"You have more than one grandfather you worthless piece of humanity."

My memories of the cigar-chewing politico were neutral at best. Still, the man standing in front of me with his fists clenched was my father and by convention I was supposed to express sympathy.

"I'm sorry."

"You'll be more than sorry if you don't get into the car and come home with me. They're expecting you at the funeral. Nobody there knows about the cesspool you've made of your life. I've kept that quiet. You got to the count of three to hustle your ass outside before I beat you to a pulp and drag you out."

"Hang on there, Colonel, this is my property and David is my guest. He doesn't go anywhere unless he wants to."

My father moved back two feet and turned his body sideways. One arm formed a right angle in front of his chest and his other arm cocked at shoulder height with his knuckles facing the ground brought forth the image of some guys in Special Forces who practiced martial arts at the base gym. A whistle that became a thin laugh escaped my father. "Big John, isn't that what they call you?"

"Mr. Jardin to you," Big John replied with a nervous tremor in his voice.

"When you came to the door you were out of breath and had to brace yourself against the wall. You also walk with a limp. From the looks of your face, you've lost more fights than you've won."

"What's your point, Ernie?"

"Just this, step away from my son."

"You don't have to go unless you want to David."

"Here's the deal I'm prepared to make," Dad said. "You keep your mouth shut and your eyes front and center at the funeral. You speak only when spoken to and only then to say thank you and yes sir or no sir to the people who come to pay their respects and I'll cut you loose when we return. You won't ever have to see me again and I sure the hell don't want anything to do with you."

"I'd get that in writing if I were you," Big John said.

"I warned you. Keep out of this, slacker."

"Where do you get off calling me a slacker?"

My father's cat like green eyes transformed to reptilian. "My friends down at the selective service bureau filled me in on how you tried to get out of serving in Korea as a conscientious objector."

"I volunteered to be a medic, but they turned me down."

"Sure. You and a thousand other shirkers."

I recognized my father's strategy. He was baiting Big John.

"It's okay Big John, I'll go to the funeral." I moved out from behind him and faced my father.

"Be a man, Colonel, promise your son that you'll keep your end of the bargain."

"I promise to have a truce until we get back from Birmingham and then you're on your own, free to do whatever your pansy ass desires."

"Get in the back," Dad whispered, as we walked out to his car. "If you sit in the front with me, I'm liable to kill you before the funeral."

Chapter 49

When Dad and I arrived at the house the gate of the stockade enclosing the backyard was open.

"Son-of-a-bitch! How many times do I have to tell Jeff to set the latch? I'm going to kick his ass until his nose bleeds. The dog's going to run away and get hit by a truck."

'Only if he's lucky,' I thought.

Dad pulled me out of the car. He flung my bag at my chest. As I started for the front of the house he yelled, "Where the hell do you think you're going?"

I didn't respond.

"You're sleeping in the rec. room. If I had my way, I'd chain you to the lamppost. Your mother will bring you your meals. We leave at 0600 sharp."

What Dad euphemistically called the rec. room was the back of a converted two-car garage.

"Anything else?"

"Yeah, keep your mouth shut. I don't want you anywhere near your brothers, infecting them with your sickness."

"That's going to be kind of hard since we'll be traveling in the same car. Unless of course you intend to tie me to the roof rack."

Dad threw his car keys at my head, missing me by a good two feet.

"Mort Ewing has been accepted to LSU," mom informed me when she brought me a tray of food. Do you know Tory? He received a partial scholarship to North Texas State. You could try for one."

"Yeah, I know him."

"His mother is such a nice person. She warned me about the company you're keeping."

Mom rambled on about the new books she was reading and recited from memory some missive she'd fired off to a local paper on insidious witchcraft sects and communist organizations that were brainwashing America's youth. At one point she even sat down next to me on the tattered plaid couch that served as my bed. She stroked my hair then sneaked her hand under my shirt and scratched my back. I moved away. She began to cry.

"You used to like me to do that when you were little. I'd ask you; do you love me. You'd hug me and say yes, I love you more than anything in the whole world. Do you remember telling me how when you grew up you were going to buy me a mink coat and lots of books?"

She had aged ten years since we left Germany. For a time, she dyed her hair but stopped when my father told her he loved the silver. Her hair was now the color of steel wool, her eyes as flat and drab as construction paper. The woman with the smile that had captivated all who knew her had become a gaunt, chain-smoking author of crank letters, a recluse in her own home.

"What happened to us, David? You're associating with bad people. They poisoned your mind against everything you were brought up to believe in."

378

At 4 o'clock in the morning Dad threw on the light switch. "Get your stinking carcass up before I beat you with a shovel. Your mother wants you to eat breakfast."

My sister was seated at the breakfast bar feeding my nephew. Jan had arrived the night before but since I was sequestered in the rec. room, I had not seen her. Tom and Jeff ate in the dining room, so I wouldn't contaminate them.

Despite the Colonel's command to ignore my presence, Janet wished me good morning. When his back was turned, she said, "It means a lot to Dad that you're going to the funeral."

"Where's Fred?"

She shrugged and slipped a spoonful of cream of wheat into Chris' mouth.

By 5:45 the Brown clan was packed into a station wagon and on the road to Alabama. The Colonel had attached his eta to a clipboard, indicating every rest stop, gas fill up, and bathroom break between Dallas and Birmingham.

"Come hell or high water we will stick to schedule," he forewarned my mother. "If any of you got any business to do, do it now because the first stop isn't for six hours."

True to form what should have been a ten or eleven-hour trip took 16 hours. We drove through East Texas, Louisiana and Mississippi, past acre after acre of muddy November fields and sharecroppers' shacks. Three and half hours away from Birmingham an explosion at the back of the wagon caused it to swerve off the two-lane blacktop onto the shoulder. The rear tire on the passenger side was split open at the white wall.

The Colonel had spent two hours the previous evening fitting every item in the station wagon like pieces of a jigsaw puzzle. In less than two minutes Jeff and I destroyed his masterpiece.

When all the bags were removed Dad shoved me aside and opened the spare tire compartment. He struggled a few minutes to loosen the wing nut that secured the jack to the spare, then jerked it out and tossed it down. The tread did not bounce like it should have. It flattened out on the gravel surface of the road.

"Goddamn," my father screamed. He hurled the lug wrench over a split log fence into a field. "Go get the son-of-a-bitch," he ordered me.

I jumped over a drainage ditch and sank to my ankles in the pure Mississippi bottomland. A watermelon truck belching oil and exhaust fumes sputtered to a stop behind us. Two black men standing in its bed leaned over a wooden fence. The driver's door yawned open, and another black man hopped onto the road. The two men in the truck kept their eyes on the ground while the driver approached my father. Although he towered above my Dad, he hunched his shoulders as if to diminish his height.

"You got a spare, Mister?"

"That is the spare," Dad said and walked to a higher point on the shoulder.

The black man's bowed head rose above my father. He nodded at the desiccated tire on the right rear side of the wagon.

My father kept looking back at my mother and sister and then at the driver's side of the car where he kept his 22 Colt Woodsman under the seat.

"That's okay. I have a CB in the car. I'm sure somebody will send help once I radio."

"Mister, you too far away from anywhere to get help. Only trucks pass this way hightailing it out of Mississippi and the only udder trucks be road gangs from the pea farm."

Dad waited until a Freightliner nearly blew him into the ditch with its air wake. "You men know a garage around here?"

"Sure do. My cousin got a place up the road. He can do that spare so it get you going where you going."

"Mind taking my boys with you?"

Dad handed me a twenty-dollar bill. The driver went around to the passenger side of the truck and untwisted a wire that held the door closed. Jeff got in first leaving me the window. I found out when I tried to roll it up that there was no glass. My mother turned her head and stared at the field as the truck pulled away.

The driver said, "Your Daddy don't smile much, do he?"

The truck pulled off the two-lane highway bouncing and rattling along a country road that was little more than a dirt path with two-wheel ruts the width of a car's axle. It threw up a cloud of dust when it skidded to a stop in front of a raw pine cabin that leaned to one side. Scattered around the yard were parts of automobiles. A red crank operated gas pump stood beside the skeleton of an old car propped up on blocks. A yellow man with kinky hair the tint of turmeric walked out of the cabin. With what might have been the only tooth left in his head he sucked and gnawed on a piece of jerky. The neck of a bottle stuck out of the bib pocket of his overalls. He pulled it out and took a swig of clear liquid that smelled like kerosene and tar.

"Can you fix it?" the driver asked.

The yellow man gulped down the liquid and started chewing on the now sufficiently softened piece of jerky.

"It gonna cost." He then held up three fingers.

I dug the twenty out of my pocket. When I tried to hand it to him, he jumped back as if I had tried to pass him a rattlesnake.

"Why you showing that to me? I look like a bank to y"?ou

The driver walked to his truck and returned with a mason jar filled to the top with coins. He carefully counted out three dollars and gave it to the yellow man. Within thirty minutes the man had inspected the tire and returned it to the driver fully repaired and inflated.

When we got back Dad was pacing up and down the shoulder smoking a cigarette. If he was glad to see us alive and whole, he didn't show it. The driver jacked up the car and changed the blowout for the spare before Dad had time to protest.

"Give me what you have left of that twenty," Dad ordered. His eyes went black when I gave him back the bill. "Who paid for the tire?"

"He did," I said.

Dad opened his billfold. "What do I owe you?"

The driver waved his hands. "What a man does for his fellow man in this life so shall he reap tenfold in the kingdom to come."

My father put away his wallet and held out his hand to the driver. The man looked down at my father's long tapered fingers then cupped Dad's hand between both of his. He pumped my father's arm for all it was worth.

*

We arrived at my Grandfather Agerton's around 10 that night. My father twisted his body, leaned over his seat, and punched me. "Your grandparents don't know about the abortion you've made of your life. You keep your mouth shut and pretend everything is fine." He aimed another fist at my chest. I blocked it and pushed his arm away. He rose from his seat but stopped when the front door of the house slammed.

"Norma, Ernest, we were beginning to get worried," my grandfather said.

"Sorry Mr. Agerton, we had car trouble."

Jeff and I removed all the bags. Dad put one of them back and closed the tailgate. He turned on the ignition. "Sorry I can't stay longer, Mr. Agerton. Thanks for letting Norma and the kids stay with you. There's not enough room over at Mother's for Charlie's brood and all of us."

"That's what family is for, Ernest. Give Mrs. Brown our condolences. We called but she didn't have time to speak."

Dad motioned me over to the car before driving away. "Remember, you keep your end and I'll keep mine."

"Want to talk about it?" Granddad Agerton asked after my father left.

"About what?"

"Down here it's the oldest boy's duty to stay by his father's side in times like this."

"A lot's changed since you last saw us, Granddad."

"No it hasn't. Your Daddy's a hard man. Be careful. Hard men breed hard sons."

*

I stood by the Chief's open casket. By late afternoon the stench of lilacs, lilies, jasmine, and roses began to turn my stomach. Tommy sat at the foot of the coffin; his eyes fixed on the floor. Every few seconds a shudder ripped through his six-year-old body and jerked his shoulders up to his ears. My Uncle Jackson, the Chief's youngest brother, hoisted Tommy in the air and forced him to kiss the waxy cheek of the corpse. A chorus of "He's here," shattered the funeral home's atmosphere of contrived solemnity.

I left my station and peered down the corridor through the open double doors, curious to know who was here. I went outside and saw Dad and Uncle Charlie crossing the parking lot at a good clip toward a doughboy figure slumped in a wheelchair. A black man in hospital scrubs steered the wheelchair. Two scowling bodyguards built like fullbacks stood on either side of the invalid. The bodyguards and the invalid were dressed identically in Dick Tracy hats, sunglasses, dark suits, white shirts and narrow ties. The old man swatted away the hand of one of the guards when he reached down to help him out of the wheelchair. Gripping both arms of the chair he grimaced and pushed himself to his feet. He stood erect long enough to wave feebly at Dad and Charlie then collapsed in his seat and gasped for air. After he had recovered his breath my father pointed to the stairs, eight in total that led to the entranceway. The old man's head recoiled. He clamped his jaw like a bulldog. His men rolled him up to the stairs and lifted the chair into the funeral parlor. He rose a few inches from his chair, peered into the oversized jewelry box of a casket, then told his men. "Get on with it. I seen what I come to see, done my duty."

"Were you coming to pay your respects, Bull, or see if he was really dead?" Louise snapped

"Let's get out of here," croaked Bull Connor, retired Public Safety Commissioner and life-long racist.

The Chief's funeral flotilla of Cadillacs and Buicks proceeded through rich and poor neighborhoods. Eventually we arrived at what had been up until 1960 a whites-only cemetery. Shopkeepers, politicians and community leaders from both sides of the color barrier joined the train of quasi-mourners.

I don't remember the eulogy. I do remember shaking hands until my palms were raw. I also recall the awful silences between my father and me. My anger toward him had softened. He was the backbone of the family. He spoke on behalf of his mother who, he said, was too full of grief to talk. He was the one in charge of doing the right thing. He clasped hands, bowed his head to everyone and thanked them for coming.

Charlie took the role of the good old boy, laughing and telling stories about his "Pappy". He invited the Chief's select group of high rollers and cronies to the house for a drink and to reminisce. The rest of the mourners ended up having dinner at my Great Aunt Virginia's, the Chief's youngest sister. Her house was full of men smoking the

Chief's Havanas. They tossed back raw shots of Wild Turkey, Johnny Walker, and clear gin chased by yarns about the Chief.

My Great Uncle Roy, a retired railroad cop, poured himself a tumbler of gin and said, "Some men accused the Chief of being a nigger lover." He drained the glass and turned it over to signal he'd had enough.

Roy held up his left hand. Three fingers were missing, severed at the knuckles when a bum slid the door of a freight car shut. "He was no such a thing though he did often say the Klan was nothing more than a bunch of white trash out to finish off what was left of the South. Black, white, Indian or Chinaman, the Chief judged a person man-by-man."

My father listened as though Roy's comment was a news flash. He turned over his uncle's glass and poured him another drink.

Next was my Great Uncle Jackson's turn to speak. "The Chief was more like a father than a brother to me. He got a place for me in the fire department. Didn't have to take no civil service exam. He told me if I messed up, I'd wish I'd never been born." Jackson had made out fine. He was a fire station captain and had started a second career as manager trainee in a savings and loan company. "Ernie, your Pap thought you'd made a mistake not sticking with the fire department until you got through dental school. Still, he was proud of what you did. You got a steel spine and a head hard as granite, he used to say. He joked that he lost count how many straps he wore out on you and how many sticks he broke over your shoulders."

"I lost count myself." Dad drained his glass of Bourbon.

"You boys are awful quiet," Jackson said. "Especially you David."

When my father looked at me, I could hear his neck crack. "He's got a lot on his mind. He has to decide what he's going to do after finishing school."

"Go. to college, boy. No offense, Ernie, but this is no time to be joining the military."

Dad continued drinking. His face became more and more flushed as the evening wore on, but his speech remained flawless. My mother told him he should be bringing us back to her parents.

It had been a long day for all of us. Dad said goodbye to his uncles and aunts. He told Louise that he would be back later to take her home. As we walked to the car my father dropped his keys. He swayed and stumbled as he stepped off the curb to pick them up.

Granddad Agerton was waiting for us on the porch swing. Mom walked a drowsy Tommy to the house and Janet carried Chris in. I started to get out but stopped when Dad said, "Where do you think you're going?"

We fell back into our seats. "Jeff, go inside. I want to talk to David, alone!"

Dad leaned over the back of the seat and pulled me toward him. The sickening stench of cigar and Wild Turkey washed over me. "You think I hate you. I don't." As he spoke, tears formed in his eyes never making it past his lower eyelashes. "I just want you to be a better man than I am. I won't have you regretting what might have been and making up for it the rest of your life."

Then, without taking a breath, Lt. Colonel E. H. Brown reverted to his old self. "I wasn't joking when I told you back in Irving to keep your sissy mouth shut. I told you to speak only when spoken to." He slapped me across the face and tried to pull me over the backrest.

I planted my feet on the back of the front seat. Kicking myself free I shouted, "I haven't said a word."

"It's not what you say it's how you don't say anything that speaks loud and clear. You don't think people know what's going on in that fucking depraved head of yours?"

"That's enough, Ernest. You best be going back to your mother." My Granddad opened my car door and helped me out. "I'm sure she'll be needing you."

"You got until we get to Irving to decide what you're going to do," Dad warned me before he sped off.

My Granddad draped his long thin arm around my neck, led me up the stairs to the porch and sat with me in the swing. "I'd let you stay here but that wouldn't do anyone any good, especially your mother. Your father might hold it against her."

"It's okay, Granddad," I said, knowing that what had happened in the car was only the preliminary round.

"Be careful David. Your mother has filled me in on some of what's been going on."

"It's not as bad as she makes it out to be. I'm not that bad, Granddad."

"It seldom is and you're not."

"Things are out of control. I don't want to hurt anyone. All I want is to-"

My Grandfather shook his head. "Don't tell me all you want to do is make your father happy. Don't try. That man was born unhappy and lives to make others unhappy."

"I thought of joining the Air Force."

"Think that's a good idea?"

"No, but it's the only one I got."

"Think that'll please him?"

"No. He wants me to join the Marines."

Chapter 50

When Dad pulled up to the house, Fred was leaning against the side of his car. Marvin Gay could be heard playing on the radio through his open window. Janet handed Chris to her husband and got in the driver's seat. They drove away without exchanging a word.

Jeff and I unloaded the station wagon and carried the luggage into the den. My father kicked the door closed behind me and dropped me with a straight right to the chin.

"Think you're going somewhere, pansy?"

I rolled to my feet. "You promised me I could leave if I went with you to Birmingham."

"You're crazy if you think I'm going to let you loose on society."

"You say there's nothing worse than a liar and yet that's all you've ever done to us!"

He closed the distance between us and punched me in the mouth. "Tomorrow you join the Marines."

"Like hell I am. You might be able to order around some enlisted man but I'm not in your goddamn army."

I reached for the doorknob. Dad spun me around and kneed me in the stomach. I stayed upright despite the pain.

"Stop it!" Jeff shouted. He grabbed Dad from behind. "You said he could leave if he went to the funeral."

391

Dad smashed him in the face with a back elbow and tossed him across the room. My eyes fell on the polished wooden handle of an ice pick. It ended up in my hand. Dad took a couple of steps forward but tripped when I flung a folding chair at his legs.

"Get up and I'll kill you," I said.

"You'll go to jail if you use that," Dad croaked.

"You'll go to hell if I do." My nerves tingled with an electric rush.

Jeff shook off Dad's blow and placed himself in front of my father, giving me a clear path to the door. "Let him go Sir."

I backed out of the den pointing the ice pick at my father. Once out in the yard, I threw the weapon into the bushes and raced down the street. I must have covered over a mile before I slid on my ass down the concrete sides of a storm ditch. It wasn't until nightfall that I dared to climb out of the culvert. Sick to my stomach, ashamed and scared, I knew I'd crossed the line. What was the punishment for violating the commandment of honor thy father? But even if it was death, it was preferable to living with the Colonel.

My first inclination was to go to Big John's house, but I could not bring myself to expose him and his family to more trouble than I already had.

With nowhere else to go I knocked on Eliot's apartment door. I expected he would turn me away, but he invited me in. Marcy was sprawled on the couch. Her pupils were dilated, and her blouse was unbuttoned exposing her naked breasts.

"Hi there," she said.

"She's not so bad when she's not on the rag and has plenty of dope," Eliot said. "You're welcome to stay as long as Marcy's happy and high."

She remained in this condition for close to a month keeping straight only long enough to complete her shift at Jack in the Box.

Chapter 51

November 1969 through February 1970 was hazy. I knew that somebody landed or didn't land on the moon and that the debate raged on whether or not Paul McCartney was dead. I'd been kicked out of school, severed all ties with my parents, and was an unwanted crasher at Eliot's place. The only bright side was that Nina ignored her father's warnings to steer clear of me.

I worked for a day-to-day manual labor agency that paid me below minimum wage. Most of the money I earned went to food and rent. I put away whatever funds were left in a gym sock to finance my escape from Texas.

"That's a dumb idea," Nina protested when I tried to persuade her to go with me. "You have your GED. You should enroll in a junior college at night."

One evening Jeff and Nina were waiting for me outside Eliot's place. My brother backed away from me when I got close. I reeked of nitrate fertilizer, sheep shit, and topsoil after hours of laying sod. Nina held her breath, pulled me to her, and kissed me.

"What's going on?" I asked.

"Dad is filing charges against you for the ice pick thing."

"That was weeks ago."

"He says he has to get you off the streets to protect society. If the courts don't throw you in jail, he's gonna have you committed."

"Come inside."

"Sorry, I have to live at home till I graduate. If Dad finds out I spoke to you, well I don't have to say more, do I?"

Nina visited me every day at the apartment despite the fact that my father had persuaded Mr. Beaudry to file a peace bond against me. If I came within a hundred yards of Nina, her old man would have me arrested. In the act as well were Lesman and Berk. They had secured an injunction forbidding me within two miles of MacArthur High. In essence, I was banished from Irving.

The doorbell rang and Johnny, Floe, and Hugh entered the apartment.

Floe hugged me. "The whole school knows about the fight with your father."

Hugh wrung his hands. "You ought to press charges."

"As soon as I walk into the police station they'll throw me in a cell."

"There's one way around all this," Johnny said. "Big John says that if you enlist, you'll be in the clear with your old man."

Nina shook her head. "I thought we were against the war."

"Nobody says he has to join the Army. He can sign up for the Coast Guard," Johnny said.

Floe kissed me on the forehead. "This is Karma, David. This is your chance to shake things up. Once in the Army you can organize soldiers against the war."

I nodded knowing that if I joined anything, it would be the Coast Guard. And that I'd lived in the military for seventeen years and had no intention of being caught protesting the war in uniform. I also thought that if I signed up, Dad might forgive me.

"It saves me the trouble of tossing your ass out," Marcy commented coldly. "Now where the fuck's the Midol?"

The next morning Johnny drove me to the recruiting station where I stood in queue at the Coast Guard office for three hours. When I finally made it to the front of the line the recruiter told me to put my name on a waiting list.

"How long is the list?"

The recruiter smirked. "Between two to three years. You could always go into the Peace Corps but the wait there is into the next decade. By that time the Army will own your ass."

Dejected, I walked down the hall. A sailor whistled at me from the Navy Recruitment door. He looked like Gene Kelley. He was wearing his cracker jacks. His white Navy cap was tipped at an angle just above his left eyebrow. I lost count of the ribbons on his chest and stripes and bars on his sleeves.

"What's wrong, kid?"

"The Coast Guard is back logged with people wanting to get in."

"Yeah, tons of guys are trying to sign up to keep from getting drafted and sent to some damn rice paddy. Ever thought of the Navy? Chances of going to Vietnam are a million to one. Even if you're sent, you'll more than likely end up floating on a ship a hundred miles off the coast."

"I'm not afraid to fight."

"Good, the Navy needs guys who aren't chicken shit. Ever heard of the Fleet Marines? They're corpsmen who serve alongside the Marines. How about UDT, under water demolition team, these guys make the Green Berets look like pussies. And then there are the SEALS. Oh man, they're scary dudes! Come in for a coffee and I'll show you some literature. You know, you can swing it to go through tech schools for almost your whole stint and when you get out, you'll have your college education paid for. Nuclear Sub sailors earn the equivalent of two years university credits in physics and engineering."

By the time I finished my doughnut I'd enlisted for a four-year hitch.

In the evening I phoned my friends and told them to meet me at the Nature Trails. Then I called the Colonel's house. My mother answered.

"You've nearly driven your father out of his mind. All he wants is for you boys to become the kind of men that he can be proud of. Is that so much to ask?"

"Mom, let me speak to the Colonel."

"Ernest, my wrist," Mom cried.

"This is none of your damn business, Norma!" Dad growled into the mouthpiece.

"I enlisted," I said before he could slam down the receiver.

"What branch?"

"The Navy."

"Figures."

"What figures?"

"Figures that you'd enlist in the only service that allows you to dress like a twinkie and keeps you out of harm's way."

I bit my tongue. "I'm leaving the 24th of November. The recruiter gave me the option of leaving then or after the New Year. I told him that the holidays don't count for much around our place."

"Makes sense," he said.

*

The campfire was blazing when I met with my friends. Johnny blamed himself for coming up with the suggestion. "When I told Big John how you intended to make waves once you were in, he freaked. He says if you make trouble in uniform you'll end up with a one-way ticket to Leavenworth."

"Don't worry I'll steer clear of trouble."

"Sure, like you did at school," Nina said.

She must have sensed that peace, love and people power were the furthest things from my mind. What I really wanted to do was lob Molotov cocktails through Lesman and Berk's picture windows. I wanted to corner the punk who threw the beer can at me and beat him senseless. I wanted to burn down the world around me.

But all I did was shrug. "What choice do I have?"

Nina rose as if emerging from the flames. She led me away into the shadows of the forest and with her body said, "You're not alone. I'll be here for you when you get back."

When I arrived at Eliot's apartment, he handed me my bag. "You better find another place to stay. Nina's father called. He said that if I'm abetting you in fucking his daughter then I'm an accessory to statutory rape. Sorry man, you gotta go."

Chapter 52

I played movable crash pads until the time came for me to leave for San Diego. On my last afternoon as a civilian, I said goodbye to my folks. My father thrust an oblong box covered in silver paper at me.

"This is for you," Dad said. "If it hadn't have been for your mother I would have had the courts lock you up and throw away the key. You want me to forgive and forget the hell you've put me through just because you enlisted. Forget it. The Navy is not what I had in mind. You belong in the Marines. You would have come back alive or dead but either way you would have come back a man."

"Cheer up, Dad. I could have joined the Air Force."

"If I thought you had any true convictions, my opinion of you might be different. The FBI came here after you assaulted me. They told me that you're a suspect in a rash of graffiti and dummy bomb attacks on government buildings. You know what I told them? I told them that you don't have the guts to carry out something like that."

"You're right. If I had any guts, I'd be in Canada right now."

"You know what you are? You're nothing. All my kids are nothing."

"You're right Sir, nothing is us."

Dad pushed the box into my hands. "Open it God damn it! Your mother told me to give it to you as a going away present."

I removed the lid. A chrome Cross pen and pencil were nested inside a puffy fake silk lining.

"From my side I don't care if I ever hear from you again. But your mother does. Do her a favor. Write to her. You haven't managed to kill off her maternal instinct yet."

That night I hitched a ride downtown. Hanging in a darkened window facing the Federal Building was an electric sign shaped like a horseshoe. The name "Lucky's" glimmered in the center of the horseshoe. Inside the smoky, piss odor lounge was a jukebox, and a few empty tables and booths and a quarter a game pool table. Bedraggled patrons balanced precariously on the counter stools.

"Show me some ID," the bartender demanded.

I ignored him.

He slapped a wet towel on the counter. "Now that I got your attention, kid, what are you doing out so late?"

"I'm shipping out at 12:00 AM for basic training in San Diego."

The rest of the night the bartender kept sliding beers down my way. A barfly hovered around a woman who chased down shots of whiskey with Coke setups. He staggered over and patted me on the back. "Good for you, boy. Too many kids today don't give a damn about this country. If I was younger and fitter I'd go with you."

The woman threw her head back. "Hee-haw you old drunk," she brayed. "You got as much of a chance of getting in the army as you do of getting in me." She slid her stool toward me and dropped a hand on my lap. "Come with me sweetie and I'll give you something to remember about Big D."

"Get away from him," the bartender said. "He don't need the kind of lasting memory you'll infect him with." He put his hand on my arm. "Kid, it's time for you to go. You don't want to be AWOL on your first day."

I crossed the street lugging my duffel bag over my shoulder. At the curb a bus idled. The driver snored with his mouth open. A lineup of young men waited outside the Federal Building. A contingent of Salvation Army women handed the recruits blue cloth sacks. In my bag were cookies, a small bottle of after-shave lotion, a can of shaving cream, a razor, a tube of roll-on deodorant, a bottle of mouthwash, toothpaste and a toothbrush, a pack of cigarettes, and a palm size New Testament.

My mind felt numb from the half-dozen brews. As I dropped my bag at my feet, I heard my name.

I turned to see Nina and Johnny walking down the sidewalk. Nina wore a buckskin fringe jacket and hip hugger jeans. Several of the recruits glanced at her approvingly then frowned when they noticed a huge peace symbol hanging from her neck. Nina kissed me until I pushed her away to come up for air.

"Peace brothers," Johnny said and flashed the onlookers a smile.

A Chief Warrant Officer dressed in a double-breasted blue jacket and a white cap with a shiny black bill walked up to the bus. Next to him stood a WAVE holding a clipboard and a stack of file folders pressed to her chest.

"Fall into line. When you hear your name, step forward, take your folder and get on the bus," the Chief ordered. His eyeballs exploded out of their sockets when he saw Nina. "Who the hell invited you here!"

Nina slipped her arm around my waist. "I came to say goodbye to my boyfriend."

"You recruits were told to say your good-byes before coming."

"We didn't have time to see each other off," Nina said. She turned her back and bent over my duffel bag then straightened up.

"Unless you intend to share your charms with every guy here, I suggest you get your sweet young ass out of here."

Nina and Johnny ran down the street to her Pacer. When her car rolled by the line of recruits Nina beeped her horn. She sang out the window, "One two three four what are we fighting for..." Country Joe McDonald's lyrics faded as she sped off.

"Brown, Ernest David," the female sailor called out.

I took my file from the WAVE and tried to get to the bus before the Chief noticed me.

"Hang on there, Seaman Recruit!" He placed his hand on my head, entwined his fingers in my hair and gave it a jerk. "I sure hope that pussy's worth it because I guarantee you when you get to Basic, they will hear about what happened here."

Chapter 53

Nine sailors wearing armbands and white helmets met us in the San Diego airport. They shouted in unison, "Shut up and fall into line you worms!" Then the order came to double-time it out of the airport and stand next to a chain of grey busses at curbside.

I took the window seat at the first bench. A black guy with hair that spread out the width of his shoulders sat next to me. We drove for twenty minutes without either one of us speaking. The bus took a highway exit and drove past a sign that read NAVSTA San Diego / Nimitz Naval Training Center.

"We finally here," my seat-mate said.

I turned my face to the glass and saw block after block of two-story white buildings along the waterfront. The bus slowed down as it approached a gate. Coral-colored guardhouses with terracotta roofs and an elaborate iron arch connecting them stood on each side of the gate. If it were not for the white helmeted sailors standing at attention, their rifles at their heels, the Naval Base could have passed for a California film studio.

My seatmate shivered. "Boy it's cold."

The endless rows of white buildings awakened me from my stupor. The hard truth of what I had gotten myself into sank in.

"Could be worse. We could be at Great Lakes," my seat-mate said. He used his fingers like a pick to fluff up his Afro.

"I'm from Bowling Green but I been to Chicago. That's no place to be in the winter. This base is gonna be like a vacation compared to Great Lakes. I made a mistake going now instead of after the New Year. Instead of nine weeks I found out we gonna be here 13 weeks to account for the holidays. Hell of a way to spend a Christmas, ain't it?"

The guy wouldn't shut up. I pressed my nose to the glass. He flicked my ear.

"What do you want?"

"Just a little conversation, home boy. When I say something, you supposed to say something back. Like I say, 'Hell of a way to spend a Christmas, ain't it?' Then you gotta answer. Otherwise, I might think you just another racist honky."

"It doesn't matter."

"Sure it does. We might end up in the same barracks and carry that bad blood over."

"No, man, I mean it doesn't matter where I spend the holidays. It's not a tradition I hold to."

"That's cool." He told me his name was Kaiser Jenkin.

"Stow the noise back there," the driver shouted.

The bus pulled up between two open sided structures resembling an outdoor flea market. Beyond them stood three white wood buildings. On the largest of the buildings a sign that rose ten feet high and stretched twenty feet in length warned or greeted the new recruits with a cryptic message.

WELCOME ABOARD
YOU ARE NOW A MEMBER OF

**THE UNITED STATES NAVY
THE TRADITION OF THE SERVICE
DEMANDS YOUR UTMOST EFFORT
GIVE IT CHEERFULLY
AND WILLINGLY!**

The door of the bus opened, and an Ensign second class jumped into the aisle. A weathered Chief Petty Officer climbed the stairs and stood behind him scowling.

"As the Chief calls your name you will stand tall and say present, then proceed off the bus and take a seat on one of the benches under the first covered section. Be sure that you fill a bench completely from left to right before starting on another bench. Do I make myself clear!"

"As clear as piss." The words escaped even as my mind warned my lips to keep still.

The Chief slipped past the waifish junior officer and strode toward me. He slapped the back of my head and pulled me to my feet. "Did I hear the Ensign give you permission to speak, worm!"

I glared at the Chief and imagined driving my matching Cross pen and pencil set through his bulging eyeballs. "Which of the two sections is the first one and do we sit from his left or our left on the bench?" I asked.

"No one gave you permission to open your fucking mouth, worm!" He slapped the back of my head again. "Are you a smart ass or just stupid?"

"Stand down Chief," The Ensign said.

The lifer held up his hand. "Sir! I struck with an open palm, Sir."

"Carry on Chief. Proceed to move these recruits off the bus and assemble them as per my order under the section to their right. First induction lecture is in 45 minutes at 0500."

"Aye-aye Sir," The Chief said as the Ensign stepped off the bus. The Chief's humorless smile said your sorry asses belong to me.

"Brown, Ernest David!" he bellowed.

"Present, Sir."

"Don't call me Sir, you low life civilian scum. I am a Chief Petty Officer in this man's Navy. Now move it. We ain't got all day."

Outside, the brackish fog of a San Diego November morning soaked through my T-shirt. Trying to breath was like placing my nose an inch away from a humidifier and inhaling a mouthful of water. The sour smell of kelp and seaweed mixed with the pervasive stench of rotting eggs and diesel fumes.

I took my place on the far end of the first bench and watched as the induction shelter filled up with hundreds of recruits.

My entire life I'd been a conscript in the private military of Lt. Colonel E.H. Brown. I didn't give a squat about "THE TRADITION OF THE SERVICE". I had no intention of giving my utmost effort cheerfully or willingly. I had done my time and was through. I didn't care who I pissed off or on whom I trampled. I intended to put the minimal effort into serving and the maximum effort into disturbing the indoctrination plan of the Naval Recruit Training Center.

A young sailor dressed in newly issued blues ordered us to stand tall and fall into two lines. "When I say double time you will run behind me to the mess hall where you will eat. You will then return here and retake your current seats."

We ran behind the newly minted sailor. The rotten egg smell grew stronger as we neared the cafeteria. The sailor blew his whistle and shouted, "Eyes down, halt!"

Running past us, six sailors wielding nightsticks chased a dozen men with shaved heads. They were dressed in dungarees with 40/50 stencilled on their denim shirts. One of the men fell down. Two of the chasers screamed at him to get up. They took feeble swipes at his legs and buttocks with their clubs.

"Get out the way you fucking pussies," the middle-aged noncom leading the group shouted. He had four hash marks on his blouse's cuff and four chevrons. He snatched a nightstick from one of the chasers and brought it down so hard on the ass of the prisoner who had fallen that I heard bone crack. "Get up!" The noncom unbuttoned the holster attached to a wide white belt perforated with rows of silver grommets. He pulled out a forty-five semi-automatic pistol and cocked the hammer. "Start blubbering and I'll blow your head off."

Then he looked at us. "Watch your step worms or you'll end up like these pieces of worthless shit."

The prisoners fell back into step and raced out of sight. The sailor leading us to chow said, "40/50" the recruit brig. You guys don't want to screw up. Once you're there, the chasers will work you over then send you back to Basic where you'll start over from day one. As a Seaman Recruit, you're nothing. You got no opinions, no privacy, and no rights. Keep your mouth shut, keep your eyes open, keep you racks made, march when you're told to, make sure your boots and shoes are spit and polish, learn to fold your clothes and stow your gear as per the Blue Jacket Manual and you'll make it through Basic. You'll be bored shitless, but you won't have any bruises."

Powdered eggs and toast the texture of asbestos shingles washed down by watery coffee and warm milk comprised our first hot breakfast. I pressed my tray flat against my chest when a mess worker tried to drop a large serving of the reconstituted eggs into one of the metal pockets of the tray and did not lower it until I reached a section of the serving line where small boxes of non-sweetened cereal were laid out beside bananas and a basket of apples.

On my way to a table a Signalman First Class and a black Chief Petty Officer were dressing down a recruit for leaving half a banana and a spoonful of scrambled eggs on his tray.

"Chief, it's bad enough that I have to watch this fucking civilian try to use a fork. I'll be goddamned if I let him waste Uncle Sam's food."

"You're right, Jones."

The Chief ordered a mess worker to bring over a dish loaded with eggs from the steam table. The rapidly cooling yellow curds were placed in front of the recruit.

The recruit hesitated but dug in when Signalman First Class Jones slammed his fist on the tabletop. "Eat and don't stop eating until Chief Petty Officer Bert says to stop." The recruit shoveled the foul-smelling glob into his mouth and swallowed. Jones and Bert walked away without telling him to stop eating.

My meagre breakfast choice proved to be wise given the fact we had fifteen minutes to eat before we were ordered to get to our feet and double-time it to the induction center. The recruit who had been forced to gorge on the powdered eggs looked like he was going to be sick.

"If you throw up, you'll spoon it up and eat it a second time," our escort warned him.

When we arrived at the indoctrination center, we had only a few seconds to catch our breaths. We assembled in front of a flagpole that resembled a ship's mast. Milling around the pole, we shivered in the early morning mist as the sun climbed over the bay.

Three sailors decked out in dress whites marched out of the main building. The sailor in the middle carried a flag folded in a triangle. The other two sailors, to the right and left of him carried M-1 carbines. The flag detail approached the mast.

"Attention!" our escort hollered.

The Ensign who'd greeted us on arrival and the two noncoms from the mess hall crossed the grounds and snapped off a salute to the detail.

The sailor carrying the flag clipped it to the mast's rope and as reveille was piped through loudspeakers, drew it up to the top of the pole.

"As you were, Seamen Recruits," the Ensign said. "Did you enjoy your breakfast?"

Before anyone could reply Jones said, "The Ensign asked you men a question. He expects an answer."

"Did you enjoy your breakfast?" the Ensign repeated.

There was a sleepy discordant chorus of "yeahs".

Chief Petty Officer Bert marched across the asphalt grinder and shoved the first person he reached. "When an officer asks you a question there are only two things that better come out of those holes you shovel food into." Bert turned around and pointed a thin baton at me. "What are those two things, worm?"

"Yes Sir and no Sir," I said.

Bert paused, perhaps debating whether he should push it further, then switched tracks and screamed, "Worms, get back to your correct bench."

"I'm happy to learn that you enjoyed your breakfast," the Ensign began. "For some of you it will be your first and last meal at the San Diego Naval Recruit Training Center. Many of the men who sign up don't really fit in for one reason or another. A few of you have engaged in political and social protests that have colored your judgment. Such preoccupations have no place in this man's Navy and may result in serious consequences should they persist. Some of you have drug addictions that could be fatal to you and your shipmates. Others, well others..." the Ensign stammered and mopped his brow with a handkerchief. His ears protruded from the side of his head like pink dessert saucers. "Others have personal problems which make them unfit to serve in an almost exclusively male environment."

"If any of you men feel that you have the type of problems I've described, drugs or the other thing, step forward now and you will be discharged without a stigma attached to your record. After you cross from this side of the base to the Nimitz Recruit Training Center it will be too late. At that point you'll be subject to military law and will risk receiving a Dishonorable Discharge and prison time. Such a stain will follow you the rest of your lives."

No one budged.

"Good. They are all yours, Signal Man First Class Jones and Chief Bert."

"You are now Seaman Recruits," the gofer announced. "For the next 13 weeks you will learn to be sailors. As I call your name you will be told to fall into line behind either Signalman First Class Jones or Chief Petty Officer Bert. They will be your drill instructors during basic training."

Kaiser Jenkin combed his fingers through his Afro. Bert charged. Leaning into Jenkin's face he showered people two seats away from him with saliva. "You better be raising that hand to ask a question, boy, 'cause if you are fixing to touch that pussy bush, I'll snatch you bald headed."

Kaiser dropped his hand. "Sir, I tuned into the drug shit but what was that man talkin' about with all that latent tendency stuff?"

I let out a foghorn laugh. Bert pushed the guy beside me off the bench, stepped up in his place and shouted down at me. "You think that boy's question's funny, Honey?"

"No Sir," I said softly.

"What did you say? I can't hear you."

"No Sir," I repeated in the same flat tone of voice.

"You're wrong. It is funny. Right, Signalman First Class Jones?" Bert jumped off the bench.

Bert crossed his arms over his chest. "It is funny. It's funny as hell. I'll tell you pieces of shit how funny. If any of you worms decide to confess to being queer when things

413

get too tough for you on the other side, we got a little test to see if you're on the level. Right Jones?"

"Sure do."

Bert pulled Kaiser to his feet. He placed a mottled hand on the recruit's collarbone. "We got a test, boy, kind of a lie detector test to make sure you ain't jiving us. We send you over yonder to Pendleton, that's the Marine base, and let you suck off forty or fifty of those gyrenes. If you puke, we know you're lying and toss your ass in 40/50 till you either come clean or get your brains beat out. If you swallow, we beat your brains out anyway before tossing you into the transitional brig to wait for your Dishonorable Discharge. That answer your question, Super Fly?"

"Yes Sir," Kaiser said.

Jones lowered his eyes from the roof beams. "Some of you recruits arrived with bags given to you by well-meaning Sally Anns. Stand up and unload all the stuff you got from those dried out biddies on the deck along with the crap from your personal bags."

"With the exception of the smokes and the bible, you're to donate the balance of your shit to the dependent relief collection. The only possessions you are permitted to bring to the other side are essentials such as bibles, photographs of loved ones, razors, shaving cream, toothbrushes, toothpaste, writing instruments, and smokes." Jones stopped talking. His eyes locked onto something on the floor. I looked down at my things and saw Nina's stained glass peace medallion. Jones raised his eyes. It was too late. Bert spotted the multicolored medallion.

Once more he was screaming in my face. "Honey, what the fuck is this?" He held up the piece symbol by its chain. "I asked you a question."

"It's a gift from my girlfriend, Sir."

"You telling me, Honey, that some cunt back home gave you this to remember her by?"

"No Sir, it was to remind me not to forget what I stand for."

"Here keep it." He made as if to hand me the medallion but instead swung it at a post, shattering it into a thousand splinters. "Jones, I guarantee you that Honey here will be spending time in 40/50 before he finishes basic."

Jones shrugged. "Recruits, Seaman Pryor will be calling out your names randomly. First name called will fall in behind Chief Petty Officer Bert. The next person called will fall in behind me and so forth until all men have been assigned to a company."

"Grady, Mike," the gofer sang out.

"Brown, Ernest David."

I felt like shouting "Thank God!" as I lined up behind Jones.

"Jenkin, Kaiser."

"Addison, Jeremy."

"Squirrel," Jones muttered as Jeremy took his place behind me. Addison's red hair was cropped to his noggin. He wore an ROTC Texas A&M sweatshirt.

"Okay worms it's time to shave your useless knobs," Bert said to his company. "Single file, march!" He tried to call out cadence but stopped when his recruits kept stepping on each other's heels. The purple veins on his thick neck throbbed as he screamed, "Start marching properly or I'll make you crawl across the base on your stomachs like the worms you are."

We arrived at a low building with candy striped columns. Four men in white smocks and matching pants sat on the stoop smoking cigarettes. A guy with a flattop haircut and an immense belly hanging over his waistband stood up. He hiked up his pants and nudged the man next to him.

Chief Bert grabbed a fistful of Kaiser Jenkin's wiry hair and pulled his head toward him. "See those men, Super Fly? They're betting on who will cry after they scalp 'em. It better not be you. Black men got enough to deal with without you giving them crackers something else to hang over us."

Bert pushed back Kaiser's head. He grabbed me by an ear and pinched it. "I'm putting my money on Honey here."

"Knock it off," Jones said rising on his toes to look Bert in the eyes. "You deal with your worms. I'll deal with my men."

"You're right Jones. This lot belongs to you. Tell you what though, if that Nancy was in my company he wouldn't last through the week before he ended up on the receiving end of a blanket party."

Kaiser asked to the guy next to him, "What's a blanket party, man?"

Bert snatched off his black billed spotless white hat and flogged Kaiser with it. "Did I give you permission to open your mouth?"

Jenkin raised his arms to protect his face. Bert backed off. His voice became very calm.

"You better be raising that arm to fend off mosquitoes recruit. Because if you are not, I'm going to spread your ass so thin against the asphalt that no one will know where the road begins and you end."

Jones ordered four guys at a time from his unit into the shop. The barbers had their routine down pat. It took them three minutes to run an electric clipper over a recruit's full head of hair leaving stubble and a razor rash on an otherwise shiny dome. Addison, the ROTC wunderkind, made a crack to the tattooed barber about how he had gotten a GI haircut before arriving. The barber frowned and applied so much pressure with his razor that it peeled away a layer of Addison's skin. He then ran the razor again over the Aggie's raw pate before dousing it with hair tonic. Addison squeezed his eyelids shut but did not let out a peep.

When everyone had passed through the shearing room Bert yelled, "That's more like it. Now you're beginning to look like men. You will fall into two lines and follow Signalman First Class Jones and me."

Jones raised his voice without screaming, "You heard the man. Double-time it."

We ended up at another clapboard building. A sign on the lawn instructed us to line up, remove our clothes, and toss them in the bins provided. A recruit who looked like he was no older than sixteen balked at stripping.

Bert said, "What's the matter Susie, you afraid of showing off your family jewels?"

"No Sir, but shouldn't we undress inside the building? It's kind of cold out here."

"Get those civilian rags off before I rip them off you. Do you know what you are? You are worms! Worms can't read! Worms can't speak! Worms can't think! Worms are only allowed to exist because we let them exist.

Get moving, strip to your swizzle stick, and march through that door. When you come out you might be dressed like sailors, but you'll still be worms. By the time you get out of basic training you will either be sailors or fish bait."

Not wanting to be marked as a candidate for abuse I entered the building with my arms at my sides and my dick swinging free. Behind a desk in the first room sat a tired looking thirty-year lifer in a rumpled uniform that resembled a streetcar conductor's suit.

He spoke without looking up from his Zane Grey western. "Recruits, take a list from the corner of the desk. As you proceed from station to station, check off the following items as you receive them: one baseball cap, two pair of dungarees, two blue work shirts, four white undershirts, four pair of skivvies, four pair of black socks, white cloth belt, ankle high black boots, deck shoes, swimming trunks, blue jacket, dress wool cracker jacks, blue pea coat, everyday whites, a neck kerchief, and most importantly, The Blue Jacket Naval Training Manual."

In the last room another worn out sailor biding his time until retirement handed out seabags to stow the goodies we had accumulated. He cleared his throat and spit before croaking, "You have ten minutes to get dressed, pack your kit, and fall in outside into whatever kind of formation you can manage. Is that clear?"

"Yes Sir," a few guys answered.

Bert shouted for his unit to fall into two lines. He started to jog. When Bert and his company had a substantial head start, maybe fifty yards, Jones turned to us and said, "Do you see those bastards? Do you see them?"

"Yes Sir!"

"Excellent. If you allow Chief Petty Officer Bert's people to beat us to the Nimitz Basic Training Center, I will lose twenty dollars. Do you want me to lose twenty dollars?"

"No Sir!"

"If I lose twenty-five dollars, I will not be happy. Do I make myself clear?"

Jones jogged behind us. We continued like this for some time until Bert slowed down.

For the first time Jones raised his voice. "Haul ass men!" He dashed past us at full sprint over a bridge that spanned a canal dividing the main base from Nimitz. We took off after him at the same insane pace. We raced past a landlocked battleship next to the road and ran through the gates of a ten-foot fence topped by concertino wire. As we closed the gap, Jones yelled at Bert, "Is that the best your boys can do?"

Bert did a 360 on the run and pushed the first recruit he came face-to-face with to the ground. He jumped up and down waving his arms above his head. "If you let those worms beat us I'll string you up by the balls. Now move it you scum!"

We stopped in front of a three-story concrete building the shape of a Monopoly hotel piece. B-149/B-150/B151 was stencilled in black letters on a large sign mounted between two metal poles. The barracks was one of several forming a quadrangle that faced an enormous strip of concrete and tar called the grinder. Aptly named as hours of monotonous marching drills and repetitive mind-numbing exercises that took place on its surface were meant to grind an individual down.

When Bert arrived at our barracks, he handed Jones two bills. "Okay, you win. Your company gets the top floor." He faced his recruits. "What are you worms doing? Get into the building and throw your gear on a bunk and get back out here. You owe me a hundred laps."

"Gentleman," Jones said, "This will be your home for the next thirteen weeks." He threw his thumb over his shoulder toward Bert. "Can't say much for the neighbors but you'll get used to them. Let's go upstairs and see what condition the previous tenants left B-151 in."

Chapter 54

Metal bunk beds faced each other across the center aisle like tombstones. There was just enough space to squeeze a locker between each pairing of bunks. On top of the wire beds were rolled up mattresses with striped, blue-on-white ticking. A set of sheets, a pillow, and a wool blanket were placed in front of each mattress. I moved quickly and claimed the bottom bunk at the far end of the room near a fire exit. I sat on the floor leaning back against the locker.

Addison dogged my steps and took possession of the rack over mine. Taller and outweighing me by forty pounds, he looked like an overgrown infant.

"Hey there bunkmate." Addison stretched out his pink hand for a shake. His palm was oily. Flecks of dried blood covered his raw dome. I wiped my hand on my dungarees.

Addison unfolded his bed linens and rolled down the mattress. He unpacked his kit and placed his newly issued belongings in the upper left-hand compartment of the locker. He kept busy while I closed my eyes, enjoying a few moments of peace. I jerked my head up when a pillow fell on my lap.

"What are you doing?"

"Making my rack. You know, just getting my area up to snuff."

"Leave it alone."

"Don't worry. I was a platoon leader in ROTC. I can make up a bed military fashion blind folded."

I closed my eyes. "Suit yourself."

A blast of hot onion breath awakened me. Jones squatted in front of me. "Are you comfortable, Brown?"

"Yes Sir."

"Good. I don't want to exhaust you on your first morning."

Jones walked down the center of the aisle. He paused a few seconds in front of each rack to stare at a recruit and move on without saying a word. He doubled back and ended up once again in front of my bunk. He glanced at my seabag, unopened on the floor.

Addison sucked in his gut, thrust out his chest and came to attention. Jones looked at the neatly made bed stretched as tight as a drum's skin, complete with hospital corners. He ran his hand over the blanket. He opened the locker and inspected how Addison had arranged his clothing. Jones picked up a pair of socks and jabbed his index finger into the small pocket created by rolling them up from the toes and folding the elastics over the tube. Addison pressed his lips tightly together, preventing himself from smiling.

"You do this?" Jones addressed me.

"No Sir, my gear is on the floor."

"It's my rack and locker, Sir." The boy from A&M blurted out. "I learned to lay out my kit and make my bunk in ROTC."

Jones grabbed the mattress with both hands and flipped it onto the floor. "What's your name," he shouted.

Addison's jaw hung to his Adam's apple. His chest caved in and his stomach flopped over the waistband of his dungarees like a deflated volleyball.

"I asked you your name."

"Jeremy Addison, Sir."

"Seaman Recruit Addison, I hate the fucking ROTC. What do you think of that?" Jones grabbed me by my arm and pulled me to my feet.

"See this guy, Seaman Recruit Addison? He is a civilian slob, don't you agree? He is a slob but he is smart enough to realize he is a slob and that he doesn't know jack all. You are a slob too, but you are too stupid to know it."

Jones stepped back and waited until Addison said, "Yes Sir."

"Yes Sir, what recruit?"

"Yes Sir, I am a slob, and I don't know anything."

Jones hopped onto the long table in the middle of the barracks. "Recruits listen up so you don't make the same mistake as Addison. I am your Drill Instructor. This means that it is my job to show you how to do things. I will instruct you on how to make your racks, how to polish your boots, how to march, how to perform the manual of arms, make you familiar with the military code of conduct and most importantly how to live by the Blue Jacket Manual. It makes me angry when people do my job for me. Do I make myself clear?"

A chorus of recruits sang, "Yes Sir!"

"One more thing I want to get off my chest so that we start off on the right foot is that I'm not like most of the DIs here. I don't bully and I don't try to break you. I don't believe you're worms. I think of you as dumb-ass civilians struggling to become sailors in the United States Navy. You tell anyone who calls you worms that you are not worms that you are Signalman First Class Jones's recruits. Okay my pep talk is finished. I want you to take an index card and a piece of official Navy stationary and an envelope from the stacks in the middle of the table. You are to write on the index cards why you joined the Navy. It's not required to sign your name. Secondly, you're to write a letter on the official USN stationary to someone back home, parents, girlfriends, parole officers, anyone who might care to learn that you've arrived safely and are not being mistreated."

I took longer listing my reasons for joining the Navy than I did composing a note to my father.

Dear Colonel,

Arrived in San Diego in the dark. It is light now. Things aren't much different here than at home.

David

When we were through with our writing assignments, we were told to go to the laundry yard. Jones warned us to take along only two smokes; regulations did not permit us to bring more. The smoking lamp would be lit for twenty-minutes. On the way downstairs we handed our letters and index cards to Seaman Pryor. The laundry yard, a concrete slab painted industrial gray was located on the left side of the barracks. A twelve-foot cement wash table occupied the center of the slab. Several feet of clotheslines were strung up between Y shaped poles. In the shaded part of the courtyard four red buckets filled with sand stood beside an equal number of wooden benches. Not a blade of grass or patch of dirt was visible.

Bert's company was running around the grinder. "Worms you owe me," He screamed at them. "You embarrassed me in front of these pussies. I do not tolerate failure."

I finished smoking my two cigarettes and trudged upstairs. Jones and Pryor were sitting at the table. From the way they moved around the letters and index cards I guessed they were matching the handwriting on the cards with the those on the letters.

Jones asked, "Which one of you guys is Clark?"

A small guy with a head that came to a bullet point raised his hand.

Jones slipped a pair of half-moon glasses from his blouse pocket, perched it at the tip of his nose and read aloud. "I joined because my father and his father had served in the Navy. Both saw action as Seabees. I want to make them proud."

"Do you mean that?" Jones asked.

"Yes Sir."

"That's as good a reason as any to enlist," Jones said and read another card.

"I feel that America is threatened by forces from within and from without and that it is our duty to serve where we are best suited. My two semesters at A&M will be an asset in Nuclear Submarine training."

"Addison, I don't know if you'd be an asset to the Submariners, but you are proving to be a real pain in the asset to me."

Jones squinted, creating a web of wrinkles around his eyes. "This isn't what I had in mind when I told you to write a letter Brown." He crumpled up my note to my Dad. He made a perfect three point shot into a waste basket. "And what the hell does this mean?" He popped an index card against his palm and read my composition.

Reasons I joined the Navy:

1. The uniforms are spiffy
2. Most Naval bases are near Universities so it makes it easier to join protest groups
3. Most Naval bases are on the coast, and I like to swim
4. Most Naval bases are within a couple of days' drive of Canada
5. If I had not joined it's likely I would have ended up in jail because I would have refused to be drafted
6. It's very unlikely being in the Navy that I will end up in Vietnam
7. Because guys in the Navy are generally more intelligent than jarheads and dogfaces, it is more likely I can convince them about the futility of the war

"Tell you what Seaman Recruit Brown. I'll give you the chance to rewrite your reasons otherwise this card becomes part of your dossier. While you're at it you can write another letter to your father."

"Thank you Sir, but I'll let things stand as they are."

"Have it your way. For a smart guy you don't think." Jones tossed my card on the table. "Lesson time boys. Seaman Apprentice Pryor and me will be instructing you on how to make your rack and store your gear in your lockers according to the Blue Jacket Manual. Seaman Recruit Brown, since you're such a smart guy, I have decided to make you exempt from this lesson. You're going to stand watch outdoors until you are relieved."

I was probably the only recruit at Nimitz assigned to stand 4 watches on his first day. On my final night on guard, at around 0100, I saw Kaiser being chased across the parade field by three 40/50 guards. His face was so battered that his eyes were swollen shut and his bottom lip was caked with dried blood where it had been split open.

"What's going on?" I yelled.

One of the chasers double backed and jabbed a nightstick in my gut. "Seaman Recruit that's not how you challenge a person. You're supposed to say halt and identify yourself!"

"Okay, halt, identify yourself. What happened to Kaiser?"

"Same thing that'll happen to you if you don't mind your business."

When I stumbled to my bed, I dimly recall wondering how my rack got made. Addison, occupying the bunk above mine, rolled his head over the edge of his mattress and whispered, "Hey, there's a stand tall inspection at 0600 but don't worry I fixed your locker for you."

I passed the morning stand tall, but I didn't thank Addison for his help. After the inspection Jones gave us permission to go for a smoke. Still woozy from lack of sleep, I sat on a bench and watched Bert abuse his recruits for failing to live up to his inspection standards. When Jones came downstairs Bert said, "I put one on the road last night."

"Who?"

"Super Fly."

"Chief, it's only the first week."

"I've told you before, Jones. If you don't hammer them from the start, they'll nail you at the end." Bert grinned at me. "You're next, Honey."

Jones shrugged and they walked away together.

A few minutes later Pryor came over. "Keep low Brown, the Chief has it in for you."

"I didn't do anything."

"That doesn't matter. If he wants you, he'll find a way to get you."

"Like he did Kaiser?"

"What do you know about Jenkin?"

"Nothing except I saw him being beaten on the run last night by Chaser assholes."

"Take my advice Brown, eyes down when you're around the Chief. You rub him the wrong way."

That evening when the smoking lamp was lit and B-150 and B-151 were down in the common area some guys from Bert's company revealed in hushed tones that Bert had been on Jenkin's case since the beginning. Because one of Kaiser's boots was more polished than the other, Bert made him stand in the running cold shower and do the manual of arms in his skivvies. Bert snatched the rifle out of Kaiser's hands and called him a worthless jack-off and a dumb black tool.

Kaiser Jenkin, from Bowling Green, snapped. He took a swing at Bert. Bert slipped the punch and executed a perfect butt stroke with the M-I, laying Kaiser out cold. When he came to, three chasers escorted him to 40/50. He would remain there until his company had cycled out and he would start over from day one with Bert.

Chapter 55

Jeremy Addison was a gung-ho squirrel but other than that he was okay. Every morning he got up before reveille and dashed off to the head to get cleaned up. He'd then return to our racks and put not only his stuff, but mine as well, in order. He was a whiz at folding laundry. Not so hot at doing the Manual of Arms or marching in step. He practiced till he made the grade. I sympathized with him. I had the tendency to walk duck-footed while marching and my inherent dislike of firearms caused me hours of extra watches and head cleaning duty.

Four weeks after Jeremy's noggin had been peeled like a potato, after he'd virtually memorized each section in the Blue Jacket Manual, Pryor walked into the head while Addison was showering. Everyone in the barracks could hear him scream, "For God's sake what the hell is all over your body?"

Pryor ran to Jones's room. Shortly afterward Addison joined them. He didn't return for roll call. Without him the company spent the day walking twice through a sealed trailer filled with smoke. The first trip through, an instructor ordered us to wear gas masks, the second pass we entered the chamber minus our masks. Several guys, myself included, tossed our breakfasts after swallowing a lifetime's worth of exhaust fumes. When I returned to the barracks Addison was sitting in the laundry yard on the edge of a bench. His seabag was at his feet.

"What's up?" I asked.

His eyes were moist with tears. "Don't go teasing me when I tell you. I went to sick bay after Pryor found out about me."

"Found out what, that you're beating your meat while everyone's asleep?"

Addison pulled up his shirt and undershirt. Welts and puss filled blisters covered very inch of his torso. He turned around and showed me the same rash on his back. "I'm allergic to wool. They're kicking me out on medical discharge."

"Jeremy, maybe I'm dense, but I don't see what all the fuss is about."

I thought he was going to belt me. Instead, he started scratching his chest and his buttocks through his clothes. "It's not fair. They should kick you out for all that anti-war, anti-American crap you've been talking."

"Addison, there are guys in the company who would sell their sisters to have your dermatological problem."

He shook his fist at our barracks. "I'll show those bastards. The Army doesn't wear wool. As soon as I get home I'm going to enlist and become a Green Beret."

I broke out laughing.

"I didn't expect anything different from you. Every man has a duty to do his bit."

"Jeremy you're right. Everyone should be content to be a bit player and die for their country."

"You should really learn to keep your opinions to yourself before you get in deep shit."

"Is there something else?" I asked.

Jeremy leaned over his seabag and dipped in his hand. The steno pad that had been issued to all recruits at the induction center surfaced. We had been ordered to carry it with us to all lectures and field demonstrations.

Mine was filled with rants against the government and the pathetic attempt of the military to inculcate its draftees and enlistees with discipline and esprit de corps. Addison held out his pad as though he was presenting the Gutenberg Bible. I flipped it open. On the left-hand corner of the first page he had printed, Seaman Recruit Jeremy Addison B-151 and his serial number as perfectly as a typewriter strikes. Under the heading, Induction Lectures, he had listed the Roman numerals from I to XII beside the name and date of every training session we had attended. Such pithy titles as Your Rifle your Friend, and Informer or Patriot stood out.

Jeremy asked if I recalled the lecture on the military code of conduct given by the wimpy Ensign who had greeted us on our arrival. Beyond the standard line about how we were obliged to give only our name, rank and serial number, the Ensign made a case for the necessity of ratting out our fellow sailors. Because of the recent conviction of 300 sailors for protesting the war while in uniform, the Navy had no tolerance for subversives.

The Ensign said that we must become vigilant in rooting out malcontents and radicals. If we suspected individuals of engaging in unmilitary conduct such as writing letters to underground newspapers, attending seditious meetings or signing petitions against the government we had a moral duty to pass along the name of the person to our superiors.

I handed Jeremy back his pad. "Thanks, but I don't want this."

"I thought about giving it to Norman," he said speaking of a kid from Indiana who was no less of a pain in the ass than he was.

"Then give it to him."

"No, he has two pads already. His and yours."

I remembered leaving my pad on the table when I went off with the company to the gas trailer. Norman was standing watch so he didn't go with us. I couldn't figure out why this milk-pure-farm boy would want my pad. He kept even more precise notes than Addison.

"When I came back from sick bay Norman was hopping mad. He read out loud some of the crap you've been writing."

"So? It's a free country."

"You should know better, your father is a Lieutenant Colonel."

"How do you know that?"

"Besides calling your old man every name in the cuss out dictionary you wrote his rank in your pad. I knew it anyway. Bert told all the recruit company leaders what a fuck-up you are, especially considering that your old man is a bootstrap officer."

"I'm not a fuck-up. I do what is expected of me."

"No, you're not a fuck-up. You just never shoulder-up to help more than you have to. But that's not the point. Norman read me the passage where you dumped on the Navy. It gets worse. You wrote that anybody who believed in the war should have his head examined. Norman was so angry about having a traitor in the same company that as soon as his watch relief reported he dashed downstairs and gave your pad to Bert. Norman told me that if the DIs didn't do something about you, he and some of the other guys would throw you a blanket party."

I did not see Jones approach us from behind. His voice startled me.

"Addison, sorry things didn't work out for you."

"That's okay Sir."

"You don't have to call me Sir anymore," Jones said.

Jeremy Addison was gone by dinner. I didn't take the time to miss him. Primarily I was concerned with dealing with Norman before he dealt with me.

I had the graveyard watch from 0000 to 0400. I paced the corridors and aisle of B-151 with a heavy metal flashlight at my hip and a nightstick in my hand. I liked the solitude of this watch. The only noises were the throaty snores of exhausted recruits. I found the chill in the air invigorating. The streetlights shone into the barracks. My breath came out like puffs of smoke when I passed by the windows.

Norman got up around 0200 to take a leak. After a few seconds I followed him into the head. Half-asleep, he rested his brow on the tile back splash above the urinal. I was tempted to cold cock him with my flashlight but just flicked his ear with my index finger. Norman jumped like he'd touched a juiced electrical wire. He sprayed an amber stream of urine on the backsplash.

I felt a sick pleasure at having this Johnny America standing in front me with his dick hanging out of his shorts like a shriveled white worm. "Keep your voice down." I pushed him against the wall and braced the length of my nightstick under his chin. "Still feel like getting some guys together and beating on me?"

"What are you talking about?"

"Jeremy told me how you gave my pad to Bert and how you've been going around threatening to throw me a blanket party."

"Brown, you're an idiot." Norman shoved me back without much effort. "You got no secrets. You leave that fucking pad on the table for everyone to see and you think people won't look at it. I've seen guys in the barracks, Jones, Bert, and even the Chaplain when he was up here last week, read it."

"Then how come Jeremy told me you gave it to Bert and that you were..."

"If I were going to throw a blanket party it would be for Jeremy. He's the biggest suck in the company and a snitch. But you wouldn't know that because you don't talk to anyone unless it's to bitch about the government."

"I'm not here to make friends."

"Don't worry, you don't have any. Half the time you go around looking like you're ready to fight at the drop of a pin. But honestly, the guys don't give a flying fuck as long as you keep your rack and locker in order and don't cost us any demerit points during inspections. One more thing, before Jeremy split he sat in the office downstairs talking to Jones, Bert, and some stiff hat wearing a badge. If I were you, I'd see Jones because when the badge left he looked madder than hell and Bert was smiling. For a DI Jones is not a bad guy. He may let you know what's going on." Norman pushed me aside and returned to his bunk.

I didn't have the opportunity to follow Norman's advice. After morning chow Pryor burst into the barracks and ordered the company to assemble outside with our bathing suits. Anyone who didn't pass the swim test by Christmas Eve would be sent back to day one of basic over and over until he did.

The front of my swimming trunks was roomy enough for a bowling ball. The butt was made without any consideration for where one's ass belonged. My dick hung out the leg opening while the fabric pulled so tight over my cheeks it crimped under my buttocks and was sucked into my crack.

A shallow end for the timid did not exist in the pool. With Addison gone my name was called first by an instructor in better fitting trunks and a baseball hat with a USMC appliqué on its front. He ordered me to climb a 12' tower to a diving platform then jump and swim the length of the pool twice. I climbed the tower, approached the platform, and did a fair dive off its edge.

When a marine tells you to jump, he means jump. To make up for my failure to follow orders I climbed that tower twenty more times that morning, jumped and swam the two lengths as ordered. I didn't mind. It gave me a chance to escape the monotony of basic training and pretend for a moment that I was having fun.

When we got back to the barracks Jones was gone. Pryor told us Jones would return after the New Year. In his absence Chief Bert would oversee both companies. Bert stormed into the barracks. He had been hiding in the head.

"Playtime is over, worms. Jones may have convinced you that you're important but you're not. You're lower than dog shit."

Maybe I rolled my eyes or gave away something in my posture. I don't know. Bert shoved me. "Honey, I got a bead on you. I took care of my Step-and-Fetch and you're next. Sneeze wrong and Jones will be minus one recruit when he gets back."

That night I pulled three watches in a row. That was okay with me. It exempted me from morning marching and rifle drills. At least it did under Jones. Under Bert it meant that when I fell in for roll call the next morning, I was told to hit the parade field and work on my manual of arms to make up for the missed drills. I ended up pulling another all-nighter.

Before going on watch Bert buttonholed me. "I don't know what your game is but you ain't gonna get no special favors from me. Your old man could be a fuckin' admiral for all I care. You either fall into step or I'll kick your ass from one end of the parade field to the other."

I glared at him and clenched my fists.

"You got something to say, worm?"

"What do you know about my father?"

"Your father must be real proud of you," He tossed the steno pad Addison had stolen at my feet.

While on watch that evening, I grew more and more morose. For some inexplicable reason I found myself caring about what my father thought. I was a failure, a complete washout. GED notwithstanding, I was a high school dropout. Not only had I burned my bridges, I'd pulled out their pilings. The prospect of going to university, getting a scholarship, or ever seeing eye to eye with my dad were as remote as my ever getting off triple watches as long as Bert was in charge. When I entered the head, I stared at my gaunt face in the mirror. My eye sockets were dark circles. My father was right. I was nothing. My punishment came at the end of my own fist. I gave myself a punch at the side of my right eye above the cheekbone. I continued to work on the eye like a boxer until a lump as big and purple as a plum rose to the surface and obscured my vision.

The next morning Bert yelled at me for not announcing his presence as he walked into B-151 but shut up when he looked at my swollen eye.

"What the hell happened to you?" He looked toward Pryor. The company gofer glanced around the room and shrugged.

"I must have fallen down, Sir," I said.

"Must have, Seaman Recruit?"

"Did fall down, Sir."

A flicker of a smile brightened Bert's face. "Maybe there's hope for you, worm. Don't give up your mates and they won't give up on you."

Bert's respect for me was short lived. He watched as Pryor posted a notice on the bulletin board announcing that we would have the twenty-fourth through the twenty-fifth of December off.

"Happy Holidays worms," Bert said. "On Christmas Day there will be both Protestant and Catholic services. Each recruit is expected to choose which service he wants to attend."

Pryor handed out note cards for people to write their preference. I wrote, "Neither!" Twenty minutes later Bert stormed into the barracks foaming at the mouth.

"Some of you pieces of dog shit think you're cute. No one here is exempt from going to services." Bert looked at me. "You got a problem with what I just said?"

"Yes Sir. I don't go to church. I'm a non-believer."

"You're going to church. This country is about freedom of religion not freedom from it. You got a problem with that?"

"Yes Sir, I do." I looked around the room for support.

"Here's how it's going to be Seaman Recruit. Either you go to church, or you pull guard duty all day until after New Year."

"Thank you, Sir," I said.

Bert glowered. "You're not making it easy on yourself. After what I read in your little notebook, you're gonna need all the help you can get from above."

Christmas morning, I stood guard duty in front of the barracks. The Chaplain stopped by my post and chewed me out. "What the hell do you think you're doing? God is your helmsman. You gotta trust the one who steers the course and show him in church that you believe in him. Now stand down and quick march to the afternoon service."

"No Sir," I said.

"Chief Bert's right, you are an f-ing worm."

When I got off guard duty at 18:00 a letter and package were on my mattress. The USO package contained a generic "Happy Holiday" greeting card, a bag of cashews, a chocolate Santa, and small pamphlet of what were supposed to be inspirational messages. The letter was from my mother. It had the rambling quality that mimicked her speech. Names of people I neither knew nor cared about were scattered throughout the letter. On the back of the letter my father had written one sentence: "Don't screw up."

Later that evening Bert came to see me. "So how'd your Christmas go? Your shipmates really enjoyed having the holiday off. They're looking forward to New Year's Day. I'm gonna bring in a TV so they can catch a couple of the bowl games. Too bad you'd rather stand guard duty than participate."

"What does it take to get out of this chicken shit Navy?" I blurted out.

"Simple," Bert said. "Just tell the Chaplain that you're not fit for the military. Tell him that besides being a communist, you're an addict. I'd tell you to tell him you're a fag, but I know that you wouldn't go for that."

"Okay."

"Okay what, Brown?"

"Okay, I fucking hate the Navy and this country. I'm a drug addict. I've done everything there is to shoot, smoke or swallow and I'm having flashbacks."

"Hang on there, sport, while I go get Pryor." When Bert came back, he had me repeat what I had said slowly so the gofer could write it down.

"First thing in the morning you go to the Chaplain and tell him exactly what you told me," Bert said.

*

The Chaplain stubbed out a cigarette in an anchor-shaped ashtray. "So you're a drug addict who has a beef against the Navy and the government," he said.

I didn't respond. I was pissed off at having to stand at attention for over an hour in his office while he read the Stars and Stripes, the official military newspaper. The photos on his walls pictured him shaking hands with admirals, senators, and just plain sailors. There was a blow-up of him conducting a service on the runway of an aircraft carrier. Several framed citations adorned the wall.

"I read the garbage you wrote on your card when you arrived. Do you believe in God?"

I let my shoulders relax and stood with my legs apart. "I haven't decided, Sir."

"No one told you to stand at ease."

He slipped a cigarette out of a pack on his desk and lit up. Sitting sideways in his swivel chair the load of his upper body was supported by the armrest. "Your father is a Lieutenant Colonel in the Air Force, a mustang."

"Yes, Sir."

The squeaking of his chair grated on my nerves when he rocked back in it. "Are you against war, Brown?"

"I'm against this one, Sir."

"But not against all wars, huh?"

"No, Sir."

"You know what I think sailor? I think you're full of shit. I don't believe you are a druggie. You're a disgrace to your father and the nation he has dedicated his life to protecting. What do you think of that sailor?"

"You are entitled to your opinion, Sir."

The Chaplain rose out of his chair and pointed the red end of his cigarette at my forehead. "Damn right I am. See these gold leafs on my shoulders? I am a military man first and a man of God second. My job is to give comfort to those brave boys ready to give up their lives for America. I have no use for punks like you."

Chapter 56

Jones returned from the holidays early. He sent Pryor to tell me that he wanted to see me right away. He pushed me back toward the wall and held me there with the palm of his extended arm. "What's the matter with you, Brown? I leave for one week and all hell breaks loose!"

"What did you hear, Sir?"

"I heard that you flushed your future down the toilet. That's why I came back, to see what I can do to help you."

"Chief Bert kept ragging me until I gave him what he wanted," I said.

"You told him that you were going around trying to get guys to protest the war and desert."

"That's not true. I told him I was against this war and would say the same thing to anybody who asked me."

"What about the drugs?"

"I told him what he wanted to hear."

"Is that what the Chaplain wanted to hear too?"

"That guy is a bigger prick than Bert."

Jones dropped his arms heavily. "You're right, he is a genuine cocksucker, but that doesn't change a thing. You're screwed."

"I don't care what they do."

"Learn to care! You got an appointment in my office in one hour with the Chaplain and the advocate. They are

445

going to ask you some questions and you better answer them right."

I began to realize that I might not be able to climb out of the hole I'd dug for myself. "I'll tell them I lied about the drugs."

Jones exploded, "How stupid can a person be! This isn't about smoking pot or downing a couple of tabs of acid. This is about encouraging other sailors to protest the war. It's about all that anti-American stuff you wrote in your journal."

"I'll say it was all bullshit, that I didn't mean any of it. What's the worst that can happen? I'll be sent to 40/50 for a couple of weeks and have to start basic over."

"40/50 is the last place you want to end up. Chief Weir runs that unit like Treasure Island. His chasers will beat on you until you can't stand up. As for the drugs, you signed a statement. You go back on that, and they'll nail you for perjury. You're liable to end up in Leavenworth. The worst part is that you were doing okay."

"What do I do?" I heard the tremor in my voice.

"Beats me. Play down the anti-war stuff and hang in on the drug stuff. If you don't make any comments like you did in your notebook about wanting to burn down America or shove the flag up your old man's ass, they might decide to get rid of you quick. The best you can hope for is a General Discharge under Honorable Conditions."

I stood at attention when the Chaplain entered Jones's office with a scowling Lieutenant wearing summer weight browns in January. His cap would have slipped over his eyes if it had not been for his ears that jutted away from his head like a truck's side mirrors. The Chaplain asked me to recount my story.

"I don't recall Sir."

He quizzed me on the sections of my notebook dealing with my father and my antipathy toward the military and government. I didn't respond.

The Lieutenant's Adam's apple bobbed up and down inside his shirt collar. His head wobbled like a dashboard puppy. "Seaman Recruit, do you know how serious this is?"

"What are you smirking at sailor? You think this is funny!" the Chaplain said.

"No Sir."

"It's the drugs sailor. You're on drugs right now, aren't you?" The Lieutenant said.

"No Sir."

"What kinds of drugs have you done sailor?"

"Everything Sir. You name it."

"Marijuana,"

"Yes Sir."

"Hashish?"

"Yes Sir."

"Cocaine, amphetamines, heroin?"

"Yes Sir."

"Which one gave you the flashbacks?" The Chaplain interrupted.

"All of them."

"All of them?" the Chaplain said.

"Yes Sir."

"You're a bald faced liar, Seaman Recruit. No one gets flashbacks from these substances. As a serious drug taker, you should know that."

"I'm serious, just non-discriminating," I said and added quickly, "Sir".

"So you insist on sticking to your cock-and-bull story about taking drugs?"

The Lieutenant appeared lost in my exchange with the Chaplain and blurted out, "Do you love this country, Seaman Recruit?"

"Obviously not enough in your opinion, Sir."

The Lieutenant craned his neck back and shouted at the ceiling, "You are a disgrace to the Navy and your father!"

Two sailors who had been waiting outside entered Jones's office. They wore white helmets, white uniforms and were carrying nightsticks painted white. The armbands circling their biceps had 40/50 printed on them.

"Get him out of here," the Lieutenant said.

The chasers ordered me to keep my eyes down when I entered the barracks. When I tried to lift my head one of them chopped me behind the neck. I could see Norman out of the corner my eye shaking his head. The chasers gave me to the count of fifty to pack my seabag. They stood on either side of me screaming, "Doubled time! Move it, move it!"

They took club swipes at the back of my legs while they chased me across the length of Nimitz at a full run. We ended up at a shabby two-story building enclosed by a twelve-foot-high chain length fence topped with roils of razor wire. One of the chasers told me to keep running in place. He pushed a button on a box attached to the fence. I glanced up at the second story of the building. Its windows were covered with black paper. The chaser opened the gate when a buzzer sounded. The other chaser rammed the rounded end of his nightstick into my back. "Get moving." He did not slack off. "Double-time it on the spot until I tell you to stop!"

I ran in place for at least thirty minutes and then a siren sounded. Twenty men dressed in 40/50 blue shirts and dungarees were herded out of the building by several chasers who looked like they were being chased as well.

Chief Weir's voice preceded his appearance. He had a typical New Orleans accent, a cross between a sharecropper's drawl and a Brooklyn cabby's whine. "Okay y'all. I better not see you pussies let these scum slack off today or I will fuck you over, under and up!"

Weir kept his hand on the flap of his side arm. He threw a hard stare in my direction. "Who the hell is this maggot scum?"

"He's the worm from B-151."

Weir spit at my feet. "So, you're the acid head commie?"

I slowed down to catch my breath. "Yes, Sir."

"Did I tell you to stop running!" His fist sunk into my solar plexus almost dropping me to my knees. "You got no right to call me Sir or anything else scum. You keep your foul trap shut and do as you are fucking told, when you are fucking told. Get this simple rule into your head and you might be able to walk out of here on your own locomotion."

Weir turned to one of my chasers. "Stick him upstairs in the observation unit. The Chaplain says keep an eye on him. He's worse than the run-of-the-mill maggot. He's out to spread anti-American messages to other sailors."

The chaser prodded me into the building with his nightstick up the stairs and into an open room that had a large cage with four sets of bunk beds inside it.

"Toss your seabag on a rack and get the hell back with the rest of the scum."

When I raced outside Weir was screaming at his chasers. "Are we running a kindergarten here or a brig? First prisoner I see goofing off today will go down hard on whoever is the lead chaser. Move it, move it, move it!"

The chasers drove the prisoners through the gates, whacking at their buttocks with their nightsticks. My chaser slapped me on the back of my head, "You heard that, catch up or I'll put you in sick bay."

I glanced over my shoulder and saw Weir running behind us. He sported a huge smile. After a while the chasers quit barking at us.

The only sounds to be heard were the slaps of boots against the pavement, the panting of prisoners and the shrill blasts from Weir's whistle whenever we slowed down. We ran two miles then turned into an empty lot the width and length of a football field.

At either end of the lot were sand piles. Each one covered an area as large as a tennis court. At the bottom of the piles were several metal buckets and a square nosed shovel. The chasers split us into two groups, one at each sand pile. On the blast of Weir's whistle, we dashed toward our respective hills and picked up a bucket in each hand. We stood in line single file with our buckets held out at arm's length. The chasers took turns filling the buckets to the top with sand. When our buckets were filled to capacity Weir blew his whistle and we double-timed it with our loads held away from our bodies to the opposite sand pile. We emptied our buckets and the process started again. This drill went on for over three hours. My arms felt like they were being torn from their shoulder sockets, but I did not falter. Any sign of weakness was license for the chasers to kick your feet from under you. They would beat you on the soft sections of your body with their white batons as you struggled to get back to your feet.

Weir looked at his watch and said, "Knock it off. Chow time."

We double-timed it across the base toward the mess hall. Inside the mess hall a chaser shouted for us to run in place while we moved through the serving line with our trays held out in front of us. Weir went off to the other side of the hall to sit with his fellow noncoms. The mess crew slopped huge portions of food into the pockets on the metal trays, mixing Jell-O with mashed potatoes, green beans with pudding. At the end of the serving line, we were handed a spoon as our sole article of cutlery. We were prodded to a table well away from other recruits.

"Sit down, keep your eyes down and wait for the whistle to start eating," the lead chaser ordered.

We held our spoons aloft. When the ear-piercing tweet sounded the prisoners attacked their food with the ravenous hunger of jackals. I picked at my food, too exhausted to eat. After about five minutes, I raised my glass of milk and brought it up to my lips just as the whistle trilled again. Before I could remove the glass from my mouth a chaser screamed, "Can't you hear worm!" He clubbed me on top of my head. My teeth bit into the rim of the glass cutting my lips. I spit out a shard and wiped the blood from my mouth. I wanted to jump up and drive the handle of my spoon through his throat but knew the beating that would follow would not be worth the effort.

"You're going have to pay for that glass, worm. It's Navy property," he said and laughed.

On the way back to 40/50 we came on Jones's company on the parade field practicing formation marching. Weir ordered us to stop. "Keep your eyes on the ground. You, pieces of shit, got no right to look directly at real sailors."

He trotted up next to me, pulled me out of the line and slapped me across my head. "Drop and give me twenty." Each time I pushed up he planted his foot on my back and shoved my face into the asphalt. "Hey Jones, look at your worm."

Jones turned his back on Weir and said, "He may be too smart for his own good, Chief, but he's not a worm."

At the end of the day a chaser locked me in the observation cage. With the exception of my cellmate, I was segregated from the rest of the prisoners. My cellmate was a kid who had gone AWOL during his first leave after having been cycled again through basic training. He didn't go out with the other prisoners on punishment drills.

Weir kept him in isolation until a space opened for him in the psychiatric ward. As a suicide risk, Weir only allowed the kid his skivvies and gave him a blanket to cover himself. He had to sleep on his back and was not permitted to bring his sheets above his chest. Every fifteen minutes a chaser walked up to the cage, shined his flashlight inside, and then dragged his nightstick along the wire.

At night the boy talked and cried in his sleep. "I'm cold it's dark. Don't hit me. Don't hit me. I'm sorry."

"Shut the fuck up," a chaser screamed when the sobbing got on his nerves. Once he opened the cage and threatened to beat him senseless but backed away when he noticed me watching. He pointed his stick at me and said, "Keep eyeballing me and I'll make sure you get hammered."

If this chaser knew how much anger deluged my being, how I had vowed I would wait outside the gates of Nimitz and waylay and disembowel each and every uniform who had laid a hand on me he would have put a bullet in my head then and there. Hate is a superb analgesic for fear and self-loathing.

*

The physical routine had some positive effects. I started putting on weight in the form of muscle and was able to fall into a real sleep. Each evening after I returned from a day of lugging buckets of sand and working out with an eight-pound M-1 non-stop, I went to the corner where the kid sat in his underwear, a blanket over his shoulders.

He always chose the same corner of the cage. His bony arms wrapped around his knees, he whined in a watery sounding way. He never looked up, didn't even twitch to acknowledge my presence. I liked to believe that he was glad to have company.

We didn't talk. I'd been told in no uncertain terms that I was to keep my mouth shut, as not to poison others' minds with my anti-American ranting. The one time I tried to talk to him the chaser on duty beat the cage with his nightstick until he made a hole in the wire grid.

I was prepared to ignore the chaser, but the kid scooted away on his ass and flattened his face against the cage. He avoided looking at me. I never learned his name. The few times I got a good look at him I understood why the isolation section was kept dark. When the door leading outside would open, it highlighted the purple bruises on his yellow complexion. The beatings he had suffered pacified him as much as a lobotomy.

The morning I was transferred out of 40/50 to the short-term misfits' unit, Weir made a special trip to the cage to see me off. In essence, I was a civilian. My discharge was being processed and I was no longer attached to either the recruit training center or the Navy. Weir stood by my rack. When I bent over to pack my seabag, he punched me in the back. I came up quickly and clipped him in the mouth with my head. It hurt like hell, but it was worth it. Weir restrained himself from laying into me. No longer in his charge, he could not touch me without facing disciplinary action.

"Your old man is a Colonel I hear."

"A Lieutenant Colonel," I answered. "And before you say it, not my old man is not going to be real proud of me and I don't really give a flying fuck."

His parting words stuck with me, "How the hell can a country like ours produce worthless scum like you?"

"Easy, look in the mirror Chief and you'll have your answer."

Chapter 57

A chaser opened the gate and spit on my boots when I walked through. No longer permitted to stay in the recruit training area, I received orders to report to the short-term processing barracks located on the other side of the base. No one accompanied me. Dressed in regulation blue work denims with a white cap, I could have passed for a full-fledged sailor. Only the lack of Seaman Apprentices' diagonal stripe on my sleeve gave away that I was less than nothing.

I crossed the same bridge that Jones made us race over to beat Bert's company. I hadn't noticed at that time that Nimitz was located on a wedge of land that jutted into an estuary. It was a nippy morning, but the sun was high, and the water sparkled. Chants of yes Sir, Drill Instructors calling cadences and the groans of sailors reached my ears. I saw recruits going through morning calisthenics and close order marching drills on the parade field. An aching feeling of despair engulfed me.

An officer walking by started to return my salute but stopped when he observed my naked sleeve. The watch bells out in the harbor rang. It was early, maybe six or seven in the morning. I imagined myself as the sailor in the Old Spice Commercial. Whistling, I hefted my seabag on my shoulder and swaggered down the road.

After a few blocks my swagger turned into a forced march. My pace slowed as I paused to read the signs on the row of faded buildings, their paint peeling from the ever-present salt mist. The further I walked the more depressing the scenery became. I jumped when rifle explosions shattered the morning stillness.

A military police jeep manned by two men pulled up next to me. An Asian looking guy hopped out. "What are you looking for?"

"The short-term processing detention center."

"You can't miss it. It's in front of the small arms firing range." He pointed at a single story building the size of three doublewide trailers laid end to end. The building had a green roof. It sat on concrete blocks in an asphalt lot.

"Thank you."

"Fuck you," he retorted. "If I had my way your kind would be used as targets on the range."

A tired looking CPO opened the door. A cigarette hung out of his mouth. "Yeah?"

"Seaman Recruit Brown reporting as ordered," I said and saluted.

The Chief turned his back on me. "You are Seaman fucking nothing. You don't have to salute me. You don't have to salute anyone, buddy. You're just parking your ass here until your discharge comes through."

The building was divided by an accordion door. Guys who claimed to be homosexuals were kept on the left side of the unit. The right side of the barracks, composed of dope smokers, acidheads, troublemakers, and hard-ass anti-war radicals, never mingled with the other side.

The Chief who headed the detainment unit was a short termer. He ran the section more like a boys' camp than a security brig. All the detainees were given duty assignments around the base.

We worked from 8 to 4 then had the rest of the day to do what we wanted and go where we wanted provided, we signed out and returned by 21:00. Most guys, myself included, stayed close to the unit. We were the target of catcalls and were pointed out as abject lessons of what awaited screw-ups.

I was given over to Kevin, a radioman who ran the laundry while waiting for his six-month tour of duty on a missile tender. When Kevin got bored reading Sci-Fi books, he would tell me about himself. He was a Hopi who joined the Navy against his elders' wishes. It was the only way out of the cycle of subsistence farming and sheep herding that his family had been sentenced to ever since their ancestors were stuck on a reservation.

"You may not believe this, but the Navy is the best thing that ever happened to me."

I kept my mouth shut as I emptied an industrial sized washer and transferred its wet contents to a dryer.

"I'm up for promotion. When on shore I take night courses. Two more years and I'll have enough credits to get a BSc. In 16 years, I'll retire. Shit, I'll only be forty. You ever thought of going to college?"

Kevin kept asking questions that I couldn't or wouldn't answer. Finally, he asked, "Have you called your parents to let them know what's happening?"

My anger was volcanic. I ripped the sheet I was folding and flung it at him. "Why don't you just tell me my old man must really be proud of me?"

Kevin put down his book. I squared off to give back whatever he threw at me in spades. He placed his hand on my arm. "You got enough problems waiting for you on the outside without my bringing up the obvious."

From that point on I knew that the relatively easy time the detainees had was out of pity. Our forthcoming General Under Honorable Discharges were in some ways worse than having a Bad Conduct or Dishonorable Discharge. We were neither fish nor fowl; neither bad nor tough enough to do time, nor strong enough morally, physically, and intellectually to stick it out.

That evening while I smoked outside, the Chief shouted for me to come to his office. He pointed to a chair, handed me the telephone, and walked out, closing the door behind him.

"David? Are you there?" my father asked when I put the receiver to my ear.

"Yes."

"What did you get yourself into? First the FBI shows up at my door with photocopies of seditious propaganda they say you wrote and then I get a call from San Diego telling me that you're being discharged. Did you write that if the Weathermen were serious, they ought to blow up the main fuel line coming into the base?"

"No."

"Are you doing drugs?"

"No."

"Then why did they tell me you were?"

"Because that's what they wanted to hear."

458

"It's not too late to take it all back."

"It is too late."

"If you don't make things right, then-"

"Then what Dad, you'll make me enlist in the Marines, you'll disown me?" I hung up without giving him a chance to bend me to his will.

At my rack a stocky guy was rummaging through my locker. He'd been staring at me since the day I arrived, making comments like, "Sure you belong on this side of the unit, sweetie?"

I pulled him away from my bunk. He punched me in the jaw and pointed his forefinger at me. "Where's my whites and peacoat?" He slapped me.

"I don't know what you're talking about."

He slapped me again. "Right punk, you have until lights out to give them back or I'll give you more of this."

I squeezed past him and went outside. There was a plank of wood leaning against the side of the building. Without judging the consequences, I drove my fist through it and hurled it over the fence of the rifle range. Next, I flipped up a bench, put my foot through it and kicked off one of its legs. When I looked up the guy who had slapped me was watching from the door. Our eyes met. He turned and went back inside. I picked up the bench leg and cleared the steps in two jumps. I aimed my first blow at the base of his spine, my next at the back of his knees. I would have beaten him unconscious if someone had not grabbed me. I managed to wriggle loose and hold onto the bench leg.

"Ever fucking put a hand on me again and I'll ram this so far down your throat it'll come out your ass," I said.

459

The guy got up as if shaking off a flea. The muscles rippled under his white T-shirt. He pointed a finger at me. "I had that coming. I found my peacoat and whites in the empty locker next to mine. I was gonna tell you outside I'm sorry."

He headed down the road to the BX and returned with a carton of smokes and a pint of Southern Comfort. He poured a shot in a paper cone from the water fountain and walked up to my rack.

"I'm Booth," he said. "No one ever got the jump on me like you did."

Booth came from Nevada. He missed the desert almost as much as he missed his old lady and got into detention because of her photo. A joint fell out of his shirt pocket as he was showing her off to a buddy.

"A BAM, a Broad Ass Marine bitch turned me in. I got to keep the photograph but not the dope."

Booth pulled a black and white Polaroid snapshot out of his wallet. A dark-haired woman was lying in bed, naked. Her legs were spread, and she was fingering herself. On the white border at the bottom of the picture she'd scrawled in ballpoint, "Keeping it wet for you baby, Kathy."

"Man, when I get out, I'm going back to my candy girl and my family."

I swallowed the Southern Comfort. My head was reeling. He poured me another three fingers. I said, "It's good to have a family that loves you enough to be there for you when you return."

Booth patted me on the head. He rolled up his sleeve. Through the tangle of wiry hair and ropes of scar tissue I made out a tattoo of Genghis Khan on a Harley with the word Mongols under it. "For a crazy mother you sure are green. This is my family," he said. "The Navy's for pussies, dude. If it weren't for the ace dope I've scored while in, I would have ditched this game a long time ago."

In a strange turn of fate Booth became my disciple. He convinced his drug-fried brain that I had answers. He would ask questions like, "What are we doing in Vietnam?"

And I would say, "That's what the hell everyone wants to know."

"How come mostly poor white kids and blacks are getting sent to Nam to be killed?"

"Isn't it obvious?" I'd answer.

Soon Booth assembled a group of like-minded dopers. While watching a TV special on the coming Mardi Gras I said, "Wouldn't it be great if our entire unit showed up in New Orleans? We could make a banner and protest the war and moon the government on national television. Maybe get totally wasted in the process."

Booth stabbed the air with his fist. "We'll be waiting for you, man. You're the leader of this revolution." He made some of the other guys pledge to meet in New Orleans after we were released.

When I walked into the Navy Justice Center to complete my discharge forms, I half expected to be grabbed by two huge Marines who would beat me before carting me off to Leavenworth. Nothing so dramatic happened. I wasn't even worth locking up. A clerk handed me some papers to sign. He advised me that my discharge didn't become official for two days. I'd be given an airplane ticket back to my point of enlistment and two hundred dollars or so in pay. If I didn't get on the plane, I'd be arrested.

As for civilian clothes, I was allowed to select an outfit from the charity clothing baskets. I could keep my navy issue socks, skivvies, undershirts, white pants, black boots, deck shoes, and windbreaker. Everything else had to be returned or their cost would be deducted from my pay. I signed the stack of forms in triplicate.

Chapter 58

There is no shame in saying I come from Texas, just in going back to it. This is how I felt as my plane taxied across Love Field's runway. I hitchhiked from the airport toward downtown Dallas. The high-rise office buildings along the Stimmons freeway blinded me with shafts of light ricocheting off their mirrored façades.

A white Chevrolet stopped. Two men jumped out. There was no need for them to flash their badges. My shorn hair, black boots, navy issue dungarees and denim work shirt gave me away as either a recent parolee or a deserter.

I handed a hatless cop a folder containing my discharge papers while his partner circled me, his beige Stetson slanted over his eyes.

"Looks like we got a slacker here."

His partner screwed up his face and spit on the pavement. "What are you, a queer or a section 8?"

"Does it matter?" I asked as I pulled my folder out of his hands.

The cowboy lifted my chin with his index finger. "It matters. Dallas already has enough–"

I closed my ears and filled in the blanks with, "Fags, dope heads, communists, goat fuckers, etc."

"Leave him alone," the hatless cop said. "He's gonna find out how tough it is for a slacker to get a job out here when our boys are laying down their lives in Vietnam."

463

"Why are you headed downtown?" the hatless cop asked. "Says on your discharge papers that you're from Irving."

"That's where my parents live."

"Yup, can see how you wouldn't be wanting to go back home right now."

"Or ever." The hatless cop told me to get in the car. "We'll drive you to a bus stop and you can make your way to the Y from there."

"Thank you."

"Don't thank me. Life is going be pretty grim from here on out, so do yourself a favor. Stay off the streets at night and steer clear of the Greyhound terminal."

After being dropped off I headed to the Greyhound station to see how much a ticket cost to New Orleans. Later I located a Goodwill clothing store where I bought a pair of used corduroy Levi's, a jean jacket, two long sleeve black undershirts and a pair of suede boots that zipped up the side. My next stop was the Army Surplus. I purchased a hunting knife and sheath and secreted it inside my waistband, pulling my shirt over it. My total expenditure left me with over a hundred and eighty dollars, more than enough for a room at a fleabag hotel and a bowl of chilli.

Most of the next day I spent at the downtown Dallas public library reading help wanted ads and browsing the stacks. Around three o'clock the librarian told me to shorten my visits in the future, space them a couple of days apart, or she'd call the cops and have me evicted for loitering. Outside the library I'd picked up a copy of the Dallas Notes. The paper asked people with a story about how fucked up the system was to submit a piece. It promised in print remuneration for any article published. On this teaser I began to write in the same notebook that got me into trouble in the Navy.

*

For three weeks I wandered the streets of Dallas. The few bucks I made working for temp agencies sometimes let me spring for a room at a cheap hotel. More often I sat throughout the night in a pay TV chair at the Greyhound station. As long as I fed quarters to the TV, I was able to catch a few winks. The money I'd allotted to survive on for a month was calculated to the penny. If I managed to hook a couple more day gigs as a laborer, I could make it to New Orleans before Mardi Gras.

One afternoon as I sat on a bench in an alley that had been converted into a strip mall, an old man dragged a ladder behind him and set it up at one end of the alley. He climbed the ladder and spread his arms and bellowed, "Do not let the wet blackness of your life extinguish the light."

I looked away from him into the window of a restaurant that masqueraded as a New York Deli, complete with aluminum trim and round bottomed counter stools. A trio of men dressed in fashions straight out of Haight Ashbury sat at the lunch counter. I went inside. A woman in a starched lime green uniform handed me a menu. Instead of coffee and the grilled cheese sandwich I'd ordered she brought me iced tea and a chilli-dog. I didn't call the error to her attention.

When the waitress came to collect, I was busy recording my experiences in 40/50. I dipped into my pocket. One of the trio who sat on a stool with his back against the edge of the counter said, "If you're short I'll help you out."

He wore burgundy leather pants and a sheepskin fur vest over a pink shirt. His collar was wide enough to use as a hang glider. His younger red- and blonde-haired Nordic companions were wearing Sergeant Pepper ensembles.

"No thanks." I slapped down enough change to cover the meal and a tip.

"What are you writing?" He pushed his fingers through his short Afro that could neither be puffed up nor combed down.

"Something for the Dallas Notes," I answered with an odd sense of pride.

"Make sure Stoney gives you money up front."

"You know him?"

"Mostly by reputation. I've met him a couple at times at SMU."

"You look too old for college."

"You're never too old, and SMU is a university, not a college. I work at their computer center as a programmer when I'm not taking classes." He pulled a pack of Kool menthols out of his boot top and handed me one. "Mind if I look?" He took my notebook and scanned my writing. "Not bad. But you should clean up the spelling and grammar."

"Thanks, but I don't have the time. It has to be submitted today to make next week's edition. I have the address, but I don't know how to get there."

"It's too far to walk. Take a bus and get off at Lee Park. You got a place to crash this weekend?"

"Yeah," I lied.

"Great, but if you do need a place to stay, look me up here tomorrow. Ask around for Van Loyt if you don't see me.

Chapter 59

I found Stoney and the mixed bag of freaks that formed his staff in various stages of undress and consciousness. The incense was thick enough to send an asthmatic into respiratory crisis but not so strong as to mask the aroma of marijuana and hashish.

"What are you doing here Narc?" Stoney asked me.

"I'm not a narc."

"You look like a narc," he said. "I know I've seen you somewhere before. Maybe you dimed out some of my friends?"

"I met you a few months ago at Ruth's house in Irving."

"Right, I was there. What do you want?"

"Your paper is calling for submissions." I handed the piece I'd written on the recruit brig.

He read it with a bored expression. "Not bad. Can I make some changes?"

The changes Stoney made were not little. He played up the violence. He stuck in some stuff he lifted from an article about sailors being suspended by their wrists in Treasure Island while Marine guards tortured them. I asked Stoney how much he was going to pay me.

"I like it, like it so much that I want to give you twenty-five dollars. Unfortunately, man, I'm tapped out. Not to worry though, I'll give you fifty-dollars' worth of this week's paper to sell. You'll make out like a bandit peddling them at the Iron Butterfly concert tonight."

That evening I stood at the bottom of a set of stairs leading up to the Fair Park's concert center with a bundle of the Dallas Notes in my seabag. The huge verandas of the Moorish styled music hall overlooked a common full of trees, flower gardens and fountains. I hawked my papers enthusiastically. "Get your Dallas Notes, the paper that tells it as it is."

After an hour of being given the dust off by every person climbing the stairs, I sat on the top step smoking a cigarette long after the last of the concert goers had entered the building.

As Iron Butterfly played "In-A-Gadda-D-Vida" I weighed my options. I didn't want to dip into my money for a room. I started walking toward the outdoor mall. I parked myself at the all-night donut shops along the way killing an hour or so over a cup of coffee in each one before being evicted. If I lasted until morning, I might be able to find Van Loyt and hang with him and his friends for a couple of days.

By 7 A.M. I was wired. My mouth tasted like I'd spent the night licking ashtrays. The streets of the commerce district were abandoned. The wind whistled through the alleys blowing trash down the pavement. The stillness reminded me of a movie I had once seen with Charleston Heston. The hero was seemingly the last person on earth. The daytime belonged to Heston, but the night was the domain of mutated humans. The difference between the hero's plight and mine was that he didn't need money to survive. He roamed the streets taking what he needed from supermarkets before retreating to a fortress like penthouse.

The idea of being on my own where no one points a finger at the kid in the crew cut was appealing. I wondered if people were whispering behind their hands– draft dodger, deserter, queer, drug addict.

It was so quiet in the fake cobblestone passageway that I trapped my head in the crook of my arms to shield my eyes from the streetlights and dozed off. When I awoke the mall was full of people. A cop approached me but turned into the New York Deli. He came out munching on a giant pretzel. He paused and stared at me but must have decided I wasn't worth his coffee going cold.

Van Loyt and his friends entered the deli. I dashed in after them and waved. The two white guys ignored me but Van Loyt tipped his head at an empty booth in an invitation to join them. His fluorescent blue satin shirt hung past the crotch of his black flaredvelvet pants and was cinched around his waist with a wide yellow sash.

"How'd things go with Stoney?"

"He's going to run my piece in the next issue."

When the waitress came, I ordered a coffee.

Van Loyt shook his head. "Bring him steak and eggs with home fries and give me the bill."

I protested weakly thanking him at the same time. For over a week, I'd hardly eaten anything that didn't have a hole in it. Van Loyt peppered me with questions until the food appeared. I barely looked up from the plate. By the end of the meal, I'd given away more than I intended. He knew that I had no place to go, no place to stay, and no one to care.

"No sweat man. At least Saturday and Sunday you have a place to crash."

Van Loyt lived near SMU but on weekends slummed with his buddies at a place they'd rented near a railroad roundhouse. Out of courtesy I asked if they minded that I stay with them.

The red-haired guy answered in a thick accent mixed with a spattering of Texas idioms. "Okay dood, you are very velcum to stash wit us."

"That's crash, Leo," Van Loyt corrected. Then he said something in a language I recognized as Dutch.

Leo and Joop were Van Loyt's cousins. Van Loyt's father was an architect from the Netherlands. His mother was from Curaçao where English, Spanish, and Dutch coalesced into a new language. His parents had moved back to Holland, unable to put up with the subtle forms of racism they found at Dallas cocktail parties.

We left the deli and started toward the seedy outskirts of the city. The sparkling clean skyline of Dallas was a mirage. Beyond the ultra-modern office buildings, past the Grassy Knoll, stood abandoned warehouses, nooner hotels, rooming houses, shooting galleries for drug addicts, and empty lots sprouting weeds. We entered the lobby of a mansion that had been converted into an apartment building. A plaster cast of Neptune hung above the entrance. The windows faced the railroad yard next to the freeway that sliced through the heart of Dallas.

That afternoon, guests came bearing drugs the same way middle-class Americans arrive at a party bringing wine and flowers. A few of the guests conversed about the war, racial conflict, and poverty in the Third World. Van Loyt held center stage. He expounded upon his vision of a universe without borders built on peace and love. I nursed a jelly jar topped to the rim with Liebfraumilch and avoided talking despite Van Loyt's efforts to draw me into his sermon as a damaged exhibit of the establishment's war machine.

The living room resembled an overturned Dempsey Dumpster. Debris crackled underfoot. The remnants of leftover pizza in flat cardboard boxes littered the apartment. Empty wine bottles and crumpled cans of Colt 45 Malt liquor dribbled onto the carpet. The day fell away.

A light switch was thrown. Blue, green, and yellow 60-watt bulbs in the lamps and overhead fixtures illuminated the room in watery pastel colors. Joop brought a small strobe light from the cloak closet and set it up on the coffee table, aiming it at the ceiling.

Van Loyt walked through the apartment door. "I'm back," he said.

I wasn't aware he'd left. Along with everyone else I applauded when he held up a plastic sandwich bag containing paper circles with one blue dot in the center of each one.

"William Blake said that when the doors of perception are cleansed, man will see things as infinite, as they truly are. Who wants to discover if he was right?" Van Loyt started a long rift on Aldous Huxley's 'The Doors of Perception'. I'd never heard of the book, but I gathered from the nodding heads and chorus of right-ons that his invitation to take a paper dot was accepted without hesitation.

"Fucking A! Let's see what's on the other side. It's magic carpet time," Van Loyt sang and passed the baggie around the room.

When it ended up in my lap, I stared at it and then reached for a circle. Van Loyt knelt in front of me. He held my wrist, keeping my hand in the baggie. "You ever dropped before?"

I didn't answer.

"Acid, especially the first time, is not something you do unless you're sure your head is in the right place. So, are you sure your head's in the right place?"

I wanted to let the dot fall back into the bag, but it stuck to my fingertip.

"Okay it's your choice. I'll be close by if things get too weird for you."

I closed my eyes and inserted my fingertip into my mouth allowing my salvia to wash the dot off its pad and down my gullet. Patiently I awaited the appearance of psychedelic flowers, neon rainbows traversing a candy-floss sky, and words of wisdom delivered by a disembodied guru. No such luck. When I opened my eyes, Joop and Leo were placing pots and basins filled with water under braided plastic bags suspended from the ceiling. Leo flicked his Bic, and the ropes went up in flames. Bits of melted plastic fell into the water where they hissed, letting off noxious plumes of chemical-laden steam. Somewhere in the room, a terrified voice whined, "What did you do that that for?"

I glanced around to see who was speaking but saw only the pied faces of the partygoers. Van Loyt who had gone from pill dispenser to trip-master roamed the apartment checking to see if everyone was comfortable.

"Got everything together. Keep it together. Keep mellow," he said to each person. Van Loyt frightened me. His head, which seemed to occupy the whole room, loomed in front of my face as he repeated his mantra. "Got everything together? Keep it together. Keep mellow."

Someone put an album on the stereo. I stared at Van Loyt with a grin seared on my lips. Procol Harum's words came at me like a nest of hornets with a message delivered for me alone.

We skipped the light fandango
You fucking low-life
And turned cartwheels across the floor
How can you bear living with yourself?
I was feeling kind of seasick
You are sick and worthless
But the crowd called out for more
You know how it should end
The room was humming harder
There is nothing worse than a liar except for a deserter
As the ceiling flew away
Degenerate, queer, coward, worm, liar, scum, junkie

"What's going on inside your head? Say something, David. Don't freak I'm here, everything's cool. Hey, where are you going?" Van Loyt asked.

Other voices in the room urged him to kick me out. "Hey man, he's really fucked up. Ditch him. Let the cops deal with him."

"I'll talk him down. I'll take care of him," Van Loyt shouted.

I found myself standing in front of the bathroom mirror. The face that looked back was as smooth and expressionless as a death mask. I felt as though someone had extracted my organs, leaving me a hollow shell. I pressed my tongue against the roof of my mouth and shuddered when it penetrated the pallet and slithered like a worm through my nasal cavity. Pain, dull and repetitive, registering as fists landed blow after blow below my cheekbones. Hands belonging to people without names pulled me from the bathroom.

"Christ's sake, look at what you've done to yourself," Van Loyt said. "Man, what's going inside that skull of yours?" Van Loyt lowered me on to the couch and put his arm around my shoulder. "Listen to me, you gotta hold on. You're having a bad trip. I'm here for you. Nothing bad is going to happen."

I moved my lips without speaking. "How do you know nothing bad is going to happen? How do you know that something bad hasn't already happened?"

The only sound that came out of me was the clearing my throat. I counted off the seconds, my connection to reality.

"David, here's a coke. Drink it slowly."

I gagged. The liquid went down my throat like sludge. I swallowed though I wanted to spew it out. I did not want to hurt Van Loyt's feelings or feel the wrath of the voice that was threatening to make itself visible and expose me to the roomful of people for what I was, a low life, a scum, a worthless piece of shit.

It's impossible to tell how much time passed before I started returning to a tenuous state of sanity. Music became audible again. But the voice less powerful continued to insert its insults between the legitimate lyrics.

She said, "There is no reason,

And the truth is plain to see"

Even that whore you call a girlfriend would tell you there is only one thing to do to make this right

And although my eyes were open

If you weren't such a coward, you'd do it

They might just as well have been closed

Put the gun barrel in your mouth, the blade against your wrist

The deep drawl of each enunciated word dropped on my head like an anvil and became recognizable. I licked my lips and heard my jaw crack. "No!" I screamed.

Van Loyt squeezed my shoulder. "Finally man, I never thought you'd come around."

"I'm sorry."

"It's cool."

He led me to the bathroom. He gave me a washcloth to wipe the dried bits of blood off my face and left. A few minutes, hours later, he returned with another washcloth and told me to hold it against the goose eggs that had formed under my cheekbones. The cloth was freezing, wrapped around ice cubes. The cold pain was a blessing. Froze out the voice of my tormentor leaving me with the last stanzas of Nights in White Satin upon which to reflect.

> *Just what the truth is*
> *I can't say anymore*
> *Some try to tell me*
>
> *Thoughts they cannot defend,*
> *Just what you want to be*
> *You will be in the end,*

When I awoke the next day, all but a few stragglers had vacated the apartment. My joints popped and my muscles burned. I pushed myself up from behind the couch where I had slept in a nest of sofa cushions and towels.

Two guys wearing only underwear snoozed away in connubial bliss. A girl with her legs folded under her was sleeping at one end of the couch. Her boyfriend's electric hair rested in her lap. On his smooth chest was a tattoo of a red and a black dragon inside a yin and yang circle. I crawled out from behind the sofa and made my way to the bathroom avoiding the bodies and refuse that covered the floor. Someone whistled in the kitchen. The sight of my battered face and bloodshot eyes jolted me awake.

The whistling grew louder as I stared at myself. Van Loyt stood outside the bathroom with his hands in his pockets. "You think you look scary now, you should've seen yourself last night."

"Did I do anything, say anything?"

"You were catatonic except for the times you got up to beat the shit out of yourself."

"Did I offend anyone?"

"Not unless they could read lips. Come with me to the kitchen. I made a pot of coffee and some toast."

The heat of the coffee radiating through the heavy white mug felt wonderful. I sipped it keeping my eyes fixed on the tabletop.

"For the record, technically I'm mixed race," Van Loyt said out of nowhere. "I do appreciate the fact that whoever was inside your head hated you for loving my kind."

I reached up to touch the lump under my cheekbone. A deep shiver chilled the core of my body.

"I was sitting next to you most of the evening and I can read lips."

"Honest, I don't know what I was doing. I don't know what was happening."

"You are the one hurting. You didn't say anything that hurt me."

My eyes stung as salty tears poured out of them and ran through the scratches and sores on my face. "Guess that's what you call a bad trip, huh?" I tried to smile.

"Not too many people can say they went toe-to-toe with their demons and came out of it with only a few lumps," Van Loyt said. "I wouldn't drop again, if ever, until you get your head straight. You got some real heavy shit to deal with. Stuff that you can't resolve sitting around with a bunch of spaced-out hippies."

He slid the Windsor knot of a conservative blue tie up to the collar stays of his white dress shirt. The Purple Haze duds had been replaced with a navy blazer and camel dress slacks. He handed me several one- dollar bills. "Some of the people last night took up a collection."

I shook my head and left the money on the table. "I have enough to get by on until–"

"Until you get punked or beat senseless on the street. You don't belong out there anymore than I do. That's twenty bucks, enough to get you a bus ticket to Irving."

"I don't want to go back."

"Maybe you don't but you have to, or you'll never get rid of the guilt eating you up. There's only one corner of the universe you can be certain of improving, and that's your own self. Huxley wrote that."

Chapter 60

There was no brass band to greet me at the Greyhound bus station in Irving. My reason for returning was not clear to me. Maybe I thought that I could turn back the clock. Or maybe I just had no place else to go. I walked down the sidewalk striking my thighs with my fists. I talked to myself drifting loudly from feverish indignation to shameful confessions like an apprentice wacko who had not yet earned the right to own a shopping cart.

Forty-five minutes of walking brought me to the plaza across from MacArthur. School was in session. I sat in the Gazebo and made myself as comfortable as possible. My jacket collar was turned up. I tucked my chin into my chest to shield my face from the late February wind.

The bell rang. I watched as students spewed from the belly of the school. Police officers still patrolled the main doors, randomly stopping kids. Lesman patted the back of one of the boys in blue with what looked like genuine affection then looked across the street and saw me. He dashed to the edge of the sidewalk flapping his arms. I made a fist and flipped him the finger. Enraged, Lesman ran back to his cop buddy. I headed down the street to the 7-11.

Three distinct cliques were gathered in the lot of the convenience store. Mort Ewing and his non-political group assembled around a white ice chest at the corner of the building.

Floe, Muffy and Hugh Swift, minus his fringe jacket and beads, sat on the curb singing and playing their guitars with other quasi-hippies. Johnny was nowhere to be seen. Tory emerged from the center of his group. He touched the prune-colored lumps under my cheekbones. "You look like you got your ass beat royally."

"Keep out of my way," I warned him.

I entered the 7-11 where I saw Nina peering through the glass doors of the drink cooler. I went up to the cash and quietly ordered a pack of cigarettes and a coffee. She didn't see me.

Tory was laying for me outside. "Hey, hero, are you here on leave or AWOL? Oh, I forgot, I heard you got kicked out before you even got started, kind of like you did here."

I slipped my hand under the flap of my jacket and clutched the hunting knife's bone handle. The bad trip at the crash pad still consumed me. Tory's voice and the guffaws of the shit kickers around him resembled the chorus that had taunted me.

My voice became monotone, as expressionless as my face. "I know where all of you live. I know the number of your lockers. I know the color of your cars. I know your mothers from a mile away."

Tory looked hard at me. Perhaps he saw something in my eyes that I did not know existed. He looked at the hand tucked inside my coat and licked his lips.

I took a sip of coffee then poured it on the concrete at Tory's feet. I began to pull my hand out from under the jacket flap. Tory squeezed his eyelids shut. He lifted his shoulders to his ears. His buddies backed away. I looked around and saw kids who were not part of Tory's group watching me. Some of them I once knew. Maybe some of them even once liked me.

"Relax Tory." I pinched his cheek.

Wandering beyond the neighborhood I ended up at a mom & pop hamburger joint far away from my old haunts. I sat a couple of hours in a booth studying the skin of milk on top of my hot chocolate. Later in the evening I broke into a public park's bathroom. I slept sitting on a toilet. The growl of a car engine awakened me. Red and yellow roof lights of a squad car splashed across the restroom's cinderblock walls. I wriggled out the window.

It was past dinnertime when I returned to the 7-11 two days later. Jeff and Nina leaned against the ice chest. Nina ran over. She put her arms around me and tried to kiss me. I turned away. I had not bathed or brushed my teeth in five days. She lifted my right arm and uncurled my fingers from its perpetual fist. When she placed her hand in mine my fingers snapped over it. She guided me to the ice chest. Jeff held out a grape soda and a tuna sandwich hermetically sealed in plastic.

"The FBI came to my house. My father would kill me if he knew I was here," Nina said.

"The cops and Feds have been busy," Jeff added. "They've been dropping in on all the old gang. Lesman summoned me to his office. He wanted to know if I'd heard from you. If it cheers you up, he's scared shitless. Someone slipped him a note warning him about opening parcels delivered to his home. Don't suppose you had anything to do with that?"

"No, not that I wouldn't, but I didn't. I just got back."

"Until I turn eighteen my father can have you put in jail if you try to see me. That's only three months away. After that I can do what I want." Nina backed away and got into a yellow mustang and drove off.

"Nice wheels," I remarked.

"Her old man gave it to her to make amends for cutting you out of her life. He also made her promise that she'd go to college back East. Do you need any money?"

"Have some, enough until I decide what I'm going to do." I lifted my shirt and showed him the bone handle of the knife.

"Christ, what are you on? Your pupils are the size of pinheads."

I wanted to break down bawling and tell him about my acid trip and how totally fucked up I still felt. Wanted to tell him how I was nothing and that my shadow had more form and substance than I did. But I kept it to myself and asked the kind of inane questions second cousins that had not seen each other for years asked one another at funerals. "How have things been going?"

"Not too bad, considering."

"School?"

"Mr. Berk has a special interest in me. He put in a word to get me on the varsity football team. He believes that you're a bad influence but that under proper guidance I'll turn out okay. He'd shit a brick if he knew I'm the main source of grass for the team."

"How are Tommy and Mom?"

"I don't know about Tommy, he hardly talks. Anyway, no one really pays attention to him. Mom's even crazier, if that's possible. She must send thirty letters a week to newspapers, radio stations, and her congressman. It keeps her busy."

"What about Jan?"

"Dad and Mom still hate Fred but they love Chris." Jeff took the sandwich out of my hand. He unwrapped it and gave me half. "Before you ask. The dog is fine, the goldfish are doing swimmingly, and the next-door neighbor has huge tits."

"That leaves the toy soldier. How the fuck is he?"

"Not good. He's been in bed since Monday. You know that he never misses work unless he's dying. He wants to see you. You guys have to get things straightened out before it gets worse. Dad promised he'll keep his hands to himself and let you leave after he talks to you."

"Like he did after the Chief's funeral?"

"I think he means it this time."

In no shape to confront the voice behind the lyrics, I said, "Not today. Tell the Colonel to expect me tomorrow after dinner. Have you got a dime for the phone?"

I called Johnny. A recording informed me this line was out of service. I went by his house and saw a "FOR SALE" sign posted in a lawn overgrown with weeds. Bare circles of earth marked where Eunice Bernier's sculptures had stood in defiance of suburban standards of decorum.

Mr. Jardin had finally had it with the death threats and garbage tossed on his lawn, that started when Johnny burned his draft card in front of network cameras.

Interviewed by reporters for his reaction, Big John sucked in his stomach and gave a thumbs up to the six o'clock news crew.

I climbed the vacant house's fence. The door of his metal tool shed was open. That evening I slept curled in a corner of the shed, dressed in layers of clothing I pulled from my seabag to keep from freezing. The next day I hung out at a shopping center on the other side of Irving, certain no one would recognize me there.

*

At 18:30 I arrived at the top of my father's street. My sister's car was in the driveway. I put down the temptation to run up to the front door and knock hoping my family was eating supper. At 19:00 I rang the bell. My mother opened the door. She wore the puckered look of disgust she reserved for people who broke wind in public.

Dad called out when I stepped into the foyer, "Who is it?"

"It's David."

"Send him in here, now!"

Mom curled her shoulders and tilted her head in the direction of the family room.

The Colonel had caught up with the rest of America. Laugh In was broadcasting from a brand new 24" RCA color television set in a simulated wood cabinet. The Colonel sat on the couch in his pajamas and bathrobe. Tommy crouched at his feet staring slack-jawed at the screen.

Dad stood up, "What are you doing here?"

"Jeff told me you were sick and that you wanted to see me."

"I am sick but not sick enough to want to see you inside my house."

"Okay, I'm leaving."

"Don't move an inch."

The Colonel disappeared into the back of the house. While he was gone my six-year-old brother scooted over and held onto my leg. I looked down at Tommy's blonde head and blue eyes and realized that I had a better visual recollection of my dog than of my baby brother.

My sister and Fred entered the den. Janet put her arm around Mom's shoulder and drew her out of the corner where she had merged with the wallpaper. Mom had become far greyer and frailer than a woman of forty-five should be.

"No Ernest." Mom's pathetic plea reached my ears. I looked down the hallway when the stomp of the Colonel's feet shook the house. The barrel of the 22-cal./20-gauge shotgun preceded him into the den. He leveled the shotgun at my chest.

"You have two choices. Either I drive you to the Oklahoma border and give you fifty bucks and you never come back to Texas, or I put you out of your miserable existence on the spot."

I was sure Dad wouldn't fire. In deference to Mom, he would not risk wounding Tommy, who clung to my legs, or splatter the shag carpet with blood.

"You can't tell me where to go or what to do. I'm not going anywhere and you're not going to shoot me because they'll throw your ass in jail."

Dad cocked the hammer. "You're leaving this state one way or the other. There is no way in hell I'll let you be close enough to your brothers to infect them."

"Colonel Brown," Fred intervened, "Janet and I talked and we agreed that David can stay with us until he gets on his feet."

"That's right Daddy," Janet said.

"It's not your decision to make. You and your husband can't even take care of yourselves. I won't have this human excrement sponging off you."

"It is our decision," Janet said.

"Ernest please," Mom implored.

Fred turned toward me, "I'll talk to my store manager to see if he has a job for you. The only thing is that you gotta keep hush on your military record."

Dad either felt a genuine moment of paternal kindness toward me, the prodigal son, or was simply too tired to maintain his anger. He let the hammer down and tossed the shotgun on the couch. "Okay, Okay. On seven conditions." He listed off the rules then told us to wait while he went to his office and typed them out. He gave Jan and me carbon copies.

Conditions for Remaining in Texas

1. Under no circumstance are you to visit this house without receiving an invitation!

2. You are not permitted to speak to either one of your brothers unless both your mother and I are present!

3. You will pay to Janet 1/3 of the rent and contribute ten dollars a week to food and essentials.

4. You are not to speak to me unless I address you first.

5. You will restrict your answers to Yes Sir and No Sir responses unless asked to do otherwise.

6. Once you are on your feet you will move out of your sister's place. At this point we will reassess our relationship and see if you have made significant moral progress to permit you to remain in Texas.

7. You will enlist in the Army.

I crumpled the paper and threw it at my father. "Your rules, not mine."

We glared at each other, neither one of us taking our eyes off the other. The Colonel made a move toward me, shifting his Bulova from his left hand to his right. I bolted out the door before he could reach me. I did not stop running until I bumped into Jeff several blocks away.

"How'd it go? Is it safe?"

"Dad threatened to blow me away with my own gun."

"That was no threat."

"You really believe he would have shot me?"

"Of course, if he'd been able to. He probably saw that the firing pin was filed down."

One day after I had left for basic training Jeff said he came home from school and my father was waiting for him behind the door with a length of board.

"He clubbed me with it until I couldn't stand up and then knelt on my chest. He stuffed a baggie of grass he found inside the attic down my pants then pulled out his pistol and rammed the barrel up my nose. I told him it wasn't my shit. He squeezed off a shot but the thing dry fired. He was so pissed, he threw the pistol on the floor and walked away. After that I unloaded all the guns in the house and fouled the firing mechanisms."

I left Jeff and started toward the bus station. I'd covered about two miles when a car honked at me. Leaning over Jan, Fred said, "Hop in."

"No, I've had it."

"Your old man's a hard ass but he doesn't call the shots for us."

I opened the rear door and tossed my seabag on the seat.

"Man you smell like someone crawled up your ass and died."

"I don't need this shit. I'm tired and hungry."

"Me too," Fred said. "I'll drop Jan off at the super market and we'll go get something. If you're going to stay with us, we need to establish some ground rules." While I scarfed a burger and a tub of onion rings Fred laid down five conditions. "You gotta get a job without delay. I'll help you out there. I want you to share the rent and food expenses and baby-sit occasionally. If you want to bang some chick, do it elsewhere or your sister will throw a fit. And most importantly, if you're going to do drugs don't bring them in the house." His last directive was funny. Fred was already on his way to becoming one of the biggest pot smokers I'd ever known.

Chapter 61

Fred loaned me a tie, white shirt, and dress slacks for my job interview at the North Dallas Sears and Roebuck where he was training to be a store manager. I got the job and started in the lawn and garden department where I unloaded trucks of fertilizer, took care of the plants and learned how to kill every sort of lawn pest from chinch bugs to aphids.

During the first month, when not responding to my boss's directives or customer inquiries, I appeared virtually mute. Off work I went for long walks along the road that ran beside the pastures and truck farms that gave Farmers Branch its name. Little by little I emerged from my seclusion. My department manager promoted me to a key employee. The new position came with a nickel an hour raise. Along with lawn equipment I sold fountains of Venus rising from a clamshell and of naked boys pouring water out of jugs. The department manager paired me with Brice who was about my age. Together we cooked up a scheme to earn some extra money. Whoever sold a fountain would recommend the other to install it for fifteen bucks, undercutting Sears's fee by ten dollars.

"I served in the Coast Guard for a year," Brice confided one day while we unloaded a trailer of sheep manure. He was inside the trailer sliding the bags down a conveyor roller for me to stack on four-by-four pallets. "How long you been out?"

I didn't respond.

"From the length of your hair it couldn't have been long."

"Did you see the new fountains that came in? They're going to be a bitch to set up, two pumps plus a lighting system."

"How long were you in for?" he persisted.

"In what, in where?"

Brice sneered as he put a rubber band around his shoulder length hair and made a ponytail. "Come on man, that blue jacket you wear to work is straight out of basic training."

"We better get working. We got another truck behind this one."

Without taking a breath he snatched up a fifty-pound bag of sheep shit and tossed it to me. "Don't worry, your secret is my secret. Fact is, I served only eight months, man. The other four months I spent in the brig before being kicked out on a medical discharge. Could have been worse considering I was caught smoking dope on watch."

"You're lucky."

I told him about my lackluster naval career but instead of becoming tighter after sharing our confessions, we regarded each other with apprehension.

My mother made the drive once every two weeks to Farmers Branch to see me. Sometimes she discussed what she was currently reading but most of the time she spent her energy trying to get me to reconcile with the Colonel. In a final act of desperation she sobbed, "You children are killing a good man. All he wants is the best for his flesh and blood."

When she crumpled on the living room divan, I agreed to make peace with my father. Mom immediately regained her composure. "I'll be here at nine o'clock Sunday morning to pick you up. Dress appropriately. I want to go to church first to pray for everything to work out."

On Sunday I waited outside the apartment dressed in a salmon-colored long-sleeved shirt and orange and black checkered bell-bottoms. I splurged on the outfit the day before to have something halfway dressy to wear. I don't recall the church. I'm not even sure if the minister was from a recognized denomination. For all I know he genuflected to Andy Warhol paintings.

The minister referred to religious figures as diverse as Martin Luther, Buddha, and Oral Roberts to make a statement about how we all worship the same God, but in different ways. As I sat through his kindergarten theology lesson, I wanted to rush the pulpit and tell him he was full of shit. If we all worshipped the same imaginary deity, why were we so busy killing each other over him/her/it? I allowed my mother to hold my hand and squeeze it whenever the preacher came near making a statement that ended in a period.

"The pastor gave us a lot to think about," Mom said as we drove to Irving. On the way, Mom picked up a tub of fried chicken, mashed potatoes and coleslaw at a KFC. She made a stop at a supermarket and bought a lemon meringue pie that had more chemicals in it than lemon. She said, "Your father is in for two unexpected treats."

The Colonel stopped mowing the grass when Mom ran over the edge of the lawn as she pulled into the driveway.

"I know you're not blind or stupid, so how many times do I have to tell you to slow down and open your eyes," he said.

He walked to the front of the car and put his hands on the hood. He must have felt some discomfort. It was a 90-degree + day and the engine's heat was working its way through the metal.

"Ernest, look who's here."

"I see who it is."

"We went to church together."

"Is that so?"

The Colonel kept his hands on the top of the hood. I got out and carried the pie like an offering toward him.

"What's this?" he asked.

"A lemon meringue pie," Mom chirped.

"I know it's a damn pie."

He kicked the box out of my hands and tore open the front of my shirt, launching buttons into the air. "How dare this piece of shit show up dressed like a pimp! He's mocking you, Norma. He's decked out like he's going to some friggin hop-head orgy."

I saw his next attack coming and slipped a punch directed at the side of my head. I wasn't quick enough to jump back before he landed a blow to my kidney. My anger was so intense it numbed the pain. I walked away.

"It's Sunday. Please come back," Mom called after me.

"Your mother's talking to you." Dad ran to the end of the driveway and grabbed at my shirt. It came off in his hand. "Get your worthless ass in the house. You may not have any respect for me, but I'll kill you before I let you abuse my wife."

My eyes fixed on a bow rake leaning against the mailbox. I grabbed it and pushed him back with its head. I wanted to swing it at my father's face, sink the metal prongs into his flesh. "What the hell do you want from me, Dad! Do I have to come back in a body bag to make you happy?"

"Look, Norma, that's what we raised. He has no respect for us. We tried to make them turn out right, and this is what we get. A whore for a daughter, a degenerate for a son, and God only knows how the two other boys are going to manage to screw up our lives."

"See what you've done to your father." Mom put her arms around his waist. "If you knew how much he sacrificed for you kids, if you knew how much he loves you, you wouldn't be able to look yourselves in the mirror."

I flipped the rake into the driveway and began the long hike to the bus station. With every step came the thought that Dad was right. Maybe I was worthless and had nothing to look forward to but failure after failure. Maybe I was as depraved and as morally bereft as he said I was.

When I arrived back at the apartment Fred and Jan were waiting.

"I spoke to Mom." Janet gave me a number scribbled down on a slip of paper. "Also, a friend of yours from work called. I fixed a plate and left it on top of the stove for you."

"Don't be so uptight," Fred joked. "We've got pot roast, not fried chicken. If you want some pie though, we could go out later."

"Very funny." I dialed the number Jan gave me. The telephone on the other end was picked up in mid-ring. I must have said something because Brice said, "Hey Brownie you sound stoned."

"I'm not."

"Too bad, man. You got plans for next Sunday?"

"No."

"There's going to be an anti-war demonstration followed by a concert. We can hear some good music and score some dope."

I started to beg off when Brice said that his girlfriend wanted him to invite me. Wanda worked hard at getting me to open up. A couple of times, she'd offered to introduce me to her girlfriends. Outside of Brice and Wanda I had no desire to socialize. Whenever I got too close to strangers there was a hollow echo inside my head and a ticklish sensation in my gut. Fearing that I might reveal a terrible secret, I kept to myself.

Ever since the night Van Loyt rescued me, the only form of escapism I allowed myself was found in books. Music heightened my unease. The bright colors and flickering images of movies provoked something akin to a panic attack. Crowds of any sort, even four people in a room, propelled me to seek safety the same way a man drowning tries to swim toward the sunlight above him. I agreed to go to the park with Brice because I thought being outdoors would give me a boost, alleviate my depression for a couple of hours.

The following Sunday Brice picked me up. Wanda's cinnamon-color braids hung down the back of her seat. The anti-war rally had already kicked off by the time we arrived at Lee Park. We stood on a bench across the street from a small artificial lake to get a better look at the gathering. A raised stage faced a fountain in the middle of the lake. Several policemen on horses patrolled the grounds. Apart from some clichéd speeches about the military establishment and chants from the peace activists, nothing aroused the cops from their apathy on a warm sunny day.

Brice whispered something in Wanda's ear. She shook her head. It didn't faze him. He hopped off the bench and ran across the open green space past a statue of Robert E. Lee mounted on his horse. He disappeared for about thirty minutes and returned with his hand stuffed in his denim jacket pocket. The speeches were winding down. A couple with guitars climbed on stage and belted out, "Give peace a chance".

Brice pulled out his hand and opened his fist. On his palm were three hits of acid. Terrified, my skin stretched as tightly as Saran Wrap across my face. I silently formed the words "no way" and walked off. Brice and Wanda caught up with me.

They squeezed me between them and herded me back to the park. Under the drooping branches of an ancient weeping willow Brice uncurled his fingers and revealed the trio of pink tablets. Wanda picked one up and stuck out her tongue, depositing it on its tip.

"Come on man, don't be a bummer," Brice said.

"No, I dropped once before and I didn't enjoy it."

"I thought you got kicked out for doing acid."

My mouth was dry, my mind in a run-down apartment across the tracks from Dallas's sterile skyline. I did not want to revisit that place.

"David, it's cool," Wanda said and rolled her tongue back into her mouth. "This stuff is beautiful. It will open your mind."

It was no use trying to explain. Wanda put her arm around my neck and pulled my face to hers. As she kissed me, she parted her lips. I did the same. She slipped her tongue into my mouth. I felt a tingle as the pill that she had kept concealed in her mouth dropped onto my tongue. I could have spat it out but didn't. Wanda went to Brice. They repeated the ritual, feeding each other hits of acid like mother birds feeding their nestlings.

Wanda and Brice pushed aside the hanging boughs of the willow and walked from under its covering into the light. I stayed back. Something told me that if I secreted myself under the cover of the willow I was protected. Leaning against the tree trunk I repeated over and over, "Stay in control. Stay in control. Don't lose it. Don't lose it."

I cried out and leaped away from the tree. White-hot needles plunged into my back and neck. I tore off my coat. A half a dozen fire ants were crawling across the collar. The intense pain persisted. I peeled off my shirt and shook it until I was satisfied all the ants were gone. The pain migrated from my upper body to my thighs and legs.

Bursting through the branches of the tree I raced past Wanda and Brice down the knoll toward the fountain. By immersing myself in the lake I thought I could drown whatever was devouring me. Brice and Wanda jumped into the pond after me. We weren't the only ones taking advantage of the coolness of the water. Other protesters had stripped to their underwear and were dancing under the spray of the fountain.

The couple on stage continued to play folk music while the party in the pond grew more boisterous. A whistle blew and a voice, amplified by an electric bullhorn announced, "It is illegal to bath in public fountains. Please get out of the water."

A policeman astride a horse as smooth and shiny as obsidian, trotted toward the crowd. The expression on the cop's face was not threatening. He didn't appear to be in any hurry to drive off the waders. He halted at the bank of the lake and leaned on the horn of his saddle, watching the nearly naked girls glistening with moisture. His smile split into a scream when a bottle thrown from somewhere near the fountain struck him in the face. The barrage of rocks that followed the bottle knocked him out of his saddle.

I heard the chant, "Revolution now! Down with the pigs!" and looked behind me. A group of people led by a familiar figure with Bozo red hair and a black beret had commandeered the stage. They wrestled the mikes out of the musicians' hands and exhorted the crowd to, "Trash this city! Kill the pigs!"

I slipped as I ran out of the lake and crawled up the slippery bank on my hands and knees. The world ceased to be jointed, ceased to be whole and coherent. Runnels of liquid light poured down the trees. The grass had turned into a field of green glass shards.

Explosions of tear gas canisters followed by waves of noxious smoke rolled across the park. The stench of sulphur, camphor and vomit permeated everything. Horses dashed by with their riders swinging Billy clubs at fleeing figures. Angry screams of "tear down the establishment" orders of "halt or else" frantic pleas of "oh God she's hurt, give peace a chance" filled the air.

I joined the throngs of people scrambling up a steep embankment to escape the suffocating clouds of tear gas, blows of nightsticks, and sharp hoofs of horses.

I tumbled down a ravine and fought my way back up the escarpment, tearing my clothes and flesh on stones, branches and stinging nettles. My voice reached me. "Fuck you, fuck you all. I'm not sick. I'm not worthless. Do want to fuck me? Fuck me then, everyone else has. I don't care if I die, if I get to take you with me. I'm sorry. I'll be better. It's not my fault. I'm dead anyway. What does it matter?" My fists and feet struck out at every form that came within a yard's length.

Through the chaos I heard Wanda. "We can't leave him here."

"Screw him, he's freaking me out."

Without being aware of where I was going or who was leading me, I was conveyed through the tumult to the other side of the park. Time passed unmarked.

Gradually forms began to assume discernible features. Wanda leaned over me. "Can you hear me?"

Cold and wet, I pressed my hands against the hard packed dirt of the baseball dugout where I lay half naked. Beyond the playing field, the sheer cliffs of Reverchon Park formed a sanctuary. Hidden trails crisscrossed in its overgrown landscape. Wanda and Brice looked relieved then Wanda screamed, "You bastard, you scared the hell out of us! We thought you were gone for good."

"What time is it?" I asked.

"Quarter past two," Wanda said.

"Time for us to shake you loose," Brice said.

"Did I hurt anyone?"

"How could you? All you did was move your lips and punch the air and roll around on the dirt like you were fighting the fucking devil."

"What did I say?"

"Who cares," Brice said.

"You didn't say anything. You just burst out with words," Wanda said. "You're scary, David. The whole time you kept your fists clenched. Once I had to stop you from hitting yourself."

"Is the riot over with? Did anyone get hurt?"

"There he goes again. The only riot we had to deal with was you."

"Can you get home by yourself?" Wanda asked. I nodded.

Brice lit a cigarette and handed it to me. "I'd drive you, but I've already had too much of you today."

"It's not your fault. You told us you didn't want to drop," Wanda said. "But Brice is right. We need to get away from you and you need to find yourself."

I sat in the dugout until I was certain they were gone. The bus was out as a means of transportation. Too many eyes would be trained on me. As it was, I felt every person I encountered was staring at me, whispering as I walked past. The voice I had heard behind the lyrics of Nights in White Satin mocked me. "Think it's over? It's not over."

I don't know how far I had gone when I spotted a police cruiser parked at a Dunkin' Donut. My invisible tormentor persisted. "If you weren't such a coward, you'd do it. Put the barrel in your mouth, the blade against your wrist."

"Officer, Officer," I yelled and crossed the street to the cop car.

A policeman on the passenger side threw open his door and struggled to get out. His stomach extended beyond his feet. "What do you want?" He peered over the roof of the car. His partner got out, handgun drawn, aimed at my heart. "I said, what do you want, boy?"

All through elementary school I had been indoctrinated to believe that when you're in trouble, go find a policeman. A torrent of words rushed out of my mouth.

"Lee Park, dropped acid, bad trip, freaking out, help me. Who stopped the riot?"

"Say what? You did what? You're on what?" the hippo-cop said. He told me to take the position. I braced my arms on the roof of the car and spread my legs so the cop could frisk me.

"This punk's been here before," the partner said. "Is he carrying?"

"He's clean." The hippo-cop jerked my arms behind me and snapped on the cuffs.

At the police station, I was stripped to my shorts and forced to stand in the breeze of the air conditioner. I gave them my name, address, place of birth, where I worked, and little incidentals like my history as a radical and the details of my short military career. When there was nothing left to say I was locked in a holding cell. After an hour or so the hippo-cop opened the door and tossed in my jeans. He handed me a T-shirt. "North Dallas Police" was printed on it.

"Get out of here. We need this cage for real criminals."

"What if he tries to off himself?" the desk cop asked as he gave me my belt and shoelaces.

"No such luck," hippo-cop said.

The cops dropped me off at the county line of Farmers Branch. "Get moving and stay moving. I better not see you in my jurisdiction," hippo-cop said.

There was a cloying odor of honeysuckle along the side of the road. The slash of whizzing cars made me dizzy. I climbed over a guard rail and hid in a culvert until my dread of dying subsided. When I arrived at the apartment, Jan and Fred were sitting by the pool talking to some neighbors. They did not see me. I entered the apartment through the sliding patio door. I was shivering and nauseous, too sick to think about filling the emptiness in my stomach.

My breath was rancid. My body gave off the stench of decay. I rushed upstairs and jumped into the shower. "It's okay. You're coming down. It's okay, you are coming down." The water pelted me like shrapnel.

"David, David are you in there?" Jan asked from outside the bathroom.

"Get straight, damn it," I commanded myself. "Yes, yes, I'm okay." The sound of the shower masked the tremor of my voice.

"Are you sure?"

"Yes, yes."

"Fred and I want to go out with our friends for dinner and a movie."

"Okay."

"Could you watch Chris while we're gone?"

"Okay."

"Are you sure you're feeling well?"

"Yes, yes I'm okay."

"He's in the crib. He should sleep until we come back. He's been fed and bathed."

"Okay."

"David, is there anything you want us to bring you?"

"No."

"Are you sure you're feeling well?"

"I'm okay, but tired. Got too much sun at the park and drank too much wine. I'll be fine."

When I stepped out of the shower, I overheard Fred ask what was wrong. Jan repeated what I had told her. I waited a few minutes after the door slammed behind them before going downstairs. As I rooted through the refrigerator for a juice, Chris's crying penetrated my trance. I went upstairs. Chris had one leg swung over the railing of his crib. He was about to do a head dive to the floor. When he rolled over the bar, I caught him. He clung to my neck and nestled his pudgy face in the space between my throat and shoulder. His corn silk hair tickled me. Holding him close I walked around the room and confessed what had happened to me since I first arrived in Texas.

"What should I do?" I whispered in his ear. "Start again. If you give up, then you've proven him right."

I put Chris back in his crib but for the rest of the evening I hovered over him. He could put his foot in his mouth without trying. He made me laugh.

Chapter 62

On Monday, Brice nodded at me but stayed on the opposite side of the garden center. I wanted to explain myself but felt that it was too late and besides was preoccupied with the appearance of a police car at the gate. Hippo-cop got out of his squad car and waddled over to a gondola I was stocking with insecticide. He picked up an aerosol can of roach killer, aimed it at me then went into the main store. Before closing time, I was paged to go to the human resources department. When I entered the H.R. office, Fred and my department manager were standing behind the personnel manager's chair. Fred crossed his arms over his chest and stared at me with a mixture of pity and anger. My department manager, Bradley, looked tired.

The personnel manager made a tish-tish noise and said, "David, I truly regret that I have to let you go."

I turned to leave.

"Don't you want to know why?"

"Not really."

He motioned me to sit but I remained standing. "A police officer came by the store. Now I'm not supposed to be telling you this, but I think it's fair you should know. The policeman told me that although he was not supposed to say anything because you haven't been charged with a crime, he felt it was his duty. He informed me you were out of your mind on LSD on Sunday."

"That's true. I guess he also spilled his guts about my military service record and other stuff."

He nodded. "I am truly disappointed. You had a future with Sears. What you've done reflects badly not only on the organization but also on Fred."

"Fred?"

"He recommended you."

"Fred doesn't know anything. I didn't tell him about my history."

"Are you trying to fool me into thinking that your own brother-in-law is unaware of your background?"

"I didn't tell him anymore than I told you."

"In your favor, Mr. Bradley says that while you have been with us, you've been hard working and have gone out of your way to help."

I glanced at Bradley whose only real contact with me had been to snort out orders: move this, ticket that, water the plants, sweep up the mess.

He lowered his eyes. "Too bad, I was gonna recommend that Sears send you to the community college course on lawn and garden care."

Sears let me go with two weeks' severance and a promise of a wonderful letter of recommendation. The same day, I went and filled out applications at every landscaping and garden center between North Dallas and Farmers Branch Texas. It was well after dark when I returned to the apartment. Fred and Jan were waiting outside.

"Where have you been?" Jan asked. "We were worried tha-"

"That I'd snuff myself? I wouldn't give the Colonel the satisfaction."

"Don't be a smart ass. Do you have any idea how hard jobs, good or bad, are to come by?"

"Real hard. I had to go to about sixteen places before I could get somebody to hire me."

The next morning, I started working at a local garden supply store owned by a snuff dipping old timer who called himself Ranger. It didn't pay much, and I worked six days a week. Ranger promised me that if I kept my mouth shut and listened, I'd learn something. I'd be able to get a job at any lawn and garden center. My first week I shoveled sheep manure and peat moss into the bags customers brought in with them.

As I filled a sack of sheep shit, Ranger slapped me on the back. "You're a natural."

The second week I learned how to care for bedding plants and bushes. It wasn't long before I demonstrated a talent for identifying and killing virtually every sort of creepy crawly thing that lived above or underground in Texas. I worked there for four months, long enough to acquire the basic lexicon of the trade and pass myself off as a garden center expert. One Tuesday afternoon Ranger called me to the picnic table he used as an office.

"You're a good worker Brown."

I took the cold can of RC Cola he handed me.

"Wish I could give you a raise but times are hard."

"That's okay."

"No it ain't. Know that Target store up the road across from Sears? They got a sign out calling for employees. Go apply."

"Are you firing me?"

"Nope, you still got a job here such as it is if they don't take you."

At the job interview at Target, I wowed Mitch Hillman, the operations manager, with my knowledge of plants, soil conditions and poisons.

"David, where do you see yourself five years from now?"

"I want to get into your management trainee program. I intend to take some night courses."

"I like to hear that. If you're an employee with management potential Target foots the tuition for business related courses."

Maybe it was my tone of eager desperation that caused him to pause, examine my application and stare at me a moment. "I'd like to hire you on the spot but I have to check your references. Do you object to my calling your past employers?"

I swallowed my hesitancy. "No Sir, I'm sure they'll give me a good recommendation."

*

I was assigned to Target's Seasonal Department. It was a mind numbing, zero stress environment. I chatted with the other workers but kept my own company outside work. I was the first person to sign up for overtime. Sometimes I would come in off the clock to finish something I had left undone. It was on one of these busman day's off that I met Perry Sanderson.

In Target's restaurant, a plate of fries and a coffee at one elbow and an El Centro Jr. College brochure at the other, I alternated between eating and reading. I jotted down ideas for stories, poems, and reflections on my life in a spiral notebook. My pencil, hovering above a clean sheet of paper, flew out of my hand when my manager thumped me on the back.

"Perry, sit here with David while I go get you a smock and name tag."

A lanky guy with solemn eyes set deep inside a gaunt face pock marked by chronic acne, slid across me into the booth. "Hey there." He smiled and his scars melted away. "Are you figuring out your class schedule?"

"What?"

"Me, I'm studying commercial art at North Texas State."

"I'm not in college."

"Anyway, El Centro's a good school." Perry raised his arms above his head, intertwined his fingers and cracked his knuckles. "What you writing?"

I closed the notebook. "Nothing."

*

I discovered at Perry's house that it is not mandatory for fathers to down a beaker of booze every night. Harold Sanderson was a jet mechanic for Braniff Airlines. He said little but always managed to say something of importance by just listening. He once asked me, "Do your parents live nearby?"

"Yes Sir, in Irving."

"Harold, call me Harold. You live on your own?"

"With my sister for right now. I pay her rent."

"Hmm, Perry says you're thinking of going to college."

"If I can get tuition together."

"Be easier if you lived at home, don't you think?"

"Not really."

"Hmm," Harold said. "Well, you're welcome here anytime."

Mrs. Sanderson treated me like a favorite nephew, lecturing me on how important it was to go to college while shoveling mounds of shepherd pie or spaghetti on my plate.

One day Perry beeped his car horn while I was sliding bags of fertilizer down a conveyor roller to another employee. It was late May. The heat and humidity were already so bad that I dreaded the prospect of what the real summer held in store for me. I jumped off the flatbed truck.

"I thought this is your day off," I said.

"It is but we don't have a lotta time to grab this deal. We can get cheap tickets to Europe."

"Come again?"

"I spoke with my father and told him how you lived in Germany and know Europe pretty well."

"Just because I lived there doesn't make me an expert."

"Hear me out. Mom's not crazy about me going to Europe alone. My dad said if you agreed to go with me, he'd arrange to get you a ticket at a discount."

"Perry, I got some money put away, but I don't know if I want to blow it."

"You'd rather do this all summer?"

Another truck pulled in with a load of peat moss to unload.

"You have to let me know by next week if it's a go."

"I'll think about it."

On Monday there was a note attached to my timecard. I put my things in my locker and slipped into a mustard yellow Target smock. Like a death row inmate on his final trek, I lumbered down the center aisle of the store. Mitch Hillman's door was closed. I rapped on it faintly then entered. Mitch sat behind his desk. A guy dressed in the grey suit of a career Fed stood behind Mitch. The Fed slapped a legal pad against his thigh and frowned. Sick to my stomach I started to lower myself into a chair.

"Nobody told you to sit," the Fed said.

Mitch stood up and faced the guy. "This is my office not yours. Dave, take a seat. This man is from the FBI."

"The Bureau of Alcohol, Tobacco and Firearms," the Fed corrected.

Mitch shrugged. "He works for the government. He's here because some guns were stolen from the store."

"That's got nothing to do with me."

"It has everything to do with you," the Fed said. "My partner and I went to your father's house yesterday."

"Is that supposed to mean something?"

"You know what it means. We told your father what we suspect you're involved in."

"What do you want from me?"

"Who'd you give the guns to and why?"

"David, go back to the floor. It's nine o'clock and you have to open the garden center." Mitch said.

"I'm not done here," the Fed said.

Mitch's round head went from bone white to thermometer bulb red. "Yes, you are."

I closed the door behind me and heard Mitch shouting at the agent. Twenty-minutes later the Fed walked into the garden center. "Kid you're in the clear. You don't know how lucky you are. Your boss sees something in you. God knows what, but something. It's kind of funny after the talk I had with your father. You know what he told me?"

"I'm not interested."

The next day two Texas Rangers escorted the receiving manager out of the store. His hands were cuffed behind his back and his cowboy hat pulled down over his forehead.

After lunch Mitch paged me. When I entered his office, he was playing a tape of CJ and the Fish. He turned off the machine before Country Joe completed his "Gimme me an F, gimme a U–" chant.

Even though my pants were covered in dirt he said, "Take a seat. I guess you heard about Rodeo Ron?"

"I didn't hear anything, but I saw the cops hauling him off."

"That was my idea. I wanted that redneck escorted down the main aisle and out the front door so everybody would get a good look at him. I don't know if he's stupid or just cocky to think he could get away with stealing guns from the dock. Even if we didn't have cameras installed in receiving, the driver he was in cahoots with turned on him to save his own skin."

"Then I'm in the clear." I started to get up.

"Sit down."

I slumped in the chair and dropped my eyes. "Can I finish out my day?" I asked. "We got a truck in and there's no one else to unload it."

"Cheer up. You look like someone just killed your dog. I don't know what you did in the past to have the Feds crawling up your ass. They tried to tell me. I told them so long as you don't have a criminal record I don't care. You're a good worker and you're smarter than 90% of the managers who work here."

"Thank you, Mr. Hillman."

"I don't want your gratitude. I'm telling you this because you're wasting your life. You're a full-time hourly employee. As soon as tough times come, you'll either be demoted to part-time or let go altogether. That's how retail works, Brown." He opened his desk drawer and took out a Target employee benefit pamphlet. "When you were interviewed you told me that you thought about going to junior college. I think you have the potential to be a manager. I'll recommend you for our trainee program provided you take some basic college courses in the fall."

The prospect of finding a way off a path leading to nowhere frightened me. Without thinking I blurted out, "Can't do it, Mr. Hillman. I'm going to Europe in August with Perry Sanderson for three weeks."

"Three weeks? You only got one-week vacation accrued. If you take more than that you'll have to quit."

"Sorry, I was gonna tell you at the end of the week."

"Okay, when you get back, I'll rehire you at your current pay and put you on the trainee program if you want."

I walked out of Mitch's office and held back hitting myself for blowing this chance. Instead, I unloaded the truck at full speed. I didn't bother to wipe away the stream of sweat that stung my eyes. When I was finished, I restocked all the skids of fertilizer and topsoil then began relocating patio flagstones from one end of the garden center to the other. At the end of my shift, I saw Perry Sanderson in the locker room.

"Can your dad still get me a deal?"

Chapter 63

I got hold of Jeff through Vince Crane and asked him to bring my passport. "Don't tell anyone. I'm flying to Europe."

"Aren't you going to ask how things are going at home?" Jeff asked when we met in the parking lot of Target.

"I doubt if anything's changed."

"Mom wigged out big time last week. Didn't Jan tell you about it?"

"No."

"She begged Jan to leave Fred, then flung herself on the floor and started kicking her legs, yanking her hair out and scratching her face. Janet and I tried to stop her, but she kept wailing and spitting. Jan finally said, have it your way and left."

"What else did Mom say?"

"The usual stuff. I want to die. Why won't God let me die? Why am I being punished? You know, all that crap we've heard a thousand times, except this time it came out all at once."

Jeff reached into the VW's glove compartment, pulled out a Mickey of vodka and killed the last few ounces in one swallow. "When she skipped from screaming to sobbing, I went outside. Dad had just pulled into the driveway. You better go in I told him. Mom's having a nervous breakdown. I almost felt sorry for him."

"You're kidding."

"Really, you should have seen him. Dad's shoulders slumped. He kind of shuffled to the house like an old man. I put my hand on his arm and said, it'll be okay. He threw me into the wall and yelled, you have no right to show me sympathy. Get out of my sight." Jeff tossed the miniature booze bottle over his shoulder. "You're a lucky bastard to get out of here."

"You'll have your chance."

"All I want is to get my diploma and split. But between those cock suckers at MacArthur and Dad, I don't know if I can make it."

"Jeff, when I get a place of my own you can crash there whenever you want."

"The worst part isn't getting beat on or put down. I know this sounds like Tommy Smother's bullshit, but Mom really does like you best. Sometimes I think I'm the fucking Anti-Christ to her."

I wanted to tell Jeff he was wrong, but I knew there was a lot of truth to it.

"Do you want me to bring you anything back?" I had asked Janet the same question when I told her I was leaving.

She answered, "What am I supposed to tell Dad?"

"That I'm gone. It's not important where."

"Fine, if he asks I'll tell him you took off and I don't know where."

"The Colonel should be happy about that."

"Quit calling him that."

"If I called him what I want to, you'd slap my face."

"Have you thought about what you're going to do when you get back?"

"I haven't even thought about if I'm coming back."

"Don't expect to move in with us."

"I don't. You have enough problems between yourselves without me adding to them."

Chapter 64

After Perry and I landed in London we caught a train to Harwich and booked a ferry to the Hoek van Holland. With every chair in the ferry's lounge taken, we squeezed into an opening along a wall. People were seated on the floor leaning against the bulkhead. Others loitered around a bar that sold booze and snacks. A few brave ones sat on the open-air deck. The people outdoors did not remain there long. Barely an hour into the crossing, the North Sea turned ugly. Waves crashed across the bow of the ship. Water sluiced under the doors and through the tiniest cracks in the rubber seals around the windows. Backpacks, ashtrays, food, bottles, suitcases, and people were tossed over-and-under from one end of the lounge to the other. From below, where the cars were held, the unmistakable sound of metal crashing into metal sounded through the skin of the ferry.

When the ferry disgorged its passengers at the Hoek of Holland, everyone reeked of piss and vomit. The early morning sky was pewter. The dampness of the North Sea breeze penetrated our bones. Perry removed a wool fisherman's sweater and a knee length raincoat from his backpack. "If it's this cold in August I'd hate to be here in the winter."

I folded my arms over my chest and squeezed my shoulders together. Perry slipped his head through the opening of his sweater. I tried not to let him see me shivering.

"Man, you're going to die if you don't put something else on," Perry said.

I opened my pack and took out a sweatshirt.

"That's it, that's all you brought?"

"I travel light."

The truth was that all the clothes I possessed were in the backpack. My letter sweater all the warm clothes I had amassed in Nebraska and Germany were stashed in a trunk in the Colonel's attic. My father also kept my academic and sports awards, early writings and report cards in a folder labeled PRE-INSANITY DAYS. In another file he had compiled an archive of my failures, correspondence from the government, my General Discharge Paper, and carbon copies of various letters he had written describing my descent into depravity.

Perry handed me his rain jacket. "Put this on."

"No thanks."

He tossed the jacket over my head. "Listen, wear the thing. Considering I don't speak German, all I need is for you to freeze to death before we get to Wiesbaden." From out of his pack, he pulled a heavier denim jacket lined with fleece. "My mom won't let me travel light."

We joined a group of people under a bus shelter. Pressed between 11x14 inch sheets of Plexiglas was a complicated routing schedule. I tried to decipher it. A young man dressed in a banker's pinstripe suit, umbrella under his arm, scrutinized the schedule. He sat down on a bench, opened his briefcase and took out a paperback. A photo of Charles Manson dominated the cover.

"Bitte," I struggled to phrase a question. "Welche autobus gehen zu Den Haag?"

The man stared at me blankly then tucked the book into his briefcase. "Would you repeat that please?" He said in perfectly enunciated English.

Perry perked up. "Boy I'm glad you came by. We want to catch a bus to the Hague."

The man raised his umbrella and pointed at a line on the route. "This one will take you there. It runs approximately once an hour. By the way, it is not a brilliant idea to speak or attempt to speak German around here. You know the war is still very fresh in people's minds."

Until the bus entered the Schilderswijk, Den Haag seemed like a gardener's paradise with parks and green pathways in virtually every direction. We stopped at a circular transit island. The only sign of vegetation was tufts of weeds growing through the pavement. The streets of the Schilderswijk were blanketed in shadows cast by the brutal collection of sterile office towers and chalk colored apartment buildings.

Across the road from the transit stop was a row of shops and coffeehouses. Perry and I walked into one of them and were driven back by the cold stares of men wearing long robes and skullcaps. They were seated around tables drinking demitasses of thick coffee. Out of a portable radio, Middle Eastern music played. Packed within the few blocks of the Schilderswijk were more cultures and ethnic groups than in the entirety of Texas. The music, voices, and mouth-watering aromas of Middle Eastern, African, and Indonesian cookery jostled for predominance.

The sound of horns, whistles, bells and cheers overwhelmed us when we approached the main drag of Schilderswijk. Balloons, streamers and crepe bunting hung from streetlamps and balconies. A banner announcing the 25th anniversary of the liberation of Indonesia from the Japanese was strung between two buildings.

We maneuvered through thousands of people partying in the streets. From food stalls that commandeered the sidewalks, vendors hawked grilled satay covered in spicy peanut sauce, fresh fruit juices, chips served in paper cones with mustard and mayo, pickled and smoked herring, cakes and cookies, and beer.

Perry and I walked down a side street, away from all the commotion. A group of freaks smoked hash and marijuana in plain view. One guy jumped in front of me and held out a joint. "It's goot sit," he said and coughed out a cloud of smoke.

"Yeah, it smells like goot sit." I plucked it away, inhaled and passed it to Perry who took a deep hit. Within ten minutes we became best buddies with the furry Niederlander.

"God I'm wasted," Perry sighed.

My voice cracked. "Me too."

My stomach gurgled and my throat was dry. My neck muscles tightened and stretched to their limit. Memories and voices from the past tried to intrude into the present.

"Perry, I need to get something to bring me down."

"Me too," he warbled.

The Dutch guy laughed and guided us into a pub where we bought a round of beers. He asked where we were from.

"Texas," Perry said and bought another round.

"Peace, hell no vee von't go!" He held up his fist in a power to the people salute.

"Go where, man?" I asked.

"Hell, no vee von't go. Vee von't go to Vietnam," he chanted.

"Don't worry, you're safe. Even Uncle Sam can't draft your Dutch ass."

He flashed me a peace sign and repeated, "Hell no vee von't go. Vee von't go to Vietnam."

Chapter 65

After visiting Amsterdam, we bought a train ticket to Wiesbaden. Young people doing Europe on the cheap packed coach class. The train had barely chugged out of the station when they abandoned their seats and sat on the floor forming temporary communes in the aisle. They shared dope, booze, and food. Someone broke out a guitar and sang antiwar songs.

Our southern drawls pretty much ended whatever potential existed for comradeship in the coach. Perry and I sat alone and watched as non-accented Americans mingled with their European counterparts. We were excluded from the party. I could not help but think that it's easy to protest the war and shout slogans from someplace safe. Let these Kumbaya baby boomers try it in Dallas or Waco.

After a long 321 kilometers trip to Wiesbaden, exhausted by the incessant plucking of guitars, I stepped off the train and smelled bratwurst, hot mustard, and beer mingled with diesel fuel. A guttural voice barked out the departures and arrivals over an intercom. The scream of train brakes bleeding steam wiped out my feelings of anger and despair. I smiled. I was home, back to a place where my family had feigned a semblance of normalcy and contentment.

We camped outside Wiesbaden on an escarpment that overlooked the Rhine. On the third day as we left a Greek Orthodox Church famous for its gold dome, Perry blasted me. "Brown, I didn't come all the way to Germany to sleep on the ground and fight off mosquitoes. If I wanted to do that I'd have stayed in Texas."

"Come on, it's an adventure. Give it one more night."

"You call lugging around a backpack and worrying wherever we go about getting ripped off an adventure?"

"You're exaggerating."

"I am not. Either you call those friends of yours to see if they can put us up or I'm finding a hotel and you're on your own."

Despite my reluctance I agreed to contact the Angermans. The Angerman's daughter answered the phone. Between Christina's bad English and my worse German, we eked out a conversation. Hans and Imegard were at their bookstore.

We walked down the main boulevard of Wiesbaden, past the gardens, fountains, the Kurhaus and the sidewalk cafes. I detoured through twisting streets with whitewashed exposed timber houses that dated back to the 18th century. The streets converged in the Altstadt at a large medieval square. Posh clothing boutiques, bakeries, restaurants, and the Angermans International Buchhandlung were located in the Schlossplazt. I opened the bookstore door. Hans back faced me. He pushed a rolling ladder down the length of the floor to ceiling bookcase. He climbed to the fifth rung and removed a book and handed it to a man standing below him.

Frau Angerman sat a desk at the rear of the store. She lifted her head from an accounting ledger and saw me standing in the shop. Her jowls shook. She ran toward me, almost bowling over a customer. She encircled me in her fleshy arms and kissed me on my forehead. "Hans, Hans—" she shouted "—look, look!"

Herr Angerman turned. The bulb of his nose was a road map of capillaries. He broke into a wide smile and lumbered over. I introduced the Angermans to Perry who stood behind me like a beanpole, his long thin arms dangling at his sides. Hans opened a cabinet and removed a bottle of Schnapps and three glasses. He handed me the first shot glass, poured, and winked. "You are old enough, yes?"

"Why didn't your parents let us know you are coming?" Frau Angerman asked. She frowned when Hans tossed back his Schnapps with a snap of the wrist and refilled his glass.

Before I could answer, Hans lifted his glass and said "Prost."

"Prost," I replied.

"Where are you sleeping?" Frau Angerman asked.

"At a campground."

"Outdoors, what will your mother say? You must stay with us. Hans will drive you to town each morning or you can explore the Taunus with your friend."

"That would be great Mrs. Angerman," Perry said.

I shook my head. "Thank you, but we have to go back to the campground. We left our gear there."

"No argument. Go gather your belongings and catch the evening train." Frau Angerman ordered. "You should arrive in Neuhof in time for das Abendessen."

*

As the train rolled through the Taunus Mountains, the fir-treed hills gave way to a patchwork quilt of farm plots outside small villages. The smoky aroma of manure and freshly harvested hay triggered a sense of remorse, of loss. I would have given anything to rewind the clock to a time in which my happiness wiped out the present and future as I envisioned it.

Perry hooted like an owl through his open mouth while he slept. I elbowed him when the train stopped at the platform in Neuhof. We walked from the station past the Geimeindehalle. I resisted going inside to see if any of the people I had once played soccer with still hung around. Had Doris finally escaped her father or was she still inside the men's toilet trolling for a moment of happiness.

We crossed the road and stepped onto cobblestones that predated the American Revolution. Flickering streetlights illuminated the display windows of the village's shops. The rampant incursion of suburbia became evident as we climbed the steep hill leading to my old house. Simple farmhouses and vegetable plots had been replaced by identical sanitary duplexes. It took me a couple of minutes to recognize my old street, and only then by an electric sign that etched "Der Freidhof" in the darkening sky.

Frau Angerman was standing at the curb when we topped the hill. She whispered as she hugged me, "I called Norma. She won't tell your father."

*

My ticket deal required me to stay a week longer than Sanderson. Herr Angerman drove me to the Frankfurt airport and stood beside me in the lineup. Policemen and soldiers carrying machine guns patrolled the terminal.

When I reached the TWA check-in counter the woman issuing boarding passes asked to see my passport. I slipped my backpack off my shoulders and reached inside it. I had hidden my passport under the pack's false bottom.

"And your ticket," the woman said in a punctilious tone of voice.

I dove into my pack again and pulled a copy of Europe on Five Dollars a Day. I opened the book to a chapter on Switzerland where I had concealed my ticket. As I searched for it, underwear, socks, a swimming suit, toothpaste and toothbrush, and other sundries flew through the air. In a panic I yelled, "It's not here. It must have been stolen!"

Devoid of any sympathy the woman said, "You'll have to take that up with the airline."

"But I'm going to miss my plane."

"Yes, you will. Please leave the queue. There are people with tickets waiting to be issued their seats."

I stormed out of the terminal and lit up a smoke. Herr Angerman tried to comfort me. "Don't be upset. I'll call your father."

"Herr Angerman, my father is the last person in the world I want involved."

In Neuhof Frau Angerman's disposition was somber. She and Hans went into the kitchen and closed the door. They came out with a false expression of cheer plastered on their round faces. "We are fröhlich to have you stay with us until you resolve this matter."

Herr Angerman lifted the receiver of his wall-mounted telephone. He dialed the operator. The only thing I made out in German was, "Irving Texas, Colonel Brown." My body grew tense when after a few minutes he said, "Ernst, did I wake you? No everything is all right. Yes, Imegard and the kinder are well. The reason I am calling is that David is here with us. Wirklich, you didn't know he was in Germany? You are making a joke. He is a good boy. Christina and Andreas love him. The trouble is that his airline ticket has been lost or stolen. You are joking again. Okay I will tell him. Yes, we want to see you and Norma again. Auf Wiedersehen."

"What did he say, Herr Angerman?"

"He says it is your problem. He hopes you are a good swimmer. He says that I should throw you out before you poison the air in my house."

"I'm sorry Herr Angerman. Things haven't been going so hot since we left Germany."

"This I could see in Texas."

"Thank you for everything. You've been really good to me. I'm sorry I wasn't up front about the rift between my dad and me." I picked up my backpack from the floor and started to walk to the door.

"Where do you think you are going?"

"I'm catching a train into Wiesbaden then I'll hitchhike to Holland."

"Holland? What is in Holland?"

"Work. I met a guy there, he said he could get me on at his hotel."

Hans slipped his arm through mine and pulled me toward the kitchen. "No, there are too many lost children in Amsterdam."

On the table Frau Angerman had set a plate of open-faced rye bread salami sandwiches, a pot of tea, and some cookies.

She pushed me into a chair. "You cannot think with your head full of nonsense and your stomach empty."

"David, I do not understand what has happened between your father and you," Hans said. "I do know that if you were Andreas and if you wanted to come home, I would welcome you. Some things cannot be undone. Those things you must live with. Other things must be undone so that you can bear those things you have to live with."

I stopped myself from interrupting. He was talking about his son who had been diagnosed with MS before my family returned to the States. I would not allow my battle with the Colonel to intrude into his precarious but loving household.

"Vati, Mutti!" Christina cried out.

We raced into the living room. Christina was kneeling in front of the television. On the screen hundreds of policemen and soldiers surrounded the Frankfurt airport. A plane had been hijacked.

We remained glued to the TV until it went off the air. A group of Palestinians had forced a TWA 747 destined for Chicago to divert to Morocco or Jordan. The plane I was supposed to have boarded had been bound for Chicago.

Herr Angerman punched me lightly in the arm. "See, you could have been on that airplane. Now your father will be grateful you lost your ticket."

For several days a drama played out in the desert. The hijackers threatened to blow up the plane and everyone in it if their demands were not met. In the end the hijackers released the passengers and blew up the empty plane, a dress rehearsal for future carnage.

I called the American consulate to explain my problem but hung up when I received a lecture about my carelessness. My next phone call was to TWA. The aloofness of the woman on the other end of the line chilled me. "You'll have to sign an avadavat swearing that you didn't sell your ticket."

"You're joking lady?"

"I am not joking. On more than one occasion young people traveling in Europe have exchanged their tickets for other things."

"I didn't."

"Very well. We'll conduct an inquiry at our end. Should it turn out that no one has used your ticket then TWA will issue you a new one."

"How long?"

"I beg your pardon?"

"I'm down to pocket change. How long will all this take?"

"Maybe two weeks, maybe more, maybe less."

Twelve days later the problem was resolved. Meanwhile I worked half days at the bookstore. In my free time I revisited my old haunts in the village and city. One afternoon I walked across Wiesbaden to check out my high school, General H.H. Arnold. Out on the football field I saw my coach. Nonstop, he barked insults at guys doing sprints up and down the bleachers.

"You run like sissies. Keep those knees pumping. I better not hear you breathing hard. This is nothing, my granny can do it with her eyes closed."

I crossed the field. "Hey Coach."

He twisted around. "Who the hell are you? This is a closed tryout!"

"It's me, Coach, David Brown."

A blank expression crowded out his annoyance.

"Track or Football?"

"Neither, the wrestling team, I broke my arm at a meet in Ludwigsburg."

"Over the years a lot of guys got hurt on the team. It's hard to tell them apart. Anyway, you look fit, so I guess it wasn't that bad a break. If you're done here, I gotta get back to work."

"Yeah, I'm done here."

Chapter 66

It caught me off guard when I saw Jeff and my mother standing beside the baggage carousel in Dallas. Jeff ran over and slapped me on the back.

"Shit Dave, I wish I had a camera when Herr Angerman called. The old man nearly dropped a load in his shorts."

"That's no way to talk about your father." Mom puckered her face like she'd bitten into green persimmon. "He's waiting for you at home."

Dad did not get up from the couch when I entered the family room. A full glass of Bourbon left a sweat ring on the side table as he lifted it and took a sip. "It isn't enough that you destroyed this house, you had to foul the nest of our closest friends."

"Is that what you wanted to see me about, to tell me what a worthless piece of shit I am?"

He hurled the glass at my head. I ducked. It shattered against the wall. "Don't stand up, Dad. If you do, one of us is going down."

He slumped in the couch. "I'm not going to fight. If I haven't been able to beat sense into you by now I never will."

"Fair enough. Why did you want to see me?"

"To give you another chance to make something out of yourself." He picked up an envelope on the table and held it out to me.

"You read it," I said keeping beyond his reach.

"It's a contract. It says that if you return home, work, and go to college, I'll pay half the tuition. But you have to agree to abide by the rules of my house and join the army when you finish."

"Dad, even if I agreed, Uncle Sam doesn't want to have anything to do with me."

"The army will take anybody."

"Real vote of confidence but I'll pass."

"That's your decision. You'll need this," he put his hand in his pocket and pulled out two hundred dollars. "It should last you a couple of months if you're careful. Don't expect to get any more help from me."

"No thanks, I don't need it. I'll make out."

"I don't want your gratitude. I'm giving it to you, so you don't end up leeching off your sister or selling your ass at the bus station."

My father insisted on driving me to the YMCA, lecturing me the whole time on how it was time I straightened up my act. Outside the Y an old black guy asked me if I needed help carrying the few belongings I owned. I said, "No Sir."

My father pulled me to the side and whispered, "You have to be careful who you call Sir. Some people might take you for a mark. Only say Sir to those people who deserve respect."

I didn't respond to his advice, didn't thank him, and did not say Sir.

Epilogue

A king had a son who had gone astray from his father a journey of a hundred days: his friends said to him, "Return to your father;" he said, "I cannot." Then his father sent to say, "Return as far as you can, and I will come to you the rest of the way."

Pesikta Rabbati found in "Renew Our Days: A Book of Jewish Prayer & Meditation" Edited and translated by Rabbi Ronald Aigen (1996)

> So close and yet so far away
> And all the things I'd hoped to say
> Will have to go unsaid today
> Perhaps until tomorrow
> Your fears have built a wall between
> Our lives and all that loving means
> Will have to go unfelt it seems
> And that leaves only sorrow
> You built your tower strong and tall
> Can't you see, it's got to fall someday

"Tower Song" by Townes Van Zandt

While attending the University of Houston in 1973, my mother persuaded me to come to Jacksonville, Florida for the holiday break. I did so reluctantly. The Colonel had retired in 1972 and moved to Florida to take a job as the field inspector of the state's nursing home system. He would later tell his friends that all his kids left home before they turned eighteen. Without giving the specifics, he pointed out how his children went through troubled times but came out on top in the end, validation that he must have done something right. My mother dully parroted his sentiments when Dad asked for confirmation.

I stepped off the bus with my moustache and long hair. My father scowled at me. "Get that damn stuff off your face and shoulders before you come home with me."

Without saying a word, I turned to get back on the bus. Dad forced a smile and waved at me. "Don't be so sensitive. I'm joking. You're old enough to do what you want."

One incident stands out that holiday reunion. On New Year's morning the Colonel grabbed my feet and shook my legs to awaken me. "Come on, let's go out on the river and see what we can catch."

It was frigid by Floridians' standards. I pushed the aluminum boat off the dock. The jonboat drew hardly a glass of water, perfect for the bayous of Louisiana and Texas but sketchy at best on the fast-flowing Saint Johns River.

Seated at the back of the boat, Dad rummaged through his tackle box. The boat rocked when he stood up to pull the motor's starter cord. Eventually the engine coughed, and the boat sputtered away from the landing. We rode the roller coaster waves driven by the winds of an incoming storm. Neither the weather nor the swells washing over the gunnels perturbed Dad. Perhaps he had jotted down on his New Year's resolution list things like cut down on smoking, get back in shape, go fishing with David.

"Get your pole in the water. The sooner we catch something, the sooner we can get back," Dad said. He killed the engine. He believed its sound frightened the fish. We drifted for an hour, carried by the north flowing current of the Saint Johns. Dad cast from one side of the boat to the other every five minutes. He brought up nothing when he reeled in the line. He lifted his head and motioned with the tip of his rod at a floating mangrove island. "Bet there's something to be had over there. What do you think?"

The bruised and swollen clouds moved swiftly. The water churned so furiously that I thought we would be lucky to make it back to shore. Dad steered the jonboat toward the mangrove. He anchored several yards off the island and made a cast toward it. Hook line and sinker got entangled in the Medusa-like vegetation. He started the motor and gunned it. The blunt nose of the jonboat rose out of the water. Traveling far too fast for him to steer with any accuracy the front of the jonboat drove into the tangle of roots and branches.

A growl, reminiscent of my childhood, issued from my father. He stood up in the boat cursing through his clenched teeth and flailing with an oar at the island beyond his reach.

"Don't just sit there!" He tossed the oar at me. "Get out and push us off."

I almost did as ordered. Almost stepped out of the jonboat onto an island of mud that could suck down a full-grown man in a heartbeat. A snake slithered through the tannin-colored water and disappeared into the vegetation holding the boat.

"Get the hell in there. We don't have all day for you to decide if you want to get wet."

"Nah, I don't think so."

"What do you mean, you don't think so!"

"I mean I'm not about to wade into that mess because you screwed up. You want to get loose that badly, you jump in. But watch out for the cottonmouths."

Dad looked like he wanted to lunge at me, but maybe the thought of taking a cold dip in the snake infested waters deterred him. He plopped down on his seat. "Then what do you suggest we do?"

"Wait."

I plunged the oar into the midst of the mangrove. Whenever a wave slipped under us, I used it to pry away the branches snaring the boat. Within thirty minutes, we drifted free.

*

After I had started a life and a family in Québec, I visited my father again. Dad now lived on the other side of Florida. He'd been promoted to the head of the agency that looked after all the state's nursing homes. He asked me to go out into the screened-in sun porch with him. He asked if I remembered our fishing excursion on the Saint Johns River. I shook my head, even though I clearly recalled that New Year's Day seven years earlier. "You told me to wait and we'd be free. Well, I've learned to be more patient, more careful I guess," he said then turned to the door when Tommy came out.

"What do you want? Can't you see I'm talking to your brother?"

Tommy shrank into his sweatshirt and retreated into the house.

Dad lit up a cigar. "I don't know what I'm going do with him. You and Jeff were hell on wheels but at least you had fire. He's just here." He gathered me into his arms, puffed smoke into my face and hugged me. I pushed myself away from him. His eyes moistened. "I know you think that I liked your friends better than I liked you. I was hard on you because I wanted you to be a better man than I am."

*

There are times the dark legacy of my father passes over me and I hear the words that his own father must have left him as an inheritance. "You remind me a lot of myself. That's not something I wished for you. I have never been satisfied, never been happy. Do you know what that's like? You're my son so you have to."

One day I will return to my father's grave and tell him, "You're wrong, Dad. It doesn't have to be that way."

E. David Brown

Montreal, 2021

Afterword

Despite Jeff's refusal to accompany Dad to Florida, enroll in college and join the ROTC, he commanded the Colonel's respect. He joined the Air Force and married his high school sweetheart. After serving 4 years he became a bodyguard for a bigwig Dallas millionaire. He later joined the police force. He remembered his time as a cop as a great gig. His career was curtailed by two events. While pursuing a burglary suspect he hopped a wall and landed on his back, screwing it up permanently. The suspect ran back and checked on Jeff before taking off. The Good Samaritan felon called 911 from a payphone to alert the police to where he had propped my brother against the wall. Jeff's stint with the force ended a few months later when he went to a party with some other off duty cops at an empty shack. He got more than a little loaded and, on a whim, riddled another abandoned shanty's front door with bullets. Neither the squatters residing in the derelict shed nor Jeff's superiors were amused.

Jeff's short career in the police force led from one high-paying job after another. The big bucks allowed him to trade up his pedestrian taste in drugs from marijuana, beer, and Jack Daniels to cocaine and Chivas Regal. Neither his first marriage nor his three subsequent tries at matrimony lasted.

He embraced his habits like illicit lovers. He did time in the county jail, lived on the streets and after a few aborted attempts, managed to become clean and sober. He replaced the solace he found in drugs and alcohol with the salvation granted through the twelve-step mantra and music. In the final analysis Jeff admitted that he would have been better off playing the guitar instead of playing for Dad's love. He died October 28, 2015; three days shy of his favorite holiday.

Tom has suffered without the benefit of being able to share his experiences with his siblings. Like Jeff, he played for Dad's love by joining the toughest branch of the Navy, the Fleet Marine Medical Corp. His commendable reviews were not good enough for the Colonel. As my mother lay dying Dad refused to sign the papers that would grant Tom compassionate leave to see her one last time.

Janet's marriage failed early on. Unlike Jeff or me, she settled down near Mom and Dad, living with them on more than one occasion. She found refuge in taking care of things: babies, stray dogs, broken people, drunks, and brothers. She is good at looking after others at the expense of her own well-being. She tended to my mother and later my father, whose cocktail of prescription drugs and booze eventually destroyed him. Mom seemed to welcome the cancer that ended her reading days. She died at the age of 59, twelve years before my father. If Mom had known that Dad would marry Charlie's widow, she would have made an effort I'm sure to send him rants from beyond the grave.

There is a photograph of my two-year-old sister playing in a sandbox on the front lawn of a clapboard depression-style house. It is a shabby little place, the kind of home that falls between real estate agents' nomenclature of starter and fix-'er-upper. It was our first house, first among many dwellings in places as far away from that sandbox as nostalgia is from the truth.

Acknowledgments

The redeeming aspect of my journey over the years is that I have encountered many people who helped me see that something worthwhile exists beyond the walls of my father's stockade. I am grateful to Roxana Nastase, publisher of The Scarlet Leaf Review, for her support of my writing and her willingness to take a chance with this book. I could not have completed Nothing is Us without the encouragement and advice of my wife, best friend, and a brilliant critic and writer, Terry Ades. I owe long overdue thanks to Professor Sylvan Karchmer (1911-1991) playwright, short-story writer, and mentor. He taught me never to let the love of my own words become more important than the story. I thank Pearl Luke, author of The Burning Ground, for her initial reading and editorial comments. I also appreciate the several people who read early versions of the book. Lastly, to my brothers and sister, we are something.

Author's Biography

E. David Brown has been writing since the age of thirteen. More than just an artistic endeavor, it has helped him go from being a high school dropout to earning a BA in English with a minor in history from the University of Houston, a Master of Fine Arts in creative writing from the University of British Columbia, and a Master of Arts in Administration and Policy Studies in Education from McGill University. Writing helped him survive when he thought he had no future, at times putting food on the table. Both figuratively and literally, it was his means of escape.

At UBC David received the CBC Award for screenplay and documentary work. There, he met his wife and fellow writer, Terry Ades. They have lived in Montreal for thirty years and have a daughter Flannery.

David is also the author of the novel *Tell You All*, a black humor retelling of the story of Lazarus.